"Eyes on the Ought to Be"

What We Teach About When We Teach About Literacy

Research and Teaching in Rhetoric and Composition

Michael M. Williamson and *Peggy O'Neill*, series editors

Basic Writing as a Political Act: Public Conversations About Writing and Literacies
Linda Adler-Kassner & Susanmarie Harrington

Culture Shock and the Practice of Profession: Training the Next Wave in Rhetoric and Composition
Virginia Anderson & Susan Romano

"Eyes on the Ought to Be": What We Teach About When We Teach About Literacy
Kirk Branch

The Hope and the Legacy: The Past Present and Future of "Students' Right" to Their Own Language
Patrick Bruch & Richard Marback (eds.)

Market Matters: Applied Rhetoric Studies and Free Market Competition
Locke Carter (ed.)

In Search of Eloquence: Cross-Disciplinary Conversations on the Role of Writing in Undergraduate Education
Cornelius Cosgrove & Nancy Barta-Smith

Teaching/Writing in the Late Age of Print
Jeffrey Galin, Carol Peterson Haviland, & J Paul Johnson (eds.)

Collaborating(,) Literature(,) and Composition: Essays for Teachers and Writers of English
Frank Gaughan & Peter H. Khost (eds.)

Rhetoric in(to) Science Inquiry: Style as Invention in the Pursuit of Knowledge
Heather Graves

Revision Revisited
Alice S. Horning

Multiple Literacies for the 21st Century
Brian Huot, Beth Stroble, & Charles Bazerman (eds.)

Classroom Spaces and Writing Instruction
Ed Nagelhout & Carol Rutz

Toward Deprivatized Pedagogy
Becky Nugent & Diane Calhoun Bell

Blurring Boundaries: Developing Writers, Researchers and Teachers
Peggy O'Neill (ed.)

Re-Mapping Narrative: Technology's Impact on the Way We Write
Gian S. Pagnucci & Nicholas Mauriello (eds.)

Unexpected Voices
John Rouse & Ed Katz

Directed Self-Placement: Principles and Practices
Dan Royer & Roger Gilles (eds.)

Who Can Afford Critical Consciousness?: Practicing a Pedagogy of Humility
David Seitz

Composing Feminisms: How Feminists Have Shaped Composition Theories and Practices
Kay Siebler

"Eyes on the Ought to Be"

What We Teach About When We Teach About Literacy

Kirk Branch

Montana State University

HAMPTON PRESS, INC.
CRESSKILL, NEW JERSEY

Printed in the United States of America

Library of Congress Cataloging-in-Publication Data

Branch, Kirk.
Eyes on the ought to be : what we teach about when we teach about literacy / Kirk Branch.
p. cm. -- (Research and teaching in rhetoric and composition)
Includes bibliographical references and indexes.
ISBN 1-57273-713-1 (hardbound) -- ISBN 1-57273-714-X (paperbound)
1. Literacy--study and teaching–United States. 2. Adult education teachers--Training of--United States. 3. Literacy programs--United States. I. title.
LC151.B717 2007
374'.01240973--dc22

2006101613

Hampton Press, Inc.
23 Broadway
Cresskill, NJ 07626

To Laura Prindiville
with love and gratitude

CONTENTS

ACKNOWLEDGEMENTS

Acknowledgements is such a mundane word for gratitude I express here. This book simply would not have been possible without the support and kindness of these people: Thank you all, as well as everyone I have accidentally omitted.

I thank all the students and staff at Goodwill Community Learning Center in Seattle, from whom I learned the most important lessons as a teacher, in particular Georgia Rogers, Hania Younis, Manuel Calloway, Rasheed Zaki, James McDade, Shash Woods, Peg Bernstein; there are so many more whose names I have forgotten but who changed the course of my life. Without that school—without those students and teachers—this book would have been impossible to write.

I also must acknowledge here several women whose influences on me as a teacher and as a person were profound. Mallory Clarke signed me up at Goodwill, and she taught me over the course of my teaching life in Seattle so much about how to remain true to a vision of teaching that embraced social justice in spite of conflicting institutional imperatives. I haven't been challenged as much by, or learned as much from, any other teacher in my career. Sandra McNeill was the director at Goodwill for most of the time that I worked there, and her extraordinary energy and vision and support and friendship were central to my excitement about working there and to my learning while I was there. No matter what, her door was always open and she always listened to me as I reflected on my classroom. She also demanded of herself and of all of us at Goodwill, students and teachers alike, that we grow and question and change, and during my time at Goodwill I learned so much about how to foster an atmosphere of openness and self-critique; only later, after Sandra left Goodwill, did I come to understand how vital her energy was in that process. Ellen Kleymann was on the staff at Goodwill during the time I taught there, and we became good friends as we discussed and critiqued each others' ideas (and more acutely, our own) over coffee and copy machines. I learned so much from her and I valued so much her approach to teaching and, especially, to learning about teaching. Melody Schneider approached her teaching with a marvelous intensity, passion, generosity, and love, and she did so with a bracing wit and embracing humor. She truly represents the sort of trickster consciousness I so admire; she demonstrated the social power of laughter and irreverence. With deep love and gratitude and friendship, thank you all.

I learned so much from Mike Caron at the Douglas County Jail in Lawrence, Kansas. The programs he has developed there, and his grace and insight about working with prisoners and correctional officers, were wonderful; he has my respect and friendship, and working with him was a highlight of my time in Kansas. I became extremely close friends with Anna Neill, a colleague of mine in the English Department at the University of Kansas, in large part as a result of our collaboration at the Jail. My work at the jail would have been impossible without her, and my friendship with her is one of the lasting legacies of that work. I regret that I cannot name the many students there whose ideas, lives, and writings continue to inspire and challenge my own.

I will never have again in my career such supportive colleagues from my own field as I had at the University of Kansas. Amy Devitt and Jim Hartman trusted me at moments in my career when I didn't; that was more important to me than they could have known. Michele Eodice and Kami Day continue to be close and supportive friends —and the godparents of my son Graham—and I have learned so much from them. Whenever this project seemed doomed or ridiculous, I turned to Michele, and she always gave me whatever time I needed, first for visits to her office at KU, and then for a series of long distance phone calls from Montana. Her faith in my work was constant and sustaining. And there is not space or words to acknowledge the degree to which Kami has enriched my scholarship, teaching, and, so much more importantly, my and my family's life. All my colleagues at KU were supportive, but I must acknowledge particularly Giselle Anatol, Byron Caminerosantangelo, Marta Caminerosantangelo, Katie Conrad, Frank Farmer, and Cheryl Lester.

Deborah Brandt has consistently been supportive of and interested in my work, and I thank her for her time and effort in many ways through my professional career. She also provided several sets of responses to this work which enriched it considerably. And everyone should have, at least once in their career, a reader like Peter Mortensen, who provided an extensive, detailed and incredibly insightful response to a draft of this book. Also deserving special notice here are Andrea Lunsford and Beverly Moss, whose early encouragement and discussions about this book made it, in large part, what it is. It was wonderful to work with them, and I will always regret that our collaboration was cut shorter than it should have been. Mike Williamson was a wonderful and supportive editor, and he provided another set of responses from an anonymous reader whose insights improved this book. Thanks as well to Barbara Bernstein at Hampton Press.

At Montana State University several people in the English Department helped this project to fruition. Thanks particularly to Michael Beehler, Robert Bennett, Susan Kollin, Michael Sexson, Phil Gaines, and Linda Karell, and generally to all my colleagues there who have supported and helped me whenever I needed it. My special thanks for the patience and help of Carolyn Steele and Teresa Klusmann. My friend Michael Reidy in the History Department read several drafts of this book and helps me keep my work in perspective. Also thanks to Billy Smith and Brett Walker and so many others in the History Department.

Thanks to my advisors at the University of Washington who were gracious enough to overlook my sloppiness and see potential where I only saw disorder: Tom Lockwood's early support literally kept me in graduate school, Gail Stygall stepped back and gave me time and space to develop my scholarship, Juan Guerra taught me a great deal about careful reading and teaching and always responded to my work with a careful and critical eye.

The Western States Conference on Rhetoric and Literacy provided me a several years long laboratory for this work. Thanks especially to Peter Goggin, Maureen Goggin, and Maureen Mathison. The International Conference on Literacy in Ghent, Belgium also helped this work immeasurably. I read some amended sections of this work at the Unitarian Universalist Fellowship of Bozeman, and I thank them for that opportunity.

So many others deserve my thanks. My brief mention here does indicate the extent of my gratitude: Patrick Sexton, Wendy Swyt, Scott Hendrix, Angela Crow, Richard Miller, Anis Bawarshi, the members of the Grote Reber Society, Diana George, David Barton, Lois Van Leer, Steve Van Slyke, my bridge club in Lawrence, Aiden Downey, Yanna Yannakakis, Bill Christmas, Hans Turley, Maggie Miller, Steve Arnold, Rebecca Merrens, Mike Clark. So many more I have forgotten to include.

To my sons Seamus and Graham Branch, whose committed lack of interest in this book provided necessary perspective for me throughout this process, I thank you for all the love and craziness you have brought to my life. My parents Tom and Katie Branch have also helped me in so many ways, offering supportive readings and mixed drinks, exactly when I needed both.

This book is a specific monument to my wife, Laura Prindiville, who has been the sustaining core of my adult life. This is your book as much as it is mine. I could never say enough. I thank you for your support, and I love you for everything else.

Introduction

In 1984, as a freshman at Marquette University, I volunteered at the Milwaukee Urban Day School's GED preparation class, run in the inner city by Sister Regina. One afternoon, Sister Regina introduced me to my new student, an African-American man at least ten years older than me who had just been released from prison and wanted to get his GED. She gave me a workbook to get us started. The first page focused on the proper use of *was* and *were*: He was to circle the correct word in each sentence. About halfway down the page, we encountered a sentence constructed to highlight the phrase *If I (was/were)*. An asterisk pointed me to a grammatical rule I had never learned before: In a hypothetical situation, the first or third person singular takes *were* instead of *was*. I spent the remainder of my session with him explaining what *hypothetical* meant and when he should use *were* with *I* instead of *was*. The rule intrigued me, surprised me, and seemed crucial to convey. I have never spoken that construction incorrectly since. My student never came back.

Fortunately, I learned more vital things from my work there. One student provided me an eloquent history of the Montgomery bus boycott when it became clear that I didn't recognize a reference to Rosa Parks in our textbook. I received a gentle introduction to the politics of race from a student supporting Jesse Jackson's presidential bid. Another student taught me simply by describing his life: In his thirties, married with five children, and studying to get his GED, he worked twelve hours a day, seven days a week, for minimum wage, then something over $3 an hour, with no overtime, meaning he brought home slightly more than $200 a week working literally half of his life. Sister Regina, listening to him tell me about his work, disrupted my sheltered suburban view of the world when she asked, "Who says slavery has been abolished?" Yet a singularly pressing memory is my voice repeating definitions of *hypothetical,* coming up with model sentences, teaching myself a rule that might be worth knowing if one were to find oneself writing a book about literacy but could not conceivably matter in almost any other situation, to me or to him.

Even in the initial encounter of a college kid with GED students, one can see themes and dynamics that, in many ways, shape the field of adult literacy education. Although literacy teaching has a history of prioritizing the minutiae of standard English grammar, the linguistic transformation emphasized in such a project has other counterparts. Conceived as vocational education, literacy instruction receives the task of making individuals employable and economies strong. Educators in prison imagine literacy teaching as a key to the transformation inherent in rehabilitation. Advocates of a critical pedagogy seek to transform social structures and to help adults recognize and accept political agency in their own lives. And the literacy crisis that recurs every ten years or so bases many of its anxieties on the dramatic need to deliver urgent educational changes to needy people, people who can't—can't read, can't speak correctly, can't work, can't stay out of jail.

Yet other kinds of transformations occurred at the Milwaukee Urban Day School. The passing of the GED marked an important event in many students' lives, often a significant accomplishment in battling a lifetime of educational struggle and underachievement. But I also changed. I had never before recognized my own racial and class position so concretely as I did when I started working at that school and had never before thought of my life as lived in relation to others, as made possible in part by people not afforded the same opportunities I had. I learned about civil rights and life in what was then one of the most segregated cities in the United States.

The reflections occasioned by such jarring experiences have shaped the questions and settings I consider in this book. Each time I have moved into a different setting of nontraditional adult education, the necessary intellectual, emotional—even physical—adjustments have discomfited and intrigued me. Moving from one institutional and discursive environment to another—community schools to vocational school to county jail writing class—has required specific and sometimes surprising changes in my pedagogical practices and theories. Because these experiences inspired the questions I ask in this book, I describe them briefly here as introduction.

I moved to Seattle after I graduated, seeking residency so that I could afford graduate school at the University of Washington. Soon after I arrived, I signed up as a volunteer at the Goodwill Adult Learning Center, where I remained as a teacher for eight years (with occasional breaks).

Central to the development and philosophy of the center were the works of Paulo Freire, whose theme-based education for Brazilian and Chilean peasants became the basis of the curriculum we learned to teach with there. Fiercely student-centered, the curriculum emphasized the lives of the students who came to the school, and we were to spend time developing and pursuing generative themes that came out of the students' own experiences. Such lesson plans would, ideally, culminate in a project that actually promoted change: students inviting a speaker to educate about AIDS prevention, for example, or organizing a meeting with a housing official to discuss a particular policy.

At Goodwill, I learned to recognize the political nature of education, to accept that something was always at stake in teaching, that teaching was always about more than encouraging the learning of basic curricular goals. Goodwill believed in teaching as a form of overt political activism, an approach that is as compelling as it is hard to realize consistently in a classroom, but while I struggled with and revised and argued with the curriculum that Goodwill encouraged, I also came to accept completely the notion that my teaching should have a social agenda, that I should see my teaching as helping students change the structures that oppressed them. I know that my interest in teaching in all settings still privileges issues of social change and political justice. My work at Goodwill committed me to that project, but my movement from location to location (including into college teaching) forced me to question as well the practical and theoretical limits of the curriculum I learned at Goodwill. At Goodwill, I was also introduced to the work of the Highlander Folk School, the subject of the fourth chapter in this book.[1]

I continued working at Goodwill after I started the graduate program at the University of Washington, where I received a Masters degree and began work toward a Ph.D. in eighteenth-century British literature. In my third year as a graduate student, I received a teaching assistantship and began teaching composition. That following summer, while I taught a particularly wonderful group of students at Goodwill, I quit graduate school and began seeking work as an adult basic education teacher. Nothing else I had ever done was as exciting and intellectually stimulating as the teaching I did at Goodwill, and I wanted to make it my career. I landed a job at the Seattle Vocational Institute (SVI), teaching adult basic education (ABE), level 1, for adults with reading skills measured by the Test for Adult Basic Education (TABE) at a fourth- to sixth-grade level.

That transition proved one of the most difficult of my working life. At Goodwill, I worked with students, volunteers, and staff on creating a learning community and fostering political empowerment through education. My mandate at SVI presented a stark contrast: I was hired to help students pass the TABE at a higher level, so that they could get into ABE level 2.

There was considerable institutional desire regarding this as well, because ABE at SVI was free; students began paying after they tested out of ABE 2 and into the vocational classes. After SVI became a pilot site for the Integrated Curriculum for Achieving Necessary Skills (I-CANS) program, for which I was the school representative, I became fully introduced to what I later realized was a discourse of vocational education in transition, moving away from a focus on particular occupations and toward a discourse of competencies, general and extensive lists of skills that employers want from employees, based on what the discourse refers to as "the high-performance workplace." I learned a great deal from participating in this project, and met some wonderful teachers throughout the state of Washington, but I also found myself responsible for implementing a curriculum that I didn't believe in, that saw my students primarily in terms of future employees and made all of their education center around that, a point of view fundamentally opposed to the student-centered discourse I had learned at Goodwill. I remember distinctly a conversation I had with one of the I-CANS organizers at a weekend retreat, who told me that the best way to assess Goodwill's performance was to see how many of their students got a job.

During my year at SVI, I became disillusioned with the notion of making a career as an adult basic educator, in part because I realized that social justice was not a central or even, in many cases, a recognizable goal of the profession, and in part due to the challenges the field posed economically and logistically (as with composition, ABE relies on the work of underpaid, overworked adjuncts who receive no benefits and typically hold jobs in two to three different schools). I quit and returned to graduate school the following year, changing my focus from literature to composition and starting with questions I had learned to ask in my teaching at Goodwill and SVI. At Goodwill, I learned to be skeptical about how I defined and understood the oppression my students experienced. No doubt my students came primarily from an economic and social underclass, but they were far savvier about the conditions of their own oppression than I could ever be, and I began to question my assumptions about what they needed to learn to produce social change. I also learned about the history of critical pedagogy at a community level: At Goodwill I first studied Paulo Freire and Myles Horton, who convinced me of the necessity to start with the students in planning a course of study. At Goodwill, my interaction with nonreading adults provided me the perspective I needed to challenge powerful assumptions about literacy made in texts like Ong's *Orality and Literacy*. My experience at SVI forced me to recognize the competing discourses surrounding education for adults and the ideological complexities surrounding literacy as a concept and inspired the questions that became the basis for my second chapter.

I continued to work at and write about Goodwill until I left Seattle to accept a job as an assistant professor at the University of Kansas in Lawrence. At the beginning of my third year there, I helped develop an educational program at the Douglas County Jail, at the behest of Mike Caron, the program director, and with my colleague in the English department, Anna Neill. For almost two years I taught there, a class hard to label. Focused on GED at the beginning, it became something else by the end—part poetry, part life writing, part bull session. I shared two and one-half hours a week with inmates I called students, some in the class for over a year, others there for only one week. Most were there for a month or two, awaiting trial, serving county time for a minor offense, or being held before transfer to the Kansas Department of Corrections (KDOC).

This was an entirely unique teaching experience for me, to say the least. My classroom was entirely male, for one thing, and made up of a population I had never had such extended contact with: mostly black; mostly poor; mostly young; so many addicted to crack or meth; abusive fathers and abused sons; most of them, as far as I knew, petty criminals (I never asked, but often learned, inadvertently, what crime had landed them in jail). Almost every week, I had a somewhat different mix of students, some who had been with me for a few weeks or months, one or two new.

When I arrived at the brand new, state-of-the-art jail to teach my class, I turned in my license and my keys, allowed correctional officers (never *guards,* Mike counseled us) to search my bags, passed through a metal detector and two large doors—electronically operated, sliding, metal and glass—took an elevator to the third floor. The door opened onto a long brightly lit corridor with doors to all the pods and to the classroom. Usually I brought with me a handout consisting of several poems, perhaps chosen for some theme but mostly just short ones I liked and hoped would engage the students, and typed-up copies of the writing students had provided me the previous week: poems, life writing, and free writes that I photocopied from their composition books at the end of every class.[2]

I had what seemed to me several privileges when I taught. No officer joined us, though occasionally Mike sat in. I picked up and dropped off students every evening at the medium pod and sometimes at the minimum. It always felt extraordinary to stand in that large two-tiered pod, at the officer's desk in the middle, greeting students in their orange jumpsuits (white in the more casual minimum pod, inmates in maximum wore red, in special protection yellow), waiting as the officer electronically opened cell doors or called in students from the enclosed basketball court, covered 40 feet up by some sort of mesh. Back in the classroom, we sat at desks arranged in a circle and succeeded, it seemed to me, however briefly, in turning a carceral space into an educational one as well (it was always, still and determinedly, a carceral space, a fact made clear by the jumpsuits, the panic button discretely hidden in my pocket, the narrow windows and thick walls, the constant background noise of clanging doors and mumbling loudspeakers.)

Why, though, was I there in the first place? When Anna and I accepted Mike's offer to begin an educational program at the jail, I would have answered this question by simply referring to my longstanding interest in teaching somewhere else, somewhere I had never taught before, outside of a university classroom. That is, I went to the jail not out of a belief in the power of education to rehabilitate, to reform, to enact positive change, but because, frankly, it sounded kind of cool. I'd always wanted to teach in a prison or jail for precisely those selfish reasons, and it met all my expectations. It was fun, it was challenging, it was destabilizing, it was surprising, it was always different. But over the time I worked there, I couldn't help but wonder about what I thought I was doing, about what I thought this would do for these students, for the addicts, thieves, armed robbers, domestic abusers, drug dealers, drunk drivers, check kiters, gang members, absent fathers, that passed through that narrow-windowed jail classroom.

This became a matter of some urgency to me one morning when I read the court report in the daily paper, a morning ritual whose meaning changed drastically after I began teaching at the jail, because now the faceless names whose sentences and crimes were closely detailed were, in some cases, my students. One morning, a month or two into my time at the jail, I read about the sentence of a student in my class, a sweet, gentle, soft-spoken, introspective, smart young man: twenty years for a rape committed in the back of a restaurant during a crack deal gone bad.

Teaching in the jail, at that moment, lost its exotic appeal, a necessary loss that made the experience richer and more nuanced, more complex, more unsettling. This was a crisis unlike any I had ever faced in twelve years of teaching, a crisis I still haven't resolved. Before he was my student, I would have been comfortable and even a little self-righteous in the revulsion I felt about his crime; before moving onto something more pressing, like making another cup of coffee, I would have very briefly contemplated his sentence with a sense of justice and just desserts. Now he was my student, and to what possible end? I was volunteering my time and expertise in the service of what? And more vitally, of whom?

Maybe like most crises, one answer came not in my thinking but in my practice. I continued teaching at the jail, he continued coming to my class until he was shipped off to KDOC, we kept doing what we did in that classroom. Whatever I thought about his crime did not change my sense that, like the other students, he must be welcome in my classroom. But I could never stop wondering what possible point this work could have beyond broadening my own perspective on my world. I still wonder this. What did I think this class would do? What role did I hope it would play, if any, in changing my students' lives? How did I know what my students needed? And was any of this even worth trying to achieve in two and one-half hours a week, when, for the rest of their time, my students were officially defined by their crimes, given little or no agency in determining how they spent any time, under continuous surveillance in an incredibly boring place?

And too, I was faced, literally, with what I had known before only as statistics representing the overwhelming racial and social imbalance of American prisons, the predominance of African-Americans and poor people, the social crisis of addiction addressed through the mandatory sentencing at the core of the war on drugs. The criminal justice system in this country is so flawed, so undeniably tilted against poor and minority populations, that the limits of any educational solution, in isolation from a reform of the system in general, are constantly apparent. Were teachers like me simply props, tokens of a rehabilitative ideal no longer operative? What effect could we have against a system so socially skewed and demographically biased, that has criminalized addiction, and that is based on tough-on-crime philosophies that prioritize overwhelming security over any hope for meaningful change? What good is it, in other words, to work to reform prisoners, when the real crisis is the prison system itself, a system that more than mitigates against any large-scale rehabilitative potential of education? Could I hope that an educational process focused on individual change could matter inside systems and institutions themselves so dramatically in need of reform?

That last question fuels my chapter on the discourse and history of correctional education, but I hope it also brings focus to everything else I do in this book. It is a question that demands that we look outside our particular classrooms, beyond the lesson plans and syllabi we bring to them. It is a question that suggests a dual emphasis to our work that can often feel—perhaps because it often is—contradictory: By working to serve individual students, do we suggest the correctness and justness of the institutions and systems that they find themselves in and that we support with our own work? Conversely, by working to address the manifest injustices in such a system, do we neglect the individual lives presently caught within it? I would argue that, at least in spirit, these are questions almost any teacher in any institution could ask about the work they do.

So, although I rarely focus on my own teaching in this book, it is a book about my teaching. Without the experience at Goodwill, the vocational institute, the county jail, and other settings, I would not have developed the perspective on this work that shapes my analysis. I hope that the passion that I have about teaching in these settings enlivens, but does not overwhelm, my explorations. Although understanding the ways that institutions and discourses shape teaching practices and theories is personally relevant to me, it's also vital for literacy educators at all levels who sign onto a project of transformation when they teach in any setting.

CHAPTER OUTLINE

In Chapter 1, I introduce two educational thinkers that are central to my work in this book. The first, Myles Horton, remains to me one of the most unsung educational figures in American history, a practitioner who disdained research and scholarship in favor of on-site work with the Highlander Folk School, developing educational programs that focused on social change and a more democratic society. The title of this book comes from a speech he delivered in which he praised Highlander's constant focus on the world as it ought to be, rather than on the world as it is. I extend Horton to argue that *all* educational practice, simply because it has in mind a future for students, projects a vision of the world as it ought to be. What that "ought to be" should be, I think, forms the center of most educational debates. Because teaching necessarily has in mind a future world, I argue that the literacy practices we teach our students also have in mind a future world, that literacy can never be wholly understood primarily in terms of the local. Although New Literacy Studies has emphasized what people do with literacy, I argue that teaching literacy practices means hoping as well that literacy will do something to people, to our students. Thus, the focus on local definitions of literacy—the focus of New Literacy Studies—remains inadequate to help teachers understand and analyze what they hope to accomplish by teaching, and what they hope their students will accomplish by learning, particular literacy practices. Educational literacy practices, I argue, always invoke a future world that ought to be. I also introduce the ideas of Basil Bernstein, whose discussions of pedagogic discourse have proven enormously valuable for my analysis in this book. For Bernstein, primary in all pedagogic discourse is what he calls the "regulative discourse," a discourse of morality and the social order, a discourse, I argue, about the world as it ought to be. Bernstein puts into the foreground the tension over control of pedagogic discourse, which is always a tension over the control of the regulative discourse, the "ought to be" behind instructional practices and theories.

In Chapter 2, I introduce the discourse of correctional education, exploring both its assumptions about the role of education in the process of rehabilitation and the way that the prison itself—as an institution and as a political concept—shapes the discourse. I explore back-to-back amendments in the Violent Crime Prevention and Law Enforcement Act of 1994—the first banning Pell Grants for prisoners, effectively ending an almost two-decade-long expansion of higher education in prison, the second requiring that inmates who have not graduated from high school pursue a diploma equivalent if they want credit toward their sentence for good behavior. These amendments highlight contradictory impulses surrounding literacy education in prison: Namely, that basic literacy education will prevent crime, but extended literacy education is a luxury. I then explore the most common theory in the field, which argues that offenders have particular social-cognitive deficits that make them more prone to crime, the correction of which should be the primary goal of teaching in prison. Because this theory defines criminality in terms of individual shortcomings, however, I argue that it must ignore the social conditions of actual prisons and the overwhelmingly skewed social and racial demographics of the penal system. I also explore other approaches to correctional education, which suggest that it is the prison itself, as much or more than the individual prisoner, that should be an object of reform in correctional education. In all cases, I claim that the prison and the criminal justice system largely shape the field of correctional education, an argument about the fundamental agency of institutions on educational practices that I return to throughout the book.

I take up the discourse of vocational education in Chapter 3, my particular interest being the ways in which this changing discourse relies on defining a world that ought to be in terms of a world that already exists. A brief history of the concept of competence within education demonstrates that it has shifted from referring to an inherent human trait—a potential for competence in several contexts—to a skill—a competency that one may or may not possess. I argue that just as early studies of literacy argued that literacy allowed for a conception of knowledge that transcends ideology, projections of competence place education outside an ideological framework by basing practice on common sense and straightforward descriptions of the world as it is. I explore this in relation to lists of competencies within two primary texts: the Secretary of Labor's Commission for Achieving Necessary Skills (SCANS) documents and a Northwest Workplace Basics Assessment System document designed for implementation within adult basic education curricula in Washington State. I argue that these texts are especially concerned with changing methods of control in the workplace and that an emphasis on the competencies workers need fosters a perception of control in the high performance workplace as nonexistent. I examine several of these competencies, paying special attention to the notion of learning to learn, which, in the British context, appears as lifelong learning, a hard-to-argue-with notion that is closely tied to the economic reality facing most workers who will need to move, and be efficiently retrained, into new jobs regularly throughout their lifetimes. I also argue that priorities and rhetorical strategies within the SCANS and NWB texts continue to shape educational reform, most prominently the No Child Left Behind Act of 2001. Throughout, rather than only engage in a critique of this discourse of vocational education, I emphasize the purpose it serves from an official policy perspective: The discourse of competency in vocational education allows for a representation of the current economy as not reliant on inequalities of wealth and opportunity, but on an abundance of workers prepared to fill positions in idealized high-performance workplaces in which hierarchical control is no longer necessary.

In Chapter 4, I turn to the history and pedagogy of the Highlander Folk School in Monteagle, Tennessee, focusing especially on the 1930s through the 1960s. I examine the ways in which educational literacy practices at the school mattered only in relation to their value in developing a more democratic society, and I look closely at the history and practice of the Citizenship Schools—literacy classes developed in the 1950s to enable African Americans to vote—as an example of how Highlander tied learning to read and write to their broadly democratic vision. I point out the ways in which the literacy practices of Highlander became understood as an official threat, and I examine the surveillance files of the Federal Bureau of Investigation—maintained, irregularly, throughout that period—as well as the harassment from various federal, state, and local agencies, which succeeded, briefly, in closing down Highlander in the early 1960s on spurious charges. I am particularly interested in the ways that a concern over literacy practices—which in Highlander's case included direct involvement in strikes and union organizing throughout the South, and later a practical commitment to integration and civil rights—became translated into a concern over who sponsored those literacy practices. To phrase this differently: How were the threats represented by Highlander's radical literacy pedagogy turned into threats of Communism? I hope, in this chapter, to suggest the difficulties of educating for literacy practices that challenge official perspectives, as well as the challenge and power of imagining, from within an educational institution, literacy practices in terms of social change, rather than as a way of accommodating individuals to some sort of real world.

In the final chapter, Chapter 5, I attempt to present some of the implications of this research for anyone concerned with the teaching of literacy practices, regardless of whether they teach adults or children, in a literacy center or an elementary school or a college writing class. My argument throughout, that educational literacy practices are necessarily embedded within particular institutional contexts that inherently shape those practices, requires that I explore this as a problem teachers must contend with. This is especially true in those cases in which the goals of teachers and the goals of the institutions they teach in are at odds, even potentially contradictory. I begin the conclusion by exploring a strong model of education as a process of social reproduction, one intended primarily to legitimize and reproduce class and social divisions in society. Understood this way, teaching becomes a sort of trap for teachers whose work primarily serves ends they must "misrecognize," to use a critical term from Bourdieu and Passeron's model of reproduction. Rather than attempt to escape that trap by claiming to work for ends separate from the institutions we teach in (an impossible ideal), we need theories of pedagogy that allow for moral action in morally ambiguous contexts, theories of pedagogy that will allow us to resist and perhaps reshape the contexts that will always shape us in return. I return here to Bernstein's discussion of the pedagogic device, arguing that his theory highlights vulnerabilities in the process of reproduction. In my conclusion, I explore those vulnerabilities, especially as they regard the construction of contexts that project, in their descriptions of the world as it is, visions of the world as it ought to be. My goal is especially to advocate an attitude toward teaching and scholarship that requires a trickster consciousness, an always grounded approach to pedagogy that resists official discourses seeking to universalize necessarily local and variable contexts.

THE (UNACHIEVABLE) GOALS OF THIS BOOK

Overall, this book is shaped by Myles Horton's belief that any goal worth working toward is one that is ultimately unachievable. He argued that if your ultimate goals were ones you thought you could achieve, you were limiting yourself. Getting disenfranchised citizens the vote was critical, but it was only a start to developing a more engaged citizenry who could work toward a more democratic society. In his autobiography, *The Long Haul*, Horton wrote

> It's important to distinguish between this goal of freedom and self-governance and the goals of the people who want only to 'Save the whales' or to 'Desegregate the South' or to organize a labor union . . . the goal I'm talking about is one that can never be reached. It's a direction, a concept of society that grows as you go along. You could go out of business if you were only for saving the whales: you'd save them, then you'd be out of work. That would be the end of it. . . . The nature of my visions are to keep on growing beyond my conception. That is why I say it's never completed. . . . In any situation there will always be something that's worse, and there will always be something that's better. (228)

Horton's argument here means that to work toward something that seems impossible to realize is not a mark of futile activity, but a sign that you might have chosen the right goal. It means that it might make sense, after all, to work toward the reform of a system so seemingly entrenched and flawed as the criminal justice system, even as you hope your teaching has some effect on a group of prisoners. Horton invokes a vision of a world that is continually shaped and reshaped by us, a world that will never be right, that will never be good enough, that will always need more. It's a world we shape by living in the present but focusing on something larger and more profound, something so big that we can't ever reach it. As a teacher, this has become for me an educational question, one almost always in some sort of conflict with the official goals of the institutions in which I teach: Why am I teaching this to students? What role will what I teach have to do in working toward a world in which we need to live? What role will my students have in shaping this world? To teach toward the world as it is, the world in which we live, is tantamount to proclaiming as a goal the neutrality Horton redefines as immoral, to accepting a world predicated on injustice and the imbalance of power, to agree with official assessments that everything is, more or less, as it should be, to set our goals so low as to see them realizable in a single lesson plan.

Of course, the location of our teaching practices within state institutions will always mean that such unachievable goals will exist in tandem with official educational goals we may not embrace or believe in. I use Basil Bernstein and Myles Horton to argue that teachers must carve out a space to act within discourses and institutions, even those that appear so restrictive as to almost determine action. The authority of a teacher typically relies on some sort of institutional credentialing in addition to, or in some cases perhaps instead of, whatever expertise or knowledge an individual teacher might have. As a relatively inexperienced graduate student at the University of Washington, I received the job of running the Educational Opportunity Program writing classes, thus having some measure of authority over other teaching assistants in the department. I remember my awareness of my utter lack of qualifications to run this program and my anxiety at meeting the first group of graduate teaching assistants (GTAs) who would use my curriculum, my textbook, my ideas about teaching, as guides for their own classrooms, and I remember, mostly, my surprise that none of them ever questioned or challenged my ability to do that, at least to my face. I recognized then what I also remember understanding less clearly the first time I entered a classroom as a teaching assistant, that the position I had been granted by the university offered me an authority that I didn't feel myself. Certainly this is an authority that I could lose, but it was also one I did not have to create wholly on my own: Much of it came from the university and the English department.

The corollary to this, as suggested by the awkward transitions I describe at the beginning of this introduction, is that what I did as a teacher and as a writing program administrator also met particular institutional goals, regardless of whether those goals were my own. I felt this most acutely when I went to work at SVI and acquired in the process an institutional mandate that I often found extremely stifling and counter to my own impulses as a teacher. I did not abandon my ideas about the potential of education to play a role in social change, but I recognized that implementing them in that setting meant doing something besides what was explicitly sanctioned by SVI, and that it meant defending what I did in language that SVI used about their desired outcomes. (The cynical reader will note that, even though I did this, I still quit, largely out of frustration with such limitations.)

This tension, too, then, is at the heart of the questions I engage in this book. I have become particularly interested in understanding how teachers might respond to the variety of often contradictory official mandates they are expected to deliver through their own teaching. Teachers working under the dictates of No Child Left Behind, for example, have become responsible not only for students in the United States achieving 100 percent proficiency in standardized measurements but also, seemingly, for dismantling economic and social barriers to equal opportunities for education. The causal relationship between increasing test scores and equality of opportunity remains, of course, an unquestioned and apparently common-sensical principle. How teachers might respond to such pressures without succumbing to what Herbert Kohl calls the "stupidity that leads to tears" seems a vital question for those of us who teach, and especially for those of us working with teachers in training. It is not enough to expect teachers to question the assumptions they are asked to accept as teachers, since such challenges will not do away with the institutional goals that inspire them. Teachers often literally embody goals they do not support, and figuring out how to teach in such circumstances matters as much as anything else we might hope to do as teachers.

So while I engage in critique throughout this book—critique of assumptions made about the relationship of education and economic opportunity, for example, or about the power of education to provide the cognitive skills that will turn a criminal into a noncriminal—I do so understanding that the critique itself is not sufficient. Critique will never do away with the contradictions that teachers experience when they find themselves teaching toward goals that not only are not their own but are in some cases directly counter to their own hopes for their teaching and for education in general. (What teacher entered the profession inspired by the vision of helping students learn to be successful at passing standardized tests so that their school retains federal funding and some degree of autonomy?) More than tools to critique official—or any—assumptions about education (as vital as those are), teachers need to learn how to teach within, and not abandon, flawed institutions—institutions like prisons, certainly, but also institutions like public schools, universities, vocational training centers, all those institutions that not only are flawed, but are destined to remain flawed, as long as they are operated by people.

This is a foreground to a theme that I return to throughout the book, especially in my chapters on the discourses of vocational and correctional education. I do not shy away from critiques of these discourses, but I also recognize their power, both within institutions and within society at large. As I note throughout this book, the power of these discourses is often political and cultural, not educational, which means, in turn, that critiquing them as educationally misguided will likely have no effect, because their educational value was never the primary purpose. It means that, while teachers need to develop both the tools of critique and the tools to develop other politically and culturally powerful approaches to education, they still likely will need to teach in places determined by educational discourses that often have education as more of a rhetorical than an actual goal.

My conclusion engages this issue directly: I am interested there in figuring out how to teach within institutions and systems that have goals we cannot wholly accept. I assume that this describes the work of a large portion of the readers of this book. In the conclusion, I use Bourdieu and Passeron's strong model of education as social and cultural reproduction to suggest that teachers, especially those of us—most of us—within official education, have space to work against such reproduction even as they, inevitably, serve it. Here, too, I have found the work of Basil Bernstein enormously productive, because Bernstein points out places in which pedagogic discourse is vulnerable, in which teachers and scholars can assume agency even in the face of increasing official attempts to limit what counts as viable theories and practices for education. My call in the conclusion, that teachers should assume a trickster consciousness, not to bring any system to its knees, but to pester, annoy, and creatively resist its simplifying impulses, I hope appears evident throughout this book. As teachers and as scholars of teaching, and as teachers of teaching, we should be encouraging more creative and interested people to enter educational arenas that appear more and more narrow, because engaging and not turning our backs on these inherently flawed systems is the only chance we have at improving them. This sort of trickster consciousness, of course, complies with the systems it resists, and in that tension, between resistance and complicity, lies a central and difficult aspect of most educational work. I hope this book suggests interesting approaches to working with that tension, even as it argues that the tension is unlikely to ever disappear.

It won't take an astute reader to note that my theoretical sympathies exist most directly with the approach put forth by the Highlander Folk School, but my intent in this book is not to read the discourse of a particular site against the discourse of another. As compelling and provocative as Highlander is, it is not an educational model that can be grafted onto teaching practices within other institutions. So I am not interested in critiquing vocational education or correctional education based on the distance they fall from the mark set by Highlander. What interests me primarily is the shape, and the shaping, of these discourses, the various claims they make about teaching and learning, about literacy, and about change. I seek in this book to explore frankly the notion that we are determined in part by the institutions we teach in and the discourses we use to support that teaching. Understanding these discourses and institutional connections is critical, but it can't provide us a place from which to teach outside of them, and although we do well to resist certain notions about teaching and learning that have come to be dominant, we also cannot pretend that these notions do not shape what we do in the classroom, as well as our reasons for doing it. I am most critical of the discourse of vocational education, but it is a discourse that educators refuse to contend with at their own peril. Likewise, I resist easy critiques of correctional education—which its focus on criminality and rehabilitation make it vulnerable to, from the perspective of someone trained in critical pedagogy—because the institutional complexities that shape the discourse of education within prisons are almost overwhelming, and an analysis that acts primarily as a critique covers those complexities in shadow. Still, as indicated by my clear affinities with Highlander's goals for education—"brotherhood, democracy, a kind of *world, in which we need to live*"—I am in the end arguing for and not simply about various ways of understanding literacy instruction.

CHAPTER 1

Educational Literacy Practices and the World in Which We Need to Live

In 1961, just months before Highlander was shut down by the state of Tennessee on trumped-up charges masking a reaction to the school's long-standing policy of promoting and practicing racial integration, Myles Horton addressed a workshop for teachers in the Experimental Citizenship School gathered at the school's Monteagle farm/headquarters. Four years earlier, at the request of an attendee of a United Nations workshop, Highlander had developed adult education classes, called Citizenship Schools, on the Sea Islands off the coast of Charleston, South Carolina, to help Black residents pass the literacy test required for voters (with the avowed intention of disenfranchising African Americans) under the South Carolina constitution. Buoyed by the success of the school and no longer able to administer the proliferating program, Highlander was now ready to pass it along to the Southern Christian Leadership Conference, headed then by Martin Luther King, Jr. At this workshop, Horton brought together teachers from the Sea Islands with volunteers who would "take the Citizenship School idea all over the South" ("Myles Horton's Talk" n. p.).[3]

He drew a circle on the bottom of a board, to represent what is in our lives.

> The situation down here somewhere is what we have to start with, because we have to start from where we are. Most programs do that. And it means they start with something specific that will help people do what they need to do at once. It may be teaching them how to write a

> check, to make a motion in a business meeting, or registering to vote. But that's where most of the programs stop—down at the "is" circle, so that the person learning never gets much away from where he is. There's no pull to anything farther along. (ibid. n.p.)

For Horton, such "small things have no value at all—they are negative, and in fact they may even produce a disservice. . . . If these specifics are learned for selfish reasons only, then they are better not learned."

He drew another circle on the top of the board, representing "what *ought to be*":

> . . . we have discovered that there was a magnetic pull up in the direction of what *ought to be*—human brotherhood, dignity, and democracy. We have kept our eyes firmly on the *ought to be*, and it seems to me that in our schools we have succeeded in making a pattern of procedure so that all the things that are needed down here, the specifics in the 'is' circle—begin to move together in the direction of what *ought to be*—and this is the difference. This is the magnetic pull
>
> . . . . we are getting results not only in terms of reading and writing but in terms of *intelligent first class citizens*—hundreds and hundreds of them—simply because we began by assuming that they *could* be citizens. (ibid. n.p.)

Without what *ought to be* as a goal to strive for, "even the best method will take you round and round in a circle. . . . The goal—and I think it is brotherhood, democracy, a kind of *world, in which we need to live*—must be constantly in view" (ibid. n.p.).

Horton's visual imagery of education as serving a sort of cultural stasis—round and round in the circle of the "is," trapped on the bottom of the page—stems from a notion that the ways in which education typically aspires to influence the environments it addresses are simply too limited, based on goals that are too small. Education *begins* to work when it provides the conditions for developing "*intelligent first class citizens.*" Critically, education could never be said to *have worked* in this model because the goals Horton had were too large: "The nature of my visions are to keep on growing beyond my conception. That is why I say it's never completed. . . . In any situation there will always be something that's worse, and there will always be something that's better" (Horton *Long Haul* 228). Teaching adults to read and write is a small thing in this model, as is getting them registered to vote. Literacy is important only insofar as it helps adults take responsibility for their own communities, to lead rather than be led. Alice Cobb, a sociologist and Highlander staff member, described the Citizenship School in such terms: "Our chief task should be to stimulate people with whom we come into contact to assume responsibilities. We should not seek to impose our institutional way or our own methods but instead should encourage people to find their own way of doing things. It is this lay leadership close to the people which will make it possible for the people themselves to assume citizenship responsibilities" (Cobb).

Highlander, then, promoted an educational approach committed to addressing social and political inequities that hamper a truly democratic society, teaching people toward this always evolving end. The world Highlander projected its education toward must always remain a social fiction, an ultimately unrealizable potential, an *ought to be* that never can be. What makes the "myth of Highlander" (in the words of Mike Clark, its director from 1972–1982 [qtd. in Glen 268]) so compelling is the circle of the *ought to be* that guided—that still guides—the practice of the school. Highlander entered one of the most contested domains in American history—the Civil Rights movement—at its geographical center, and they fought against and survived constant attacks from an angry and powerful opposition, at the same time that their committed political approach to education trained leaders and Civil Rights educators and registered, ultimately, thousands of African American voters throughout the South. What educator interested in social change can resist that story, can tire of hearing it? It's a story in which the circle of the *ought to be* carried the day, and of course that is exciting to hear and to tell.

Horton's way of distinguishing Highlander from other programs—Highlander focused on the future and other programs focused on the present—appeared regularly in the school's representations of itself, and it's a compelling distinction. At that point in operation for three decades, Highlander was certainly a unique educational program. Highlander opened in 1932 as a center for labor education and was, throughout most of the 1940s, the official school for the Committee on Industrial Organization (CIO). In the early 1950s, when unions started distancing themselves from anything that had acquired, rightly or wrongly, the reputation of being Communist, the CIO officially broke with Highlander which, almost since its opening, had been consistently, and wrongly, accused of operating under, at best, the aegis of the Communist Party and, at worst, as a sort of Russian sleeper cell subverting the American and Southern way of life from its Tennessee mountain home. When labor unions stopped using Highlander, the school shifted its attention from union activities to civil rights; labor had been its initial focus because the school saw unions as critical to the expansion of democracy, their ultimate goal, and when they could no longer work with unions, they opened another front. By the time Horton addressed this group of students, current and future civil rights leaders like Rosa Parks, Septima Clark, John Lewis, and Marion Barry had attended classes and workshops at the school, and Highlander had established itself as the educational center of the Civil Rights movement. Certainly there was no school like it, and, I think, there has been no school like it in the history of the United States.

The extensive differences between Highlander and other educational programs, however, are not accurately summed up by the claim that the other programs teach toward—and become mired in—a world that *is* whereas Highlander teaches toward a world that *ought to be*. Central to my claim in this book is that educational rhetoric of any sort relies on a construction of a world that *ought to be*, a future world that justifies the educational practices and theories advocated within particular discourses. Highlander's vision of the future is certainly distinct, as the continuous attacks on the school throughout its first forty years would suggest, but I argue here that any educational program projects and teaches toward a world as it ought to be, a world in which we need to live. In this regard, what makes Highlander distinct is not that it founded its approach on a world that ought to be, but that the school acknowledged doing that as a central part of their enterprise.

More commonly, as in the case of the dominant discourse of vocational education, educational rhetoric evades articulating an *ought to be* by relying on a description of reality to support its action. Historically, vocational education emphasized a set of particular job skills—welding or operating a ten key, for example—directed toward a particular trade. In the last several years, however, the discourse has begun to emphasize what are commonly called competencies, a general set of skills that employers value in their employees. Several official documents, most notably the Secretary of Labor's Commission on Achieving Necessary Skills (SCANS), have gone to great lengths to list these competencies, which in some cases number in the hundreds and include categories such as critical thinking, group effectiveness, and personal qualities. Underlying this discourse is a representation of what is referred to as some variation on the high performance or the twenty-first-century workplace. So, according to SCANS documents (U.S. Department of Labor *What Work Requires*), "In this new environment, work is problem-oriented, flexible, and organized in teams; labor is not a cost but an investment" (3). This new environment, quite unlike the nineteenth- or twentieth-century workplaces, is nonhierarchical, in which entry-level employees express their opinions on an equal level with management; it's all about working as a team to foster the success of the company; it's organized around creative and unorthodox solutions; and it's incredibly flexible, reorganizing quickly to address changing customer demand and improved technology. It's also, in a word, pretend, that is, it doesn't exist. However, by representing this as the new, standard, already-existing workplace, the discourse of vocational education can present itself as neutral. It is, after all, just helping students work better in a world that already is. To acknowledge the high-performance workplace as a construction, an ideal that vocational education strives for, would entail a very different discourse, because then the values it promotes would also be constructions, and when educational values are recognized as constructions and not as what is, they are suddenly open for argument. However, just to prepare students for a workplace that already exists, that is simply, and neutrally, providing a necessary service, focused, to quote another SCANS document, on "real things in the real world" (U.S. Dept. of Labor 1991 *Skills and Tasks* p. 22). In turn, this discourse presents a portrait of a world in which unemployment is the result of a lack of skills, in which high technology jobs are proliferating across the country, hindered only by employers' inability to find qualified workers. In the world of the high-performance workplace, there are no divisions between labor and management, because everyone works together as a team, so control in the workplace is also unnecessary. Vocational education promises to address the problems of unskilled workers and their inability to live up to the high cultural and social requirements of the twenty-first century workplace.

The ideal of the high-performance workplace, then, promotes industrial efficiency and employee dedication to quality and company profit, and vocational education quite naturally promotes this as its outcome. As an *ought to be*, this is strikingly different than the goals of Highlander, whose students—union members and civil rights activists—learned to question and challenge the rights of government and industry to determine oppressive social and industrial standards. My intention in this book is to highlight the struggle for the *ought to be* within particular areas of adult and literacy education, as well as to explore how that *ought to be* becomes defended, attacked, hidden, and potentially threatening. I mean this in part as a challenge: I want teachers to recognize that the work they do is in service of a social project, a future world with moral implications. Moreover, teachers rarely have full control over determining that social project; typically, they teach within institutions and systems that powerfully assert their own goals, their own *ought to be*. The strongest versions of reproductive theories within education—those of Bourdieu and Passaron or Bowles and Gintis, for example—suggest that no matter what teachers believe they are doing, as employees of an official educational system they inevitably work to reproduce an unjust and inequitable social system and make it appear normal; they wholly serve, in other words, the goals of the systems in which they teach. I also intend this book, then, to explore the tensions teachers often—in some cases constantly—experience between their own ideals for education and the goals of the institutions or systems in which they work, tensions that at times seem insurmountable. Whatever hopes teachers have for education, whatever ideals support their faith in their work, they must also contend with the hopes and ideals of institutions, systems, and societies often starkly at odds with their own.

My metaphor for this tension—one I rely on throughout the book and especially in the final chapter—comes from a description of the first teachers allowed into jails in the United States. The annoyed warder of the Walnut Street Jail in Philadelphia, required against his will in 1787 to allow two ministers to teach and preach in his jail, demanded that a cannon be placed next to them on the platform from which they taught, aimed at and ready to fire on the assembled inmates. The cannon served as more than a security measure: It also acted as a continuous reminder that the students were inmates, that the ministers worked in a jail, that the institution still held sway during the educational process. Over two hundred years later, the panic button I was required to carry at the Douglas County Jail—resembling a garage door opener and hidden in my shirt pocket—more subtly conveyed a similar message: My students were dangerous people under the charge of the jail, and if necessary jail authorities would take over. That the cannon was never fired, that I never used the panic button, matters less to me than the fact that no matter the goals of those ministers, no matter my own goals in my jail classroom, the institution could forthrightly assert itself as primary. In the history and discourse of correctional education, this relationship is especially stark: Education in prisons has always been inextricably linked to social trends and academic theories about imprisonment, rehabilitation, criminality. A classroom in a prison, then, is always defined fundamentally—often overwhelmingly—by the building it is located in. I suggest throughout this book that the institutions most teachers work in, and the discourses supporting and supported by those institutions, similarly assert themselves in individual classrooms, not in overt ways like a cannon or a panic button, certainly, but strongly and determinedly nonetheless. This is the cannon in the classroom, perhaps present in the form of federal testing mandates or competencies that students must learn to become good workers. Most of us who teach, I argue, have some kind of cannon in our classrooms, some kind of continuous reminder that the institution employs us to achieve its own goals, even when, or especially when, we see our individual goals as primary. This creates unresolvable conflicts for many teachers; how we handle such intractable conflicts is a central question in this book and an ongoing challenge for me in my own teaching.

In the discourses and institutions I examine in this book, literacy acts as a primary term, a marker of everything else. The reliance on statistics surrounding illiteracy in discussions of correctional education and vocational education, in discussions of education at all levels, emphasizes the ways in which a lack of literacy becomes a standard and convenient marker of difference. That marker hides, even explains away, other differences that are more uncomfortable and less amenable to educational solutions, such as race or class. If a lack of literacy is the reason for unemployment or criminal behavior, teachers can address these issues as a series of individual problems that can be fixed with the right education. In the face of the overt racial and economic imbalance within American prisons, an imbalance made more insidious by the soaring level of incarceration in the last thirty years, explaining imprisonment as an educational problem sidesteps the need to address out-of-control penal and criminal justice systems. To describe unemployment as the result of a lack of skills provides an easy enough answer: Teaching skills will reduce unemployment. To recognize that proportionally more African Americans and Hispanics and immigrants are unemployed, that class position remains a constant factor in job opportunity and potential income, that the jobs will not be there even for students with all the competencies, because the jobs have moved overseas or been lost through technological innovation, means that education cannot fix or solve the problem of unemployment. Teachers in prisons and vocational schools almost always become defenders of the idea that education can solve these problems, even if they understand that education cannot. This sort of tacit support, however, which most of us who teach engage in on some level, does not mean that teachers should not work in those settings, nor does it mean that teachers should not teach job skills or teach toward reducing recidivism. It means, rather, that teaching is almost always a great deal more ethically and politically complicated than most teachers are willing or able to recognize.

In this chapter, I introduce aspects of educational rhetoric I see as primary to those complications. I am especially interested in how educational rhetoric often evades the *ought to be* by representing its goals and processes as objective and neutral, which in turn means teachers can similarly sidestep challenging ethical considerations. Representing literacy as nonideological and objective allows for literacy education to appear as a wholly positive activity as well, devoid of moral and political complexities. However, within educational discourse, literacy's meanings are always intrinsically tied to an *ought to be,* stemming from the futures that literacy is supposed to enable. As such, understanding educational literacy practices requires more than the focus on the local that has long been the emphasis of new literacy studies. I also suggest tensions around definitions of *adulthood* and *citizenship* in the discourses I explore, arguing that these definitions often project very different ideas of what it means to be an adult and a citizen and thus what sorts of goals adult education ought to have. Finally, I introduce the work of Basil Bernstein, whose model of what he calls *the pedagogic device* has at its very center a *regulative discourse*, a moral discourse about the social order. For Bernstein, this discourse is fundamental, shaping all instructional practices and goals. In this chapter, I examine Bernstein's description of pedagogic discourse and the primacy of regulative discourse within that. I return to other ideas of Bernstein's throughout the book, and especially in the last chapter, because his pedagogic device also provides a way to understand how teachers might act ethically at the same time that they serve social projects they may not support.

Readers may have discerned what I want to acknowledge up front, that I am skeptical of official rhetorics of education, wary of their claims and goals and justifications. I argue, sometimes rather stridently, that literacy teachers and experts—those of us within English and composition studies and teachers and scholars of literacy at all levels—must intervene and take a vocal position in what I see as a sophisticated educational battle, which uses definitions of literacy and literacy practices as a primary tool—and sometimes weapon—of social reproduction. However, the necessity of taking a moral position should never be equated with an ability to take the moral high ground, to claim we are somehow above more petty and complex ideologies and conflicts within education. If we teach in official settings, we are as engulfed as any other teacher in morally vexing and sometimes contradictory projects, and to pretend otherwise simplifies and degrades the work we do. How we do that work, and why we might continue, is a central concern of this book.

EDUCATION WORKS: NECESSARY FUTURES IN EDUCATIONAL RHETORIC

> Having spent the past four years following the post-release careers of 654 Canadian federal prisoner-students, we can now assert definitively what most of us knew intuitively all along: education works. By *education* we mean the traditional kind built around the idea of arguing about facts and values within a curriculum centered on a set of subjects—not just skill acquisition and certainly not cognitive skills therapy programs thinly disguised as education. By works we mean reducing recidivism and inhibiting a return to crime after release from prison. (Duguid "Confronting" 153)

All the discursive sites I examine in this book contain some version of the claim that Duguid opens his article with: "education works." But as Duguid clearly recognizes, it's a claim that immediately requires context. On the simplest level, my interest in this book is on what has to happen to justify the claim that education has worked. Unless you teach in a prison, it's unlikely that you've focused on "inhibiting a return to crime" as the primary way to assess your success, but you won't teach long, or at least very well, without some way of arguing that education works. As a claim, "education works" requires some sort of transformation, which in turn requires a starting point (for Duguid, prisoner students who are high-risk offenders, likely to offend again), an ending point ("reducing recidivism"), and a theory about how to get from one point to another. I deliberately choose a linear metaphor here, because those starting and ending points are also, in many cases, physical places: That is, claiming that education works often entails claiming that it helps students move from one physical space to another, say, from prison to the outside, or from welfare offices to a workplace. Both the points defining the boundaries of transformation and the process by which transformation is achieved are rhetorical necessities in educational discourses.

I am interested in this book, focusing on the discourses of correctional and vocational education and the theories and practices of the Highlander Folk School, in how these sites construct a world for which the recommended educational practices are relevant, a world often but not necessarily, presented as real. I also am interested in how these sites construct the students and the environments that they are supposed to act upon and within. How do these discourses conceive of transformation? Where does it start, where does it end, and what role can education play in transformation? Who or what gets transformed? In what way are these discourses relevant? All educational rhetoric must construct and justify the conditions under which education works. To put it another way, at the center of educational rhetoric is a construction of its own relevance: Education must justify itself by pointing to a world in which it matters, and that world, I argue, is always rhetorically constructed. Sometimes that construction, as in the case of Highlander, is acknowledged and even embraced as a construction, as an ideal world that education aims for; in other cases, more commonly, that construction is claimed as real, already existing, already in place. It's still a construction, but it is eagerly presented not as a construction but as a fact.

These discourses must also take a kind of stance toward the presents and futures they address, a position about what project is entailed in education, but they often seek to represent that position as unbiased, socially useful but politically neutral. By arguing that a high-performance workplace is either the standard or inevitable, for example, the dominant discourse of vocational education can claim that it simply works toward helping students live better in a world that already exists. Claims of a lack of bias also support recent official discourses about public education, most prominently the No Child Left Behind Act of 2001, which relies heavily on teaching methods "grounded in scientifically based research," approaches which thus can be argued as objective and neutral. Correctional education, necessarily focused on a moral outcome because it seeks to change criminals into noncriminals, nonetheless works extensively to define criminality in scientific and psychologically valid ways. The disciplinary focus on rehabilitating criminals, moreover, often corresponds with a relative silence regarding the racially and socially imbalanced state of the penal system or the staggering growth in prison populations over the last thirty years. In these examples, educational rhetoric strives to appear as uncontroversial, a transparent medium for unproblematic social improvement.

At Highlander, the point of education was to foster citizens capable of working toward democratic social change. When Horton argues that neutrality is "a code word for the existing system" and, therefore, immoral, "nothing to do with anything but agreeing to what is and will always be" (Horton and Freire 102), he thrusts into the foreground the notion that all educating is a political act. Highlander promoted not narrow educational outcomes (for example, teaching someone to read) but nothing less than ongoing social change in service of a more democratic society. By openly enlisting education in a process of social change opposed to dominant racial and industrial practices, Highlander rejects the notion that supports most dominant approaches to education, the idea that schools and teachers should be objective, unbiased, neutral. A perspective that justifies educational action by defining it as nonideological and objective dismisses any openly biased discourse as politically driven and so noneducational. In this view, Highlander could not be understood as a school. For its opponents, Highlander functioned as a center of Communist and anti-American indoctrination, complete with horrifying and wholly fabricated stories of students required to salute the Russian flag after every class. Even for its supporters during Highlander's early history, the school was more a center of social and political activism than an educational institution. By proclaiming as its goal a more democratic society, emphasizing rights for workers and racial equality, Highlander clearly marked its mission as more ideal than real, more *ought to be* than *is*, and so, seemingly, more ideological than educational.

In each site I examine, literacy education becomes a central project in working toward its desired future. Again and again, tests of unemployed adults and prison inmates demonstrate that they have literacy abilities below the mainstream, a correlation that easily slips into a causal relationship, which asserts a lack of literacy as leading directly to unemployment or criminality. For vocational and correctional education, then, literacy can become the sine qua non of success, a necessary if not always sufficient individual corrective. Highlander, however, rejected the notion that African Americans suffered disenfranchisement and marginalization because they could not read or write; a lack of literacy simply provided official justification of state-sanctioned racism, a racism that would exist regardless of whether or not these adults could read or write. Literacy education on its own, then, had no intrinsic value in terms of Highlander's goals. It mattered only insofar as it helped adults work toward becoming more democratically active, first-class citizens enacting broad social change. In each of these cases, what matters is the *right* kind of literacy. Literacy means something very different in each of these settings, tied to being a good worker in vocational education, rehabilitation in correctional education, social activism for Highlander. These are some of the things we teach about when we teach about literacy. I began this project several years ago by asking how literacy comes to have varied and sometimes radically opposed meanings across educational settings, how literacy connects to a wide array of social projects and individual futures. What literacy *is* becomes in part a function of how education *works* in these settings, and how education *works* is always in part a rhetorical construction. Although recent literacy studies has prioritized ethnographic explorations of local literacy practices, I argue in this book that understanding literacy in educational settings requires a rhetorical focus, because literacy in these settings takes its meaning, not from local uses, but from its connection to the world as it ought to be, the world in which we need to live.

TOWARD A MODEL OF EDUCATIONAL LITERACY PRACTICES

In a discussion of the priority of literacy learning in a newly independent Namibia, Uta Papen notes that one of the dominant slogans in the government-sponsored campaign, appearing on a banner at a Literacy Day Rally—"Literacy—your key to a better future"—highlights literacy's transformative agency:

> That literacy does lead to a better future is an unquestioned assumption. The sentence refers to a goal most people can easily identify with: a wish to change and a belief in the future. The banner directly addresses its readers, and appeals to their responsibility in making that dream happen: literacy is *your* key. At the same time, the slogan offers the means to achieve the dream: *literacy*. The use of the second person signals the difference between the addresser, presumably the government, and the addressee, the people, since it is assumed that only the latter need the remedies advocated for. (44)

Literacy appears in this campaign as the educational agent of transformation, the tool that the people will use to get from where they are to a better future. Literacy, in its simplest and most common sense of being able to read and write, often takes on this power within popular approaches to adult education (a term that easily gets conflated with *adult basic education*, thus emphasizing adult learning not as a continuous process but as a kind of catch-up to proper adulthood). Literacy moves the narrative in the discourse, providing the engine that drives the story from where we are to whatever world the discourse posits as its end goal. Stories about how non-reading adults have been transformed by learning to read and write are common news features, celebrating both literacy and, usually, the volunteers who teach it, but these stories mask the fact that any site of literacy instruction is a site of conflict over what literacy means and how it should be taught, about what literacy practices should be valued. This occurs no more in sites where literacy's potential is valued only insofar as it helps empower intelligent first-class citizens to address social injustices than it does in sites where literacy is apparently valued tautologically, because it's an individual or social good to be able to read and write. In each case, the transformations supposedly engendered by literacy are in service of something.

So, underlying all these sites and discourses are questions about the transformative powers connected to the gaining or improving of literacy, an issue that has long been a central theme of literacy studies. Early scholarship in the field proclaimed the various cultural and psychological effects literacy imparts, arguing literacy as the cause of or necessary precondition for, among other things, economic development, democracy, science, history, urbanization, industrialization, abstract thought, objectivity, analysis, intellectual growth, and so forth.[4] Ethnographer Brian Street has argued that approaches such as these define literacy as "an autonomous variable whose consequences for society and cognition can be derived from its intrinsic character." Instead, as Street and dozens of recent historians, anthropologists, and theorists have argued, literacy must be understood in particular contexts.[5] It cannot be understood as a universal "it," but as changing depending on who uses it for what reasons under which particular historical and cultural conditions. The study of literacy, then, becomes the study of literacies. Understanding literacy from this perspective means recognizing that literacy always exists within particular ideological contexts. As Street argues, "[literacy] is a social construction, not a neutral technology: it varies from one culture or sub-group to another and its uses are embedded in relations of power and struggles over resources" (*Cross-Cultural* 29).

But the idea of literacy as a neutral technology, however effectively challenged by New Literacy Studies, seems to have lost none of its official appeal. Shirley Brice Heath, in her new introduction to the second edition of Harvey Graff's *Labyrinths of Literacy*, suggests an earlier optimism that has proved unfounded:

> In my foreword to the 1987 edition, I naively wrote: "Finally, he [Graff] has put to rest simple correlations linking literacy with higher earnings, increased civility, great citizen participation, and higher forms of thought" (p. vii). Certainly, in the past decade, these notions and their more simplistic companions [crime and illiteracy, literacy and employment] have not been "put to rest." Many programs still struggle to let their students know that in the economy of the final decade of the twen-

> tieth century, literacy skills alone will not offer even a job, and certainly increased literacy skills will not necessarily bring higher wages. In an era when fewer and fewer voters exercise the privilege of the ballot in the United States, citizen participation in voting does not correlate with literacy rates. When the best-educated societies in the world have the highest crime rates, it is hard to claim that literacy brings civility or positive attitudes toward one's family members and neighbors. (viii)

However untenable, these are links that are repeatedly invoked in these discourses, and they rely, I think, on a paradoxical argument about literacy that trumpets literacy as both neutral and as capable as producing enormous and intrinsically beneficial social change; paradoxical, because literacy is objective, but it's also really really good.

To explore this idea more fully, I turn to the early history of literacy studies, which fostered what Brian Street (*Cross-Cultural* 5) called "autonomous" theories of literacy. These theories argued that the cultural or individual acquisition of literacy produced enormous socially progressive changes, but that it produced those changes outside of an ideological framework. So, literacy can enact massive changes but neutrally, unfettered by politics or culture, for the inherent betterment of individuals and society in general. It is this combination that holds such particular appeal. Because a dominant and, from my perspective, successful project of literacy studies for the last twenty years has been to argue the shortcomings of such an autonomous perspective, I see no need to repeat those claims here—claims that I accept as standard and that stem from accepting literacy as always having an ideological function. I turn to early representations in the field of literacy studies not in order to critique them but to highlight certain ideas that, notwithstanding the two-decade challenge from literacy studies, continue to have enormous appeal for educational policy. In effect, I ask why those ideas have such official power even though within scholarly circles they have been largely abandoned as simplistic and overly decontextualized. My focus, then, is not on the theoretical weaknesses of an autonomous approach to literacy but on its enduring strength as a policy instrument.[6]

Part of literacy's seemingly inherent emotive power comes, I think, from the near necessity of transformation in its narratives. As a term, literacy easily invokes a story: It narrates personal, social, and cultural development. Like requited love in a romance novel, literacy signals movement into social and personal fulfillment. As with most persistent genres, the literacy narrative (Eldred and Mortensen) reflects dominant cultural perspectives, many of them in this case fitting under what Harvey Graff has called "the literacy myth": "The rise of literacy and its dissemination to the popular classes is associated with the triumph of light over darkness, of liberalism, democracy, and of universal unbridled progress. In social thought, therefore, these ideas relate to ideas of linear evolution and progression; literacy here takes its place among the other successes of modernity and rationality" (*Literacy Myth* xv). Evolution, progress, even rationality triumphing over irrationality, invoke a process of conversion, rebirth, inevitable change.

These are, of course, narratives of transformation, and transformation lies at the heart of most definitions of literacy. With the Citizenship Schools run by the Highlander Folk School, people used literacy to develop the skills they needed to become active citizens, emphasizing the agency of communities rather than of literacy, but in early academic discussions of literacy, literacy itself appears as the fundamental agent of change. Literacy changes the nonliterate on individual and social levels. Walter Ong, for example, writes the story of literacy acquisition as analogous to religious conversion:

> There is hardly an oral culture or predominantly oral culture left in the world today that is not somehow aware of the vast complex of power forever inaccessible without literacy. This awareness is agony for persons rooted in primary orality, who want literacy passionately but who also know very well that moving into the exciting world of literacy means leaving behind much that is exciting and deeply loved in the earlier oral world. We have to die to continue living. (35)

In Ong's description here, literacy itself acts as the agent of transformation, and people without it live lives of yearning. Such an approach decontextualizes literacy at the same time that it makes it almost concrete and palpable, an existing object ready to be picked up. It's part of a paradox in such representations of literacy: It is at once a neutral technology, a skill, but its acquisition changes everything, ultimately for the betterment of all.

Given this, identifying the ways in which literacy enacted transformation was an early concern of the field of literacy studies. In their pioneering essay "The Consequences of Literacy," Jack Goody and Ian Watt attempted to define the cultural and historic consequences of literacy. They proposed literacy as the crucial player in several social advances that occurred in ancient Greece at about the time that literacy became widespread. Literacy, by allowing for a permanent record through writing, made it possible to sift the cultural inheritance into two distinct categories: "fiction, error, and superstition"; and "elements of truth which can provide the basis for some more reliable and coherent explanation of the gods, the human past and the physical world" (49). Literacy put into the foreground the objective over the superstitious, so one consequence of literacy was that it facilitated the separation of truth from nontruth, history from myth. They also argued that literacy allowed for the development of logical thought: "it is difficult to believe that such a large and complex series of arguments as are presented in the *Republic*, for instance, or in Aristotle's *Analytics*, could possibly be created, or delivered, much less completely understood, in oral form" (p. 53).

The syllogism, which dissects thought into abstract categories, is, they argued, only possible with literacy, and such dissection leads to "the ordering of all the elements of experience into separate areas of intellectual activity" (p. 54). From this comes both "autonomous cognitive disciplines" and, crucially for my purposes, "the notion of the world of knowledge as transcending political units" (p. 55). Literacy, then, enacted massive social and epistemological changes, but it also transcended the messy world of human interaction, creating an idea of knowledge as "transcending political units."

In *Orality and Literacy*, Ong attempted to do for psychology what Goody and Watt did for culture—to demonstrate what literacy does to individuals who receive it in turning over their primarily oral (and thus contextually mired) culture. For Ong, as for Goody and Watt, literacy's effects are monumental and extensive, and literacy effects a psychological and cognitive reorientation. Ong often qualified the orality he discussed as a primary orality, one that has had no contact with a literate culture, but he went to some length to make his ideas about such orality relevant for contemporary readers. So, "to varying degrees many cultures and sub-cultures, even in a high-technology ambiance, preserve much of the mind set of primary orality" (11). Characteristic of "the psyche in oral cultures not only in the past but even today" are such features as "lack of introspectivity, of analytic prowess, of concern with the will as such, of a sense of difference between past and future" (30). This is a crucial move, because it allowed the historical cognitive distinctions between orality and literacy to be applied in contemporary cases. Literacy's consequences become not only a matter of historical concern, but a way of understanding and justifying present social dichotomies.

Ong's major distinctions between orality and literacy revolved around the idea of permanence. Oral peoples "commonly and in all likelihood universally consider words to have magical potency" (52) and rely on mnemonic devices for recall and knowledge transmission. Ong listed a number of characteristics of oral thought and expression, but more interesting than these characteristics are the ways he offset them from literacy and the claims he made for literacy. So, orality privileges the additive over the subordinative, while literacy provides "the analytic, reasoned subordination that characterizes writing" (39). Or, in making the claim that orality is "agonistically toned," Ong argued that "Writing fosters abstractions that disengage knowledge from the arena where human beings struggle with one another. It separates the knower from the known. By keeping knowledge embedded in the human lifeworld, orality situates knowledge within a context of struggle" (43–4). This fascinating description literally has literacy rising above the more petty arena of history, where conflicts distract from the discovery and identification of true knowledge. Like Goody and Watt, then, Ong attempted to rise above ideological concerns, aided by literacy's transcendent powers. At every step, literacy trumps orality's weak hand. In both arguments, literacy conferred the ability to escape ideology, to detach from day-to-day political and social struggles. One of literacy's transformations appears to be the development of objectivity, of analyzing outside one's subject position. Literacy's extraordinary power, in this case, stems from the idea that it literally changes the course of human history *and* the minds of the humans who make that history, but it does so as a neutral agent. On the one hand, without literacy, societies and individuals are doomed to exist in some sort of reduced state, whether economically, psychologically, or culturally. On the other hand, the radical transformation literacy allows is neutral, one that exists outside of local conditions and circumstances. As James Collins notes, "literacy is viewed as *sui generis,* as a socially neutral 'technology of the intellect' that in itself produces significant transformations in cultural orders as well as individual cognition" (70–71). Literacy's appeal in this formulation lies in its paradoxical ability to transform but to do so without transforming in the service of anything but itself. Literacy is an unvarnished and untainted good, acting outside political and partisan interest. On a fundamental level, then, advocating literacy is above argument, a position itself of considerable cultural power.

With the exception of Ong's caveat about the losses associated with moving from orality to literacy (something similar in his representation to a nostalgia for childhood), the transition is ultimately cause for considerable celebration. It follows, then, that to promote literacy as such an agent is inherently positive, because literacy will in turn promote overwhelmingly desirable changes. If, in turn, that literacy lies outside "the arena where human beings struggle with one another," then teaching literacy lies outside that arena as well. Like the knowledge it makes possible in Goody and Watt's description, teaching literacy transcends political units. From a policy perspective, then, promoting such a literacy has tremendous advantages, because it is the literacy and not the interests of individuals, institutions, governments, or businesses that matters. Whoever supports literacy education simply helps by creating a setting in which literacy can work its inevitable powers. Part of the appeal of this model of literacy is that literacy as an agent is morally neutral, carrying no inevitably controversial vision of an ought to be; it simply and straightforwardly improves cultures and individuals.

From an official perspective, this also means that what Deborah Brandt calls the "sponsors of literacy" will shine brightly as advocates of social progress and individual human betterment. Brandt describes such sponsors as

> any agents, local or distant, concrete or abstract, who enable, support, teach, and model, as well as recruit, regulate, suppress, or withhold, literacy—and gain advantage by it in some way . . . [I]t is useful to think about who or what underwrites occasions of literacy learning and use.

> Although the interests of the sponsor and the sponsored do not have to converge (and, in fact, may conflict), sponsors nevertheless set the terms for access to literacy and wield powerful incentives for compliance and loyalty. Sponsors are delivery systems for the economies of literacy, the means by which these forces present themselves to—and through—individual learners. They also represent the causes into which people's literacy usually gets recruited. (*Literacy* 19)

Brandt's description sketches the ways that sponsoring literacy works powerfully to advance the goals of the sponsor. However, when advocating literacy is necessarily positive for everyone, sponsors appear as altruistic agents of constructive social change. In the terms of the discourse of vocational education, businesses certainly stand to benefit, but their gain is everyone's, promoting national economic power, job satisfaction, and increased employment. Sponsoring literacy is a politically neutral act inherently improving society and its members, and sponsors of literacy are thus unassailable, unproblematic instruments of beneficial social transformation. Viewing literacy and its provision as a neutral *and* extremely positive agent thus carries enormous power from a policy perspective. Workplace literacy programs, GED education in prison, teaching adults and children to read and write in any context is always laudable, always good.

The idea of sponsorship, the idea that literacy might take its definition in part from the agents or agencies that promote it, suggests a level of analysis beyond what has been the longtime focus of New Literacy Studies. More or less developed in reaction to discussions that made literacy the necessary foundation for all that is progressive and good about western civilization and schooled ways of thinking, New Literacy Studies has emphasized an ethnographic methodology that focuses on what people do with literacy in particular local settings. This approach puts human agency, and not literacy, as an autonomous agent, at the center of literacy studies. Literacy, in effect, is defined by the people who use it, and it is always variable, always grounded in particular ideological and cultural contexts. This has proven an enormously valuable line of research and many of its conclusions are now more or less completely embraced in the complexity of ways scholars have come to understand literacy. However, it is, as Deborah Brandt and Katie Clinton argue, a limited perspective. Arguing that "Figuring out what things are doing with people in a setting becomes as important as figuring out what people are doing with things in a setting"(348), Brandt and Clinton propose the concept of "literacy-in-action" to develop a fuller representation of literacy as a social practice:

> The double meaning of our term is intentional. We want to retain attention to the role of literacy in human action: how readers and writers

> mediate their social world through literate practice (i.e., literate action as part of our action). But we also want to consider the additional question of how literacy acts as a social agent, as an independent mediator (i.e., literacy, itself, in action). (349)

Literacy practices not only take place in particular settings, but "historically have been embedded in the objects" that exist in those settings, objects such as documents, machines, and instruments involved in getting a loan at a bank, which emphasize the loan not only as a local activity but one tied to a much larger economic framework. Analyzing such objects as actually having literacy practices embedded within them can allow for an examination of "how they deliver meanings from other places and transform local actions into meanings bound for or relevant to other places" (349).

One of Brandt and Clinton's points, as I read their article, is that the turn to the local has engendered a myopia about the meaning of literacy practices, which have been emphasized as primarily local activities with local meanings. That perspective perhaps helps explain what Joyce Kim calls a "serious limitation of New Literacy Studies, . . . its evasion, in many cases, of concrete suggestions for literacy practitioners, especially classroom teachers." Kim argues that NLS does not provide a way for teachers to negotiate the demands made upon them by "the increasingly narrow constraints of the school system," which still operates with an autonomous model of literacy. However, I would argue further, following Brandt and Clinton, that another reason such models have been difficult to translate into understanding literacy within a classroom context is that the emphasis on local meanings of literacy does not reflect in helpful ways what necessarily occurs in a literacy classroom. In such settings, almost by definition, literacy takes its meaning not from the actual classroom but from something, or some place, outside that classroom, not only from sponsors but also from a whole host of cultural expectations surrounding literacy. That is, the meaning of literacy practices in a classroom is never only, or even primarily, local. Pedagogy is a deictic act, always pointing somewhere else. That somewhere else, I think, is toward the constructed world, the world in which it can be said that education works, a rhetorically created world that justifies the teaching of particular literacy practices.

All of which is to stress, again, that understanding what literacy practices mean in educational settings requires that we make a rhetorical turn in addition to whatever empirical turn currently favored in ethnographic studies of literacy. This is not to malign those ethnographic studies, because they have exquisitely demonstrated the central proposition that literacy is not a monolithic and stable entity, that people use literacy for different purposes, that what people do with literacy fundamentally shapes what literacy is. But as Brandt and Clinton note, literacy can act on people just as people can act on literacy; in educational settings, literacy is *supposed* to act on people, and turning to the educational rhetoric that shapes any classroom (regardless of whether a teacher is aware of it) can help us understand how literacy practices become wrapped up in educational understandings, whatever they are, of the worlds in which we need to live, the worlds we teach about when we teach about literacy.

This calls, I think, for an understanding of educational literacy practices that always links those practices to the futures they are supposed to enable. I understand literacy instruction as more than helping people learn to decode and encode print. For me, literacy instruction means teaching particular sorts of literacy practices, which David Barton and Mary Hamilton define as "the general cultural ways of utilizing written language which people draw upon in their lives . . . they are not observable behaviors since they also involve values, attitudes, feelings, social relationships" (7). From this perspective, I am a literacy instructor as much in my freshman writing courses and my graduate seminars as I am in a community literacy class of mostly nonreaders. In all these settings, I am teaching literacy practices as Barton and Hamilton define them. Although I do not agree with the arguments that Ong and Goody and Watt make about the inherent power of literacy, it is useful to remember that we teach literacy practices because we want those practices to make a difference, to effect some sort of positive transformation in our students. I study the teaching of literacy practices outside the university, but perhaps uniquely, literacy practices are the content of English and composition studies, my home disciplines. Above all we study and teach ways of understanding, analyzing, and producing written language, all of them involving "values, attributes, feelings, social relationships."

As such, a very brief look at moments in the history of composition and English studies highlights ways in which conflicts and anxieties about literacy practices have been central to disciplinary formation. Trying to define and defend proper literacy practices—the ones we should be teaching and enacting and expecting from our students—has been a central part of what has driven research and teaching in the field. Here, for example, Adams Sherman Hill describes the causes of failure for almost half the 316 students taking the fifth Harvard admissions exam in English composition in 1879:

> Some of the unsuccessful . . . avowed or displayed an utter ignorance of the subject-matter: several, for example, confounded Steele with Sir Roger de Coverly, others the period of Queen Anne with that of Richard Coeur de Lion, others the style of "Henry Esmond" the novel, with the manners of Henry Esmond, the hero of the novel. Some . . . showed such utter ignorance of punctuation as to put commas at the end of complete sentences, or between words that no rational being would separate from one another; and a few began sentences with small letters,

> or began every word with a capital letter. Many, a larger number than usual, spelled as if starting a spelling reform, each for himself. (49–50)

Hill then lists dozens of words misspelled on the test, "including vain attempts to reproduce proper names that were printed on the examination paper itself," and concludes:

> Of these mistakes some are evidently much graver than others; but some of the worst were found in several books, and not a few are apparently due to an unconscious effort to represent to the eye a vicious pronunciation. Many books were deformed by grossly ungrammatical or profoundly obscure sentences, and some by absolute illiteracy. (50)

I quote Hill at length here for two purposes: First, the chronicle of student failures, ending with a claim that some exams demonstrated "absolute illiteracy," itself becomes a definition of proper literacy practices. Literacy in this sense encompasses correct identification of literary figures, periods, and terms, proper punctuation, correct spelling and mechanics, clear prose, and even standard pronunciation. Second, Hill, and other writers, represents these failures as a social threat, creating what has been called "the first literacy crisis" (Spear 335). Later evaluations of Harvard's writing program repeat what is a general theme in Hill's early report, that such ill-prepared students are hobbling a respected university. As an 1892 report put it, "The College, instead of being what its name implies—a seminary of higher education,—becomes, in thus far, a mere academy, the instructors in which are subjected to the drudgery of teaching the elements" (Adams, Godkin, and Quincy 96). The solution, for Hill, the 1892 report, and generations of subsequent critics of basic instruction in whatever form, was clear: Students needed to be better prepared for college before they arrived, so that universities could concentrate on the work they were supposed to do.

This sort of representation of "deformed" literacy practices as a threat to the scholarly integrity of academic institutions, and sometimes social structures themselves, has been standard in the history of composition and English studies. As Thomas Miller argues, the formation of English studies can be traced to a wider readership stemming from the development of the periodical press in eighteenth-century England and to a dramatic change, especially in provincial areas, in the demographics of the student body. Educators could no longer assume an elite language usage, and part of the early mission of English education in such settings became teaching students a proper orientation to language and literacy. The development of English studies in Great Britain throughout the nineteenth and twentieth centuries can be tied to anxieties about class-based and feminized ways of reading (see, for example, Ball, Kenny, and Gardiner, and Sampson). Anne Ruggles Gere notes that the personal and informal ways of reading literature advocated within early twentieth-century women's clubs became useful feminized foils for definers of English studies in the United States, and the development of basic writing in the 1960s and 1970s is replete with discussions, which carry on to the present, about the sort of institutional and social threats basic writers present (as well, of course, of the reverse: of the ways in which basic writing programs support an egalitarian and democratic belief in providing educational opportunities across social divides). Robert Scholes's argument about New Criticism, that it "functioned to construct for literature a safe place outside the pressures of the marketplace and the strict demands of scientific study (and above the realm of politics and strife as well)" (27), suggests a regular pattern in institutionally condoned approaches to reading: that they are often in part a response to ways of reading that appear debased or threatening.

In all these cases, anxiety about or valorization of literacy practices entails a particular conception of the social order, a conception that becomes inscribed into the curricula and its instructional practices. Thus, Hill's lament about the literacy impairment of incoming freshmen, while superficially focused on errors, also plays directly into, among other things, a debate about the proper goals of language education in secondary schools and university, being specifically an attack on a classical curriculum that doesn't prepare students for facility in their native language. At stake in Hill's discussion are the very principles of higher education, which becomes threatened by the need to teach what should have been taught elsewhere. There is always something at stake in educational discussions of literacy practices, thus, there will always be a conflict within them. To state otherwise, to claim literacy as a neutral set of skills that can be taught in value-free ways, is more than simply naïve, it is itself a strong and even dominant ideological argument within current debates about literacy.

I emphasize the development of English studies as part of a claim that an analysis of discourses of literacy merits attention from scholars concerned with the teaching of literacy practices (such as those within English studies). Understanding our teaching of literacy practices as ideologically located in relation to other literacy practices and pedagogies presents a way of viewing our teaching that takes us significantly beyond the classroom; it also provides us a way to critique and resist the discourses that, even so, continue to shape our practices. In the process, this model of what I am calling educational literacy practices shifts the orientation of the study of literacy practices, away from the focus on local settings that has been the primary emphasis of New Literacy Studies over the past quarter century, and toward the rhetorical construction of the future world, those literacy practices are designed to facilitate.

Although, then, the discourses I examine typically move well beyond an emphasis on teaching adults to read and write—that is, well beyond the notion invoked by the phrase *adult literacy*—they always remain discourses about literacy, discourses which value particular literacy practices over others and that support that valuing in part through their various constructions of the "world in which we need to live" ("Myles Horton's Talk" n.p.). The discourses about literacy practices within these sites cannot be seen as separate from the lived literacy practices on the workplace, say, or in a prison (though, as I shall argue, the differences between the discourses and the lived experiences are important); rather, these discourses are literacy practices in themselves, constructing, but also constructed by, the institutions and societies they seek to enact. The ability to read and write might be presented, in some cases, as an inarguable and inherent social good, but that ability by itself always remains a "small thing" (ibid. n.p.) next to the visions of social order these discourses intend to invoke.

THE ADULT AND THE EDUCATION IN ADULT EDUCATION

Breaking down the phrase *adult education* allows us to see claims made about adulthood and education implied within practices and discourses. Straightforwardly, of course, adult education is simply definable as any education that occurs with a student or students over eighteen. However, the phrase is considerably more loaded than this and somewhat more exclusive as well: College professors rarely label themselves as adult educators, nor do yoga teachers or master-gardener instructors. There are great and particular resonances around the idea of adulthood and the idea of education, resonances that suggest as well goals for the societies we imagine students living in and enabling.[7]

What is the education in adult education? These discourses often set themselves apart from traditional types of education, relying on a trope common in the history of adult education, namely, that adult education is an improvement over other sorts of education, and that to engage in adult education, then, is to play the role of both social and educational reformer. Adult education transcends traditional forms, because the education is more practical, or because the students are more intrinsically interested, or because the teachers have overt social goals.

Who is the adult in adult education? In addition to a simple chronological definition, the adult can be understood to refer not to the students themselves but to the goals of education: That is, adult education teaches people how to assume roles implied by various concepts of adulthood. This is certainly apparent in my exploration of vocational education, correctional education, and Highlander. Each discourse makes central the social role the student is supposed to assume because of the educational process—worker, noncriminal taxpayer, first-class citizen. Behind those roles, of course, are social visions, goals about the world in which we need to live.

In his groundbreaking *The Meaning of Adult Education*, published in 1926 and recognized as a central text in the history of adult education, Eduard Lindemann highlighted the definition of adulthood and the notion of adult education as reform:

> . . . *education is life*—not a mere preparation for an unknown kind of future living. Consequently all static concepts of education which relegate the learning process to the period of youth are abandoned. The whole of life is learning, therefore education can have no endings. This new venture is called *adult education*—not because it is confined to adults but because adulthood, maturity, defines its limits. (6)

Lindemann is careful here, and throughout his book, to emphasize the positive ways that adult education is different from static concepts of education. For Lindemann, a good deal of the power of adult education stems from its challenge to a moribund educational practice. Such a position gives adult education an inherent theoretical power, imagining as it does an educative practice that presumes interest in learning and relevance as primary values, and it's a position common in the discourses I examine, which often represent themselves as anathema to standard ways of understanding education. This is increased by the fact that typically (although not for Lindemann) adult education emphasizes populations that have been identified as marginalized. Lindemann is also concerned here with adulthood and maturity, recognizing that these things must mean *something* for adult education to have any meaning. The discourses I examine rely—often but not always implicitly—on particular ways of understanding what it means to be an adult, a concept linked as well to what it means to be a citizen. The differences in approaches highlight the notion that adulthood and citizenship are themselves cultural constructions. How both get defined is a central issue for the discourses I examine.

For Lindemann, adult education required an understanding of learning that challenged education at all levels. Traditional models emphasized an overreliance on "texts and secondary facts" over experience (11), on "pecuniary gain" (13), and on specialism as a central aspect of the curriculum. Such models could never truly educate adults because they narrowly defined education as a youthful enterprise important only insofar as it helped students prepare for adulthood. The focus on *adult education* meant that education could not be parceled off and defined differently according to the age of the students. Rather, education needed to think in terms of an adult who could act and participate socially in ways that reflected self and group interests: "Orthodox education may be a preparation for life but adult education is an agitating instrumentality for changing life" (165). Adult education's lack of familiar institutional constraints allowed a space from which to reconsider exactly what it is that education should aspire to: "Adult learners attend classes voluntarily and they leave whenever the teaching falls below the standard of interest. What they learn converges upon life, not upon commencement and diploma. The external tokens of education are removed so that the learning process may stand or fall on its intrinsic merits" (178–79). In short, adult education is everything that Lindemann claims traditional education is not, starting with educational.

Like most ideals, Lindemann's portrait of adult education in *The Meaning of Adult Education* exists in part to demonstrate the shortcomings of actual practice, stemming from a "desire somehow to free education from stifling ritual, formalism and institutionalism" (xiv), a "hope that some day education might be brought out of college halls and into the lives of the people who do the work of the world" (xv). This has been part of the power and the meaning of adult education throughout the twentieth century and to the present: By emphasizing the ways in which it is an improvement over traditional models of education, theorists, and practitioners of adult education position themselves, not only as teachers, but as reformers, educationally and socially. For many (including me), that position is a compelling draw. Like others, I have been attracted to teaching in sites of nontraditional adult education for precisely the reasons that Mary-Ellen Boyle notes is common in the field: "The field attracts those who are disillusioned by the politics and rigidity of the traditional educational system, yet those who see themselves as providing a much-needed service to a population that has been marginalized" (33). Working as an adult educator has offered me a chance to practically and theoretically re-evaluate assumptions about education I learned from my own schooling and my teaching in official institutions at the same time that I have believed that my work has a positive social outcome. From a practitioner's perspective, this combination can be one of the most attractive aspects of involvement within adult education.

Of course, adult education can be understood to serve marginalized populations in often conflicting ways. As Alan Rogers puts it in *Teaching Adults* (2002): "we need to decide whether the education we provide for adults is to help them to reconcile themselves to their lot in the slums (make them happier), to help a few of them to escape the slums, or to help those who live in the slums to change those slums in their own ways rather than in our ways. I know where I stand in this scenario" (3). The rhetoric of reform and service can easily elide these differences, however, emphasizing the practice of adult education, especially tied to adult literacy programs, as an inherent social good. Boyle (48–60) notes that workplace literacy programs, a critical component of the recent discourse of vocational education, accrue benefits for employers based upon the symbolism of providing classes for undereducated adults, even with a lack of evaluative measures of success. Programs thus carry importance for the image of altruism and commitment to employees which they convey, even if, as Boyle suggests, "literacy education may be the mechanism of choice because of the messages it imparts about educational deficits and the 'kind of person' needed in contemporary workplaces . . . [T]he new schoolhouse thus creates consent to continued inequality" (105). In Rogers's terms, this is probably closer to an education designed to reconcile than one designed to help people escape. In any case, it is not (and, frankly, could hardly be expected to be, given that it is sponsored by an employer) an education based on helping adults change fundamentally the conditions of their own lives. Still, simply invoking the idea of adult education can enhance the notion of reform, of involvement in an inherently socially positive process. Borrowing from Lindemann's title, that connotation has become one of the meanings of adult education.

Lindemann's idea that adult education be considered as such "because adulthood, maturity, defines its limits" (6) highlights the notion that the field has necessarily been concerned with how education should be understood differently when its subjects are adults and not children. Malcolm Knowles proposed, in fact, that teaching in the field be considered *andragogy* rather than *pedagogy* to resist the roots of the term *pedagogy* in its focus on children, a proposal that has been taken up by many in the field of adult education. Adults, Knowles wanted to emphasize, are different from children, and approaches to teaching them should reflect that. The differences Knowles proposed—noting that, for example, adults are more self-directive than children, that they learn more from experience, and so forth—often do not seem like clear distinctions (see Jarvis 90–94), but I am less interested in pointing out the shortcomings of Knowles's definitions than I am in pointing out the necessity for theories and practitioners in the field to somehow define adulthood and citizenship, implicitly or explicitly. Definitions of adulthood are, in part, discursive constructions, and they change according to the discourses addressing the issue. One could claim that all of the discourses I examine emphasize the necessity of adults to take responsibility for their own lives, but this merely shifts the ambiguity away from *adulthood* to what it means to be responsible. Horton's conception of responsibility, for example, included two possibilities at odds with ideas of responsibility in vocational and correctional education: A citizen truly working toward democracy, Horton believed, should be willing to both risk a secure job and, if necessary, go to jail. The definitions of *adulthood* and *citizenship* that define the limits of the dominant discourse of vocational education are primarily economic: mature adult citizens work, and their work is in service of national economic priorities. In the dominant discourse of correctional education, the defining limits emphasize an individual morality. Mature adults take responsibility for their decisions and recognize the effects they have on others, and they become productive, tax-paying, noncriminal citizens. In any case, the kinds of people adults should be becomes a critical part of the process of transformation entailed by educative acts.

Likewise, the role that education has in creating citizens is fairly contentious across these discourses. Official definitions of citizenship reflect, obviously, official priorities, and these include a strong economy, a reliable and economically supportable workforce, control of crime, and punishment of criminals. Official definitions of citizenship do not, typically, privilege dissent and activist challenges to governmental and industrial power, both essential in the conception of citizenship fostered at Highlander. Likewise, the discourses I explore must be clear about what students lack as proper citizens, and how they go about this, too, is highly various. Constraints on citizenship from the perspective of Highlander come from official limits on democracy, within communities (as with the literacy laws disenfranchising African Americans) or within workplaces, and to claim citizenship means actively resisting such constraints by struggling against them. Within the dominant discourses of vocational education and correctional education, students are not proper citizens because of individual shortcomings that are also obstacles to official priorities. They are unskilled, or they have particular cognitive deficits that incline them toward criminality; they are, in effect, students who can't. They become citizens when those shortcomings are remediated and they can better work in service of those priorities. These discourses, then, engage in struggles over what it means to be a citizen and how education plays a role in creating adults and citizens.

Teachers, too, must engage in this struggle, for how are we to understand the relationship of our work as teachers to our responsibility as citizens? Should we accept official mandates that determine the sorts of work we should do and the kinds of approaches that are not legitimate? Should our teaching challenge those mandates and help develop students who are more likely to engage in the critique of official systems? For most of us, these last two will appear as rhetorical questions with obvious answers (respectively, "of course not," and "of course"), but most of us will always be pulled, in practice, between those two poles, especially those of us who teach in official educational institutions. How we understand and deal with that tension—a tension that will not go away—is central to how we see our citizenship reflected within our teaching. In part, I see this book as suggesting the permanent obstacles in the way of achieving an activist ideal of citizen-teacher, as well as trying to figure out how to work toward that ideal anyway, even though we'll never reach it.

BASIL BERNSTEIN, PEDAGOGIC DISCOURSE, AND THE WORLD IN WHICH WE NEED TO LIVE

Throughout this chapter, I have argued that educational discourse always implies a social order, always has in mind a future world toward which it is relevant. Myles Horton's idea that Highlander keeps its "eyes firmly on the ought to be" ("Myles Horton's Talk" n.p.) shapes my claim that all educational discourse focuses on an *ought to be,* and I have attempted to explore that vision of the future as a necessary rhetorical feature of educational discourse. Educational literacy practices likewise involve themselves in working toward those futures, and what 'literacy' means, then, changes, according to those futures. Likewise, I suggest that complexities around the meanings of "adult" and of "education" in adult education are intrinsically connected to an idea what an adult should be, what social function an adult should fulfill. These social prerogatives for education I have also referred to as the cannon in the classroom, present in our classrooms because no matter what we aspire to teach and why we teach it, we are also teaching with discourses and inside institutions that project their own goals, their own *ought to bes*, into our classrooms as well.

In all these discussions, I have been highly influenced by the work of Basil Bernstein, whose theory of the pedagogic device explores the creation and movement of what he calls pedagogic discourse. I have come to understand Bernstein's pedagogic discourse as a close synonym for educational rhetoric, and his model provides a detailed description of the centrality of a moral vision, ideas about the proper shape of the social order, within pedagogic discourse. Several aspects of Bernstein's last work are critical throughout my book, and because Bernstein's ideas, and prose, are so complicated, I withhold other discussions of his work until I am sure they are directly relevant to my own analyses. Here, I will discuss two concepts within Bernstein's work—regulative discourse and recontextualization—both of which have shaped my understandings in this chapter and throughout this book.

Briefly, before a fuller explanation, pedagogic discourse appears whenever a question about how one teaches something arises. At that moment, a disciplinary or professional discourse (Bernstein's typical example is the discipline of physics) changes fundamentally, so that the discourse of teaching physics is not the same as the discourse of physics. This movement and change, central to Bernstein's theory, he calls recontextualization, the knowledge from the primary field recontextualized as it becomes a subject for teaching. Pedagogic discourse consists of two parts, Bernstein argues: An instructional discourse focuses on the methods and structures of teaching and learning, but that discourse is embedded in what he terms a regulative discourse, a moral discourse, a discourse of the social order. This regulative discourse shapes and directs the instructional discourse, which is to say that in Bernstein's model, the vision of the social order grounds our understanding of how, what, whom, even where to teach. Bernstein, then, provides a comprehensive perspective on the arguments I have been exploring throughout this chapter: that education always points toward an *ought to be*, that the meanings of education and of literacy and adulthood within educational discourse can *never* be understood without exploring the vision of the future, that what we decide to teach, and how we decide to teach it, is always shaped by claims about the sort of world in which we need to live.

Before I turn to a fuller analysis of Bernstein's pedagogic device, I will illustrate some of its general principles broadly using basic examples. Imagine a visit to a knee specialist following a knee injury. Your doctor projects an X-ray of your knee, using a diagram or perhaps a plastic model to describe the extent of the injury; you learn some technical terms, some basic leg anatomy, and a bit about the physical process of repair and recovery. You leave the specialist's office having been taught something about the knee and knee injuries and something about the related medical discourses. You also leave the office—especially if the visit goes well—having reconfirmed certain ideas about the authority of medical doctors, about proper doctor/patient relations, about your distance from particular forms of specialized knowledge, lessons about your own relationship with this doctor, about the medical system and the shape of your social role within it.

This situation presents a simplistic description of recontextualization: Here, the knee specialist takes knowledge learned in medical school or in further specialized and ongoing training and experience, and turns it into knowledge for you, the patient. That recontextualization changes the knowledge significantly, because it is not knowledge only about the knee but also about the social situation within which the knowledge is communicated. It becomes, in addition to being what Bernstein calls an "instructional discourse" (*Pedagogy, Symbolic Control* 13) about the knee, a discourse about the social order, what Bernstein calls a "regulative discourse." (ibid. 13) It is a moral discourse because it defines the proper sort of ethical relationship between you and your doctor, it suggests the correctness of the boundaries that separate you, and it sanctions knowledge as properly belonging with some actors and not others. Both the instructional and the regulative discourse are aspects of what he refers to as pedagogic discourse, and he argues that within the discourse, the regulative discourse is primary: The regulative discourse, that is, determines the shape of the instructional discourse.[8]

Now, imagine an elementary school reading teacher. This teacher relies on ideas, theories, and methods learned in part through teacher education programs (and of course from other teachers and from personal experiences). However, that knowledge about teaching reading, learned in teacher education, has to be brought into a specific reading classroom, a process that changes it fundamentally. Likewise, the knowledge as it appeared in the teacher-education courses also has been recontextualized from another site, a specialist site focused on the production of knowledge through, say, research done regarding children's brains as they learn, or theories about cognitive development, or controlled studies about particular ways children learn to read. This list could of course go on, but my point here is that movement of knowledge from the site of knowledge production (for Bernstein, the "field of production" [ibid. 13]) to the site of teacher-training and educational programs (Bernstein's "field of recontextualisation" [ibid. 13]) changes that knowledge significantly, a change which occurs again when the knowledge moves into the classroom—for Bernstein "the field of reproduction" (ibid. 13). And as with my example of the knee specialist, when the discourse moves from the field of production to the field of recontextualization, it becomes shaped primarily by a regulative discourse. In this case, teachers in training learn what kinds of knowledge are valid to consider as teachers, which methods are sanctioned and by whom, how to understand their goals as teachers, how to think about teacher-student relationships (as well as a host of other relationships in school). For Bernstein, these are more than tangential considerations—they are, rather, ideas that fundamentally shape the knowledge presented, primary, determining the shape of the instructional discourse.

I present this brief and simplified model of Bernstein's terms the pedagogic device as an optimistic introduction to a more detailed discussion, because trying to paraphrase and selectively quote Bernstein, I have found (both as a reader of texts attempting to do that, and especially as a writer aiming at accessibility), is nearly as difficult as initially reading Bernstein. I certainly find it intimidating even to attempt a summary of any aspect of Bernstein's rich and extensive theories. For one thing, when he was alive, he kept careful watch over his commentators, often responding at great length to essays about his work with detailed refutations of their interpretations. It's hard not to imagine his ghost scanning my own discussion for its inevitable shortcomings. For another, Bernstein's models are developed from, and refer back to, four decades of research in which each idea became the starting place for his next exploration, and thus to write about his latest work requires a perspective on his own intellectual history. He described the point of each paper he wrote as creating what he called "productive imperfection . . . a conceptual tension which provides the potential for development. So for me the papers are the means of discovering what I shall be thinking, not what I am thinking"; he acknowledged, in an understatement, that while this helped him, "it can lead to difficulty for those using the work" (ibid. 211). Finally, that research, up to his last work, is often written up in prose that even fellow sociologists have called "virtually unreadable" (Walford, qtd. in ibid. xv); unreadable is too strong a word for me, but the density of his prose makes reading his work arduous and adds to the anxiety of interpreting and summarizing it. In addition to summarizing Bernstein, I am also recontextualizing his work, moving it to another context in which I find it productive, a process that no doubt produces inherent changes to the meanings of his work. The history of what Parlo Singh calls "monstrous readings" (571) of Bernstein (particularly with regard to his early theories about elaborated and restricted codes) and Bernstein's own caustic criticism of commentators who suffer from what he calls "reading omnipotence," which denotes "a clinical condition which renders texts which disturb one's own interpretation unread, even when they are [read]" (ibid. 177), simply adds to the riskiness of reinterpreting Bernstein.

Bernstein's final work included an extensive discussion of the pedagogic device, described by Parlo Singh as "a model for analyzing the processes by which discipline-specific or domain-specific expert knowledge is converted or pedagogised to constitute school knowledge" (572). The pedagogic device, according to Bernstein, "regulates fundamentally the communication it makes possible, and in this way it acts selectively on the meaning potential. The device continuously regulates the ideal universe of potential pedagogic meanings in such a way as to restrict or enhance their realisations" (*Pedagogy, Symbolic Control* 27). The meaning potential refers to "the potential discourse that is available to be pedagogised" (ibid. 27). So, the pedagogic device turns potential meaning into pedagogic discourse; simply stated, the pedagogic device chooses, from seemingly limitless possibilities, what will be taught and changes it into something that can be taught. For an act of pedagogy to occur, something must be taught, to someone, in some fashion, with some way of assessing success. The model of the pedagogic device provides a way of exploring how this process occurs.

Bernstein's pedagogic device has three primary fields: the production of discourse, its recontextualization, and its reproduction, each of which operates according to particular sets of rules. My primary interest at this point is in recontextualization, but I return to a fuller discussion of the entire pedagogic device in my conclusion, to understand how teachers and scholars might act to resist, even as they involve themselves within, official processes of social and cultural reproduction. I will withhold, then, a description of this until it becomes necessary to understand my argument, simply to avoid overloading my readers with technical explanations for which the purposes will only become clear in my conclusion. (Readers who want to know now, of course, can turn to the conclusion.)

My interest in recontextualization stems from the fact that I am primarily studying texts that Bernstein would likely locate in this field. (This becomes more complicated in the case of Highlander, perhaps because in

Highlander's case the boundaries between the fields are not as clearly defined.) In the field of recontextualization, recontextualizing rules "regulate the formation of specific pedagogic discourse" (ibid. 28). These rules describe the "process of delocating a discourse . . . that is, taking a discourse from its original site of effectiveness and moving it to a pedagogic site" (32). Through the process of recontextualization, a clear distinction arises between, for example, "physics as activities in the field of production of a discourse, and physics as a pedagogic discourse" (34) in such a way that "Pedagogic discourse is not physics, chemistry, or psychology. Whatever it is, it cannot be identified with the discourses it transmits" (32). Here's a fuller description of this process:

> As the discourse moves from its original site to its new positioning as pedagogic discourse, a transformation takes place. The transformation takes place because every time a discourse moves from one position to another, there is a space in which ideology can play. No discourse ever moves without ideology at play. As this discourse moves, it becomes ideologically transformed; it is not the same discourse any longer. I will suggest that as this discourse moves, it is transformed from an actual discourse, from an unmediated discourse to an imaginary discourse. As pedagogic discourse appropriates various discourses, unmediated discourses are transformed into mediated, virtual or imaginary discourses. From this point of view, pedagogic discourse selectively creates *imaginary subjects*. . . . Pedagogic discourse is constructed by a recontextualising principle which selectively appropriates, relocates, refocuses and relates other discourses to constitute its own order. In this sense, pedagogic discourse can never be identified with any of the discourses it has recontextualised. (33)[9]

Within pedagogic discourse, Bernstein argues, are two discourses, an instructional discourse, "the discourse which creates specialised skills and their relationships to another," and the regulative discourse, "the moral discourse which creates order, relations and identity . . . [T]he instructional discourse is embedded in the regulative discourse, and . . . the regulative discourse is the dominant discourse. Pedagogic discourse is the rule which leads to the embedding of one discourse in another, to create one text, to create *one* discourse" (32).

It's this embedding of the instructional within the regulative—which I read as similar to the embedding of educational methods within educational goals, the *ought to be*—that I find such a compelling aspect of recontextualization. Under Bernstein's model, the regulative discourse "produces *the order in the instructional discourse*" and thus constitutes "the whole order within pedagogic discourse" (34). So, when a discourse is removed from its original site and transformed into a pedagogic discourse, it must address questions such as: How should the discourse be presented to novices? How fast? In what order? What material should be used? While these are aspects of an instructional discourse, they are also, according to Bernstein, aspects of the regulative discourse. The transformation must also take into account, among other issues, the setting in which teaching and learning will occur, the social distribution of teachers and students, the methods of evaluation and mastery, and the legitimate uses of the discourse once acquired. Recontextualization "not only recontextualises the *what* of pedagogic discourse, what discourse is to become subject and content of pedagogy. It also recontextualises the *how*; that is *the theory of instruction* . . . Both are elements of regulative discourse" (34-5). To study a pedagogic discourse according to the model that Bernstein provides is to study, primarily, a regulative discourse, a discourse of the social order. As I state it here, to study educational methods, theories, and practices is to study, primarily, a rhetorical construction of the world as it ought to be.

Bernstein's visual representation of pedagogic discourse emphasizes that relationship:

$$\frac{\text{INSTRUCTIONAL DISCOURSE (ID)}}{\text{REGULATIVE DISCOURSE (RD)}}$$

He uses this model to show that the instructional discourse is embedded within, and an outgrowth of, the regulative discourse. Thus, fundamental to any pedagogic discourse, be it of physics or of literacy, is this regulative discourse. That regulative discourse, of course, has everything to do with the world for which the pedagogies are presumed relevant. It's a projection of that world, I would argue, which is why I would say that in the case of Highlander's discourse and practice, the regulative discourse is foregrounded, acknowledged, and embraced as primary, while in the dominant models of vocational education the regulative discourse is avoided, shaded by a discussion of an instructional discourse that corresponds directly with a supposedly existent world of work. Or, to restate this, in the case of Highlander, teaching adults to read and write has no intrinsic value but is meaningful because it will enable those adults to play a role in a democratic society; in the case of the dominant discourse of vocational education, increasing students' literacy skills—broadly defined as competencies—will help them fit in better to a world already in place, will make them more secure in their employment, and will help maintain the economic superiority of the United States.

A fuller example from the field of correctional education might clarify my point here. Correctional education, by definition, is supposed to *correct*, and typically that correction is emphasized on an individual level, the changing of a criminal into a noncriminal. There is virtually no attempt, at any level, to avoid the moral nature of education in prison; rather, the central tensions revolve around exactly what moral project—what regulative discourse—should shape the field. On one level, of course, prisoners are, by virtue of having been imprisoned, socially defined as criminals. But the extent to which criminality is an individual attribute is a central issue in the field. In the most extreme representations, something exists that could almost be called a criminal mind, a set of psychological characteristics that all criminals share, especially regarding their relationship to others in society. A much less extreme and more widely accepted version of this also exists, whereby prisoners are said to share—not universally but typically—what become referred to as social cognitive deficits, which include a lack of empathy for others and a lack of understanding of the consequences of one's actions. In either of these versions, correction, that is, rehabilitation, is a process that works on an individual level. Others in the field, however, include the prison itself as an object of correction. For education to work in prisons, these writers argue, prisons themselves must be restructured to provide more opportunities for individual decision making and communal living, among other issues. Finally, another strand in the field, heavily influenced by critical pedagogy, makes the injustices of prisons and the criminal justice system a central issue of schooling; teaching in this model is a process of helping students confront and change an inherently corrupt system.

What each of these approaches has in common, however, is that the moral project they embark on openly shapes the instructional practices they advocate. That is, the regulative discourse, the vision of the social order, makes what happens in the particular classrooms relevant. One of the reasons the field of correctional education is such a rich discursive site, in fact, is that the relationship between a regulative discourse and an instructional discourse within the field is especially vivid and powerful. Within the discourse of correctional education, the differences about the sorts of worlds the educational process seeks to invoke, the worlds in which we need to live, are especially stark, but the overtly moral dimension in each of them is always apparent.

I'll return to my earlier example of the elementary reading teacher as a way of describing why control over the pedagogic device can be understood as a central struggle within education in general. Read the No Child Left Behind Act of 2001 (NCLB) and you'll likely be struck by the constant repetition of the phrases "scientifically based research" and "scientifically based reading instruction." These phrases point to the field of production, and research engaged in there becomes legitimized by the degree to which it meets the demands of "science" as defined within NCLB.[10] The legitimization of pedagogical methods and teaching directives through science proclaims them as neutral and objective, but it also serves to control what is acceptable and unacceptable within the fields of recontextualization and reproduction. If it passes muster as science, it is acceptable. I interpret this as a fairly transparent attempt to assert official control over how reading gets taught in individual classrooms. Bernstein suggests why control over the pedagogic device should be such a contentious issue:

> Essentially the pedagogic device is a symbolic ruler, ruling consciousness, in the sense of having power over it, and ruling, in the sense of measuring the legitimacy of the realisations of consciousness. The questions become whose ruler, what consciousness? In this way there is always a struggle between social groups for ownership of the device. Those who own the device own the means of perpetuating their power through discursive means and establishing, or attempting to establish, their own ideological representations. (*Pedagogy, Symbolic Control* 114)

Bernstein's caveat here, "attempting to establish," is critical, I think, for teachers to understand how they might act in educational situations within which official ownership is asserted more and more forcefully. He hints there at what I will examine more closely in the last chapter—that there are places where teachers and scholars can act to resist initiatives designed in large part to limit their own agency.

The focus on recontextualization also becomes a way of understanding what happens when literacy becomes recontextualized into a pedagogic discourse. This is a different process than, say, the recontextualization of physics into a pedagogic discourse of physics, since literacy is not primarily practiced within a specific specialized field (although my discussion of NCLB earlier suggests one way of thinking about literacy within a specialized discipline). However, literacy is nonetheless recontextualized. In all the discourses I examine, literacy is *imagined* as an aspect of the transformation that education can potentially engender, and that imagined literacy becomes the basis for the literacy practices encouraged within the educational discourse. Part of the way literacy is imagined in these discourses is in relation to literacy practices within noneducational sites. Teaching literacy practices, that is, matters because those practices matter somewhere else, outside of school. I see the justification of the educational literacy practices as typically falling in a sort of continuum. At one end, educational literacy practices have significance because they reflect directly literacy practices in particular sites. Within vocational education, for example, teaching particular literacy practices is important because they correspond with literacy practices within the high-performance workplace. As Gemma Moss notes, pedagogic discourse often "seeks to replicate itself elsewhere. It looks outside the confines of schooling, only to find confirmation of what it already is" ("Informal Literacies" 51), confirmation and, I would add, justification. However, given Bernstein's discussion of pedagogic discourse, such a correspondence is impossible. By definition, literacy practices recontextualized in a pedagogic discourse cannot be the same as literacy practices (or even representations of literacy practices) within a particular site, such as the workplace. At the other end of the continuum, educational literacy practices serve as a corrective to actual literacy practices. My brief reading of the history of English and composition studies—in which the fields develop in part to address the threat of particular literacy practices—suggests this process, as do the Citizenship Schools, which challenged literacy practices that justified disenfranchisement. Whether reflective or corrective, literacy itself becomes recontextualized into the educational discourses. This process of recontextualization suggests that to teach literacy practices at any level, in any setting, is to necessarily take a position within a regulative discourse, one that we communicate in various ways, but certainly through the ways we define, teach, and enforce particular literacy practices. Following Bernstein, the skills we teach—the instructional discourse—are embedded, and necessarily, within a discourse of the social order, a regulative discourse. Considering pedagogic discourses—and the literacy practices encouraged within them—in this way means, necessarily, recognizing them as sites of conflict, as discourses that take a position about the social order by privileging particular regulative discourses.

Understanding our teaching of literacy practices as grounded in particular visions of the social order, as ideologically located in relation to other literacy practices and pedagogies, presents a way of viewing our teaching that takes us significantly beyond the classroom; it also provides us a way to critique and resist the discourses that, even so, continue to shape our practices. In this book, I use the concept of recontextualization to examine the regulative discourses within various sites of nontraditional adult education. The sites that I explore go well beyond traditional concepts of adult literacy, and they emphasize much more than teaching adults to read and write. Thus, I focus instead on literacy practices as they are represented in the discourses and histories of the sites I explore, on ways in which literacy practices are directly tied to the regulative discourse. This means understanding, for example, how literacy is tied to rehabilitation (in the case of correctional education) or to civil rights and community development (in the case of the Highlander Folk School). This focus allows for an analysis of what is at stake in the various discourses and how particular literacy practices connect to visions of the social order projected by the regulative discourse, and it provides a way of understanding how literacy instruction at any level always projects an argument about social relationships and ideological commitments, an argument about the world in which we need to live.

CHAPTER 2

Make Them Wise to Salvation

Literacy and Literacy Practices in Correctional Education

When the first educational programs entered American prisons, John Reynolds, warder of the Philadelphia's Walnut Street Jail, initially refused entrance to the two ministers who planned to offer religious instruction and sermons. After he was ordered to let them in by the sheriff, Reynolds warned the men of their potential for injury and loss of valuables. "In a final, desperate act of intimidation, Reynolds had a cannon placed on the platform next to the clergymen with a lighted wick, ready to fire into the assembled crowd should the occasion demand" (Silva 19). Aiming the cannon toward the inmates must have served as more than intimidating. The cannon would have been a visceral symbol of where this class took place and who had the ultimate authority in that classroom. It emphasized a criminal over a student identity, likely reminding the ministers that no matter their intentions, the fact of the prison and its institutional dominance would always matter more.

As such, it doesn't matter that the cannon was never fired; what matters is that it could have been, indeed, was perpetually ready to be fired. It serves, then, as an appropriate symbol for the conflict between penal and educational priorities within the prison. On the one hand, prisoners are potentially students whose lives can be positively altered by education; on the other hand, prisoners are criminals whose history of law breaking makes them an ongoing social and institutional threat that must be continuously quelled. Sarah Matthews's description of the uneasy place of education in prisons underscores the contradictions between these two perspectives:

> Nestled within the heart of every prison facility is an education department made up of teachers, counselors, and administrators. These professionals, trained to be part of a helping profession, are charged with the duties of educating prison inmates—within a system designed for punishment. People from opposing ideological backgrounds must somehow work together in order to accomplish a very difficult mission. (179)

Inside such a facility, Matthews reminds us, are people who are "part of a helping profession," people typically of "opposing ideological backgrounds" from those involved in the design and function of the overall prison. The educators in this prison can't be seen apart from the prison itself, located as they are within its imposing structure emphasizing security and surveillance and punishment. Even if the teachers in this prison are lucky enough to teach a class in which no correctional officers are present, there will never be any doubt that they are teaching in a prison. As they engage in a social act inevitably hinging on some sort of transformation, these teachers are surrounded by the instruments and semiotics of restraint.

Inside an extremely sophisticated institution of punitive security, such teachers occupy a unique position as educators. They teach within what one historian of correctional education in prisons has referred to as "anti-education institutions" (Gehring 1989 166); that is, their very professional mandate comes into conflict, in most cases, with the mission of the prison in which they teach. Anyone who has taught has no doubt felt some version of that conflict, but for a prison educator, more often than not, it is the basic condition of employment. Education, as George Carey puts it, often appears to correctional officials as "a run in the knit of institutional life" (91).

This palpable tension exists not only within physical institutions—in the form of literal cannons or guards quietly standing in the back of classrooms—but within the professional discourse of correctional education as well, a discourse itself positioned within the larger context of what some commentators have termed the prison-industrial complex in the United States. Located as it is, the discourse and its educational literacy practices cannot be separated from the idea and reality of the modern prison. So, correctional education must respond not only to theories of learning and teaching, but to theories and controversies surrounding crime and criminality, rehabilitation, the function of imprisonment and the economics of the prison industry. All of these become central, unavoidable aspects of the regulative discourse of correctional education, and their roles in that discourse are one of the reasons that, for my purposes, correctional education is so worthy of study and exploration.

Inspired by my limited experience, my interest in correctional education has to do with the extent to which it must deal with the physical and rhetorical power of its location, the extent to which it is shaped by, even through resisting, the prison. Correctional education takes place in institutions characterized by extremes and contradictions, and the theories developed from this institutional positioning engage in debates wholly unfamiliar in other pedagogical location: The definition of criminality, for example, has been a necessary and extremely thorny issue for the field, because it labels what needs correction. The discipline maintains a strong argument that education has the power to transform people in identifiably positive ways, holding out hope against obstacles that most of us (and most of our students) rarely confront in other classrooms. Correctional educational is often labeled a success or failure based on whether students recidivate, return to prison having committed another offense. Correctional education takes on explicitly a goal for education that most of the teachers I know and whose works I read speak about in muted and reluctant voices: to socialize students, to help them buy into the social and cultural norms of society enough so that they no longer resort to crime. As a field, correctional education is primarily dedicated to the principle that education can affect fundamental changes in character, behavior, and personality. For educators in other locations, the extent of this principle as a guiding aspect of their pedagogies is a challenge, because it frames the educational mission of teaching in ways that many of us have come to believe as suspect. Here's a blunt statement, one common in the field, about the mission of correctional education: "correctional educators are literally in the business of salvaging lives and changing families for generations. We must find more effective ways to meet the education (and other) needs of the offender, so that he can be returned to society, not to re-offend, but to become a productive, tax-paying citizen" (Lynch 36). This is an educational goal I have never specifically attached myself to, at least not with the pride of a vocation. Correctional education, however, explicitly holds out the successful socialization of its students as a central goal of the field.

This is not, I should make clear, the opening salvo of a critique of the field, pointing out shortcomings in its theoretical and pedagogical stances. I don't have the experiential background to engage in a grounded critique. I taught only as a volunteer, I have no experience as a professional in the field, and I only have worked in a brand new, clean, and efficiently run county jail. Likewise, professional correctional educators must defend their work against particularly powerful forces. Having experienced major funding cuts in the last decade and having watched programs of higher education dry up with the withdrawal of Pell Grants for prisoners, they know that political funding in the field relies on rhetorical compatibility with an excessively punitive society. As Howard Davidson has argued, "The more correctional educators can represent schooling as quasi-punitive, the more likely it is that they will be spared severe cutbacks" (7). But most importantly, to examine correctional education primarily in the language of critique would be to miss what I see as its fundamental insight for educators within any institution:

Pedagogic discourses are intrinsically linked to their institutional locations, the regulative discourses necessarily and fundamentally shaped by those institutions and their goals. This is one reason Myles Horton insisted that Highlander operate independently, outside the aegis of any union or civil rights organization, never allowing the label of a political party or philosophy to be placed upon the school. He understood the limiting consequences of working within formal systems, of accepting their goals, in part, as your own. Unlike Horton, most educators do not teach within institutions promoting goals they can fully embrace. Witness, for example, the regular hand wringing among teachers regarding the practices of assigning grades (especially troubling, in my experience, for new teachers), based, I think, on the recognition that our teaching practices and our theories about them are strongly determined, often in ways we perceive as detrimental, by where we teach. Within correctional education, as with everything else about prisons, this relationship between institutional setting and educational theory is especially stark.

In this chapter, then, I explore the extent to which the regulative discourses within correctional education are fundamentally linked to the institution, to the very idea, of the prison. Like the cannon in the classroom at the Walnut Street Jail, the institutions and politics of imprisonment continually shape the practices and theories within the field. A discussion of literacy education within prisons, for example, cannot be undertaken without an examination of the historic and current ways in which illiteracy and criminality have been connected, and the value of any curriculum within prisons often becomes measured by its ability to improve things like moral reasoning among inmates. As I argued in chapter one, pedagogy is a deictic act, always pointing somewhere else. Pedagogy, and thus educational literacy practices, points to a future in which those literacy practices are relevant, and that future is primarily a discursive construction. Understanding the meaning of educational literacy practices requires an understanding of how, according to various pedagogic discourses, they invoke and create the conditions for change and transformation. Who or what is being changed? What is the process of change? What is the goal of that transformation? Pedagogic discourse must address these questions, and the various answers it provides shed particular light on the often conflicting expectations placed upon literacy in a given educational setting, and across educational settings. Like any pedagogic discourse, the discourse of correctional education must project a hope for education, must believe that education can work toward some sort of better future. The challenge for correctional education, as for any pedagogic discourse, is to determine what that future should be and to describe the role education has in realizing it.

Most commonly, that future has focused on the individual rehabilitation of prisoners, a belief that education can, in the words of one nineteenth-century prison chaplain, "make them wise to salvation" (qtd. in Gehring "Characteristics" 53). How that salvation, that release into a noncriminal mentality, will come about has changed over the more than two centuries that the prison has emphasized correction as one of its goals, from, in the chaplain's case, engendering a belief in and acceptance of the Christian God to, more recently, remediating a range of "social-cognitive deficits," "inadequacies which may limit [the offender's] ability to function effectively in a prosocial manner" (Ross and Fabiano 117). Because recidivism is the most common measure of success or failure for the field, determining what sort of education is likely to change inmates from criminals to noncriminals is perhaps the central issue in the discourse, a determination predicated on the belief that such a change is possible. Thus, the field must always contend with cultural beliefs and attitudes toward crime, criminals, and imprisonment that dramatically affect such issues as funding, resources, and the professional respectability of the field. Such issues are central in conceptions of literacy and educational literacy practices within the field, which I examine at length in this chapter for the perspective they provide on the goals the field promotes as well as the means for achieving them.

I begin this chapter by looking at consecutive amendments to the Violent Crime Prevention and Law Enforcement Act of 1994, the first denying prisoners access to the Pell Grants largely responsible for the growth of college programming within prisons, and the second mandating that federal prisons provide basic literacy education. The second amendment plays off the ubiquitous and seemingly common sense notion that illiteracy is causally linked to criminality, making urgent the provision of a particular kind of literacy education. This amendment relies on the familiar terms of the literacy crisis, a manifest fear of the social disaster caused by illiteracy. The first amendment suggests, however, that beyond a basic sort of literacy provision, further schooling actually serves, at worst, as an actual inducement to crime and, at best, as an unwarranted luxury gotten at the expense of more deserving, law-abiding citizens. I explore the tensions reflected in these amendments first by looking at how literacy and criminality remain commonly linked in discussions of correctional education, then by discussing the ways in which educational provision beyond the most basic level abruptly turns from a social necessity to a social threat. I then examine the ways in which educational literacy practices, however named, reflect a range of conflicting goals in the discourse. In the cognitive skills approach I referred to earlier, for example, educational literacy practices address the individual social cognitive deficits of prisoners, changing the ways they think to take into account a more prosocial perspective and behavior. The prison itself—as well as an exceedingly and increasingly punitive and racially imbalanced criminal justice system—recedes into the background from such a position, the central issue being the correction of individual deficits that lead to criminal behavior. Many correctional educators, however, look beyond individual prisoners to the prisons themselves, arguing that meaningful rehabilitation can only occur within a social setting that fosters it. Educational literacy practices in this approach work toward the creation of a social structure that emphasizes meaningful decision making and the democratic process, rather than individual transformation. In this perspective, educational literacy practices should play a central role in the reform of an ineffective and unjust penal system. What's notable about these perspectives is that, although they require dramatically different theories about learning and education and advocate fundamentally different literacy practices, they are all necessarily located in relation to the prison itself. The differences between them stem from their conceptions of the world as it *is*—a function of individual cognitive deficits, institutional limits, or social injustice—as well as the world as it *ought to be*, whether that *ought to be* should focus on individual prisoners, on prisons, or on society itself.

I position my examination of correctional education before my discussions of vocational education and of the Highlander Folk School in part because I suspect arguments within the field will be more unfamiliar to readers. Also, however, I focus on the discourse of correctional education because it highlights issues of institutional positioning that any teacher must contend with. Correctional education puts into stark relief the influence of institutions upon educational literacy practices and suggests the necessity of commitment to working within systems we might find overly constraining at best and oppressive at worst. As I argued in Chapter 1, a metaphoric cannon exists in all our classrooms, as the institutions in which we teach shape and even enforce particular practices and theories that might oppose our own ideas about the methods and goals of education. But I am not only interested in using the discourse of correctional education as an analogy, something to think with, about teaching in other locations. The discourse of correctional education places educators and educational literacy practices at the center of one of the most vital social and civil rights issues in the United States today. At present, the racial and class imbalance in American prisons is overwhelming, and the statistics bearing this out are boggling. According to the Bureau of Justice Statistics, for example, by 2002 roughly 12 percent of black men in their twenties were in jail or prison, and according to a 2004 report by the Sentencing Project, "At current rates of incarceration, one of every three black males born today can expect to be imprisoned at some point in his lifetime" (5). Over the past thirty years, the number of prison inmates in the United States has increased over sixfold, from about 350,000 to now well over 2 million inmates. How the discourse handles this imbalance and growth, how it addresses its roles, its goals, its present and its future matters because the criminal justice system and the penal system shapes the daily experiences of millions of Americans, not simply inmates and correctional staff, but their families and their communities. The discourse itself reflects issues surrounding punishment, justice, and control that, like the impulse of the prison system "to isolate itself, to place prisons in rural or deserted regions or regions of high unemployment where criticisms might mean local job loss" (Duguid *Can Prisons Work?* 81), most Americans are content to locate as abstractions far from the center of their intellectual and moral concerns. In exploring those reflections, I do hope teachers of literacy practices might see their own work and their own positions in a different light, but I also hope to offer readers another way of thinking about the goals, the shape, and the systematic injustices of the prison system in the United States. This should matter at least as much as—probably more than—any perspective the discourse might offer about teaching in other locations.

CRIMINALITY, "BLIND HOGS," AND THE CONTRADICTIONS OF LITERACY EDUCATION IN PRISON

Political debates about education in prison, debates that directly impact the professional lives of correctional educators, highlight some consequences of understanding literacy in basic and functional terms. Because of the historic and current correlation between a lack of education and incarceration—that is, prisoners, by and large, are far less officially educated than the general population, likely by the standards of any test to prove well below culturally acceptable literacy levels—a simple but unwarranted conclusion commonly follows: Illiteracy, or low literacy, causes crime. This assumption makes the provision of certain kinds of literacy education appear as a matter of some urgency, for to allow prisoners to leave prison without a basic education, often represented as necessary for postrelease employment, fails to address an easily identifiable impetus toward continuing a criminal career. It is a duty of the state, then, to provide basic literacy education for prisoners, not because it addresses a fundamental human right, but because it is an integral part of the process of correction, of turning criminals into noncriminals. To not support the provision of basic literacy education would be officially shortsighted.

But there are limits, apparently, beyond which literacy instruction seems to become counterproductive. The teaching of literacy practices arguably falls under what Roger Matthews refers to as "the principle of 'less eligibility,' such that conditions in prisons must be no better than those experienced by the poorest sections of the working classes, otherwise members of the lowest social strata will not be deterred from committing crimes"

(*Doing Time* 10). So there appears no contradiction between a correctional policy that makes basic literacy not only available but mandatory, as Davidson points out, "making education punitive" (20), while at the same time decrying the availability of more advanced literacy education as sending the wrong message to and causing increased hardships for law-abiding degree-seeking students.

This tension appears dramatically in two back-to-back amendments to the Violent Crime and Law Enforcement Act of 1994. The first, Section 20411, prohibits prisoners from receiving Pell Grants, thus ending a more than twenty-year financial assistance program that had fostered an enormous growth in college education within prisons. The second, Section 20412, requires that the Federal Bureau of Prisons make GED education available to inmates and makes work toward a GED mandatory for inmates hoping to credit toward their sentence for good behavior. The full text of these two amendments is as follows:

> SEC. 20411. AWARDS OF PELL GRANTS TO PRISONERS PROHIBITED.
>
> (a) IN GENERAL- Section 401(b)(8) of the Higher Education Act of 1965 (20 U.S.C. 1070a(b)(8)) is amended to read as follows:
>
> '(8) No basic grant shall be awarded under this subpart to any individual who is incarcerated in any Federal or State penal institution.'.
>
> (b) APPLICATION OF AMENDMENT-The amendment made by this section shall apply with respect to periods of enrollment beginning on or after the date of enactment of this Act.
>
> SEC. 20412. EDUCATION REQUIREMENT FOR EARLY RELEASE.
>
> Section 3624(b) of title 18, United States Code, is amended—
>
> (1) by inserting '(1)' after 'behavior- ';
>
> (2) by striking 'Such credit toward service of sentence vests at the time that it is received. Credit that has vested may not later be withdrawn, and credit that has not been earned may not later be granted.' and inserting 'Credit that has not been earned may not later be granted.'; and
> (3) by adding at the end the following:
>
> '(2) Credit toward a prisoner's service of sentence shall not be vested unless the prisoner has earned or is making satisfactory progress toward a high school diploma or an equivalent degree.
>
> '(3) The Attorney General shall ensure that the Bureau of Prisons has in effect an optional General Educational Development program for inmates who have not earned a high school diploma or its equivalent.
>
> '(4) Exemptions to the General Educational Development requirement may be made as deemed appropriate by the Director of the Federal Bureau of Prisons.'

In this section I examine the impulses guiding both these amendments. I start by looking at the assumptions the second amendment draws on, namely the historic and current links made between illiteracy and criminality, by which the obvious correlation between being imprisoned and having a limited education becomes framed as a cause—illiteracy—with a criminal effect. Basic literacy education, then, becomes a curative for criminality. I then look more particularly at the debate ending in the prohibition of Pell Grants for prisoners, which has had the consequence of severely curtailing opportunities for prisoners to receive a college education.

Illiteracy and a Lack of Education as a Cause of Criminality

In requiring that federal prisons provide basic literacy education and that inmates enroll in such programs if they hope to receive credit for good behavior, lawmakers drew on popular conclusions that explain criminality as stemming from low educational achievement. Such explanation, of course, conveniently elides other perspectives on causes of imprisonment, perspectives that may often involve issues of social and economic inequality. Promoting an educational solution, especially one that ends with the equivalent of a high school diploma, suggests that imprisonment stems primarily from shortcomings located within an individual and precludes a larger social examination. Correlations between illiteracy and imprisonment become more important in the process than other equally dramatic correlations between, for example, race or class and imprisonment.

In his discussion of the nineteenth-century Canadian linkage of criminality to illiteracy, ignorance, and a lack of education, Harvey Graff notes that two arguments, seemingly in contradiction to each other, were often advanced at the same time. In one formulation, "learning to read led naturally to the inculcation of restraint and morality," while the other "stress[ed] morality as independent of literacy or intellectual training" (*Labyrinths* 209). The former was useful in using data about the literacy levels of prisoners to promote public schooling as having a central role in diminishing criminality. When public schooling did not, in fact, succeed in lowering the crime rate, the latter argument became useful in promoting the right kind of public schooling, one that explicitly emphasized morality. Reformers presented data on illiterates in jail to bolster an argument that literacy was sufficient to reduce crime, even as they argued that ignorance and not illiteracy caused crime, making a moral education of primary importance: "The role of literacy was to provide the vehicle for the efficient transmission and reinforcement of morality and restraint" (*Labyrinths* 209). The right kind of literacy education, so the argument went, grounded in a proper morality, would serve to reduce crime.

Graff, however, challenges the causal link between illiteracy and crime. By investigating the jail records of one county in Ontario for 1867–1868, Graff demonstrates that instead of illiteracy, convictions were related

> to patterns of discrimination and social prejudice against the Irish, the lower class, and women—these individuals were convicted most often regardless of their level of literacy. Punishment was of course more frequent for the least educated members of these groups, and illiteracy related more directly, perhaps, to arrest and successful prosecution than it did to guilt and criminality. Social inequality was the root of both illiteracy and conviction, and the actions of the courts were based in the social hierarchy. (*Labyrinths* 214)

In this case, illiteracy becomes a defensible and addressable substitute for more deeply rooted inequities, one that can be more easily dealt with structurally, through the provision of the right kind of literacy education, whether within schools or within prisons. As we will see, too, in the discourse of vocational education, literacy becomes a decontextualized marker that explains, and justifies, social differences more predicated on issues of race and class.

This linkage between criminality and low literacy, of course, does not exist solely in nineteenth-century Canada. Often, the link becomes inferred through studies such as the National Adult Literacy Survey, which presented data about prisoners' literacy, claiming that "Their proficiencies are substantially lower than those of the household population" (Kirsch, Jungeblot, Jenkins, and Kolstad xviii). There are reasons to be skeptical of such results, as Anita Wilson suggests in commenting that the criteria for evaluation in such work, based solely on a document/prose criteria, "hardly does justice for the skills required for maintaining correspondence links with the outside world" (97), nor does it take into account the vast contextual difference between literacy's uses and meanings within prison and its uses outside prisons. Even so, such data certainly reflect a real disparity between the educational level of prisoners compared to that of adults in the United States in general, a disparity claimed in almost every study done in prisons regarding education and literacy. The identification of the disparity, however, easily slides into an explanation of one of the causes of crime, as in this excerpt from an article by Montross and Montross. After citing several studies demonstrating the "strong positive correlation between the lack of education and the incidence of criminal behavior," they take this one step further:

> If education is the key to economic success and a lack of education leads to unemployment, one may assume that a lack of education feeds crime. What is not so clear in correctional education is how best to offer remedial programs to incarcerated students. This confusion may result from a lack of understanding who these students are and how they fit into the traditional education system. What is clear is that the expanding prison population results at least in part from a lack of education and that correctional educators realize they must develop a body of knowledge unique to the correctional education system. (179)

Two things occur in this passage: First, a hypothetical relationship between a lack of education and crime—"one may assume that a lack of education feeds crime"—becomes an open claim of a causal relationship, at least between increased incarceration and a lack of education. This requires putting aside other clear reasons for an expanding prison population, the war on drugs, for example, which has fueled an unprecedented racial imbalance within American prisons through such initiatives as mandatory sentencing, or the increasingly punitive ideas about retribution and justice behind such laws as "three strikes and you're out." (This is a fairly stunning rhetorical elision, one I will return to later in this chapter.) Second, that claim means that correctional education, to meet its rehabilitative ideal, must focus on what these authors call "remedial programs," the medical metaphor itself highlighting the curative benefits of education.

As Roger Matthews points out in a discussion of how unemployment relates to criminality, "even a strong correlation . . . need not imply causation" (111). Still, a focus on the illiteracy of criminals leads writers, likely better trained in statistical analysis than I, to make claims such as this one, in *Prison Literacy*, published by the National Center on Adult Literacy in 1993: "Because illiteracy and criminality are umbilically joined, it stands to reason that greater literacy would have a dampening effect on criminality" (Newman, Warren and Beverstock ix). One of the strongest arguments for literacy education within prisons, then, becomes the association of illiteracy with criminality. (Often, the link between illiteracy and criminality is unemployability; thus literacy education in prison will reduce criminality by providing offenders with the skills necessary to gain employment after release.)

This argument has the powerful advantage of framing literacy education in stark terms that no doubt provide compelling political reasons to fund literacy programs in prison. However, it gets writers, and teachers, caught in the sort of rhetorical conundrum Graff points out in his discussion of nineteenth-century Canada. Although Montross and Montross and *Prison Literacy* suggest that a correlation between illiteracy and criminality implies causation, they don't follow that by advocating the sort of literacy education that would help students pass the tests that marked them as deficient in the first place. Rather, like Graff's reformers, they advocate the right kinds of literacy education, in the case of Montross and Montross one that addresses the cognitive and moral deficits evidenced by student-offenders, and, in the case of the authors of *Prison Literacy*, a specific set of broadly defined literacy practices designed to address criminal tendencies and traits. This calls for

> growth in literacies that include moral education, democratic self-rule in the 'just community,' instruction in the humanities, with a strong appeal to the cognitive, delivered by means of andragogical instruction, in company with training in a variety of skills to enable the inmate to cope with the personal, sexual, familial, chemical, economic, vocational, and social problems of life, thereby to gain a realistic sense of one's individual worth as a human being. (Newman, Warren, and Beverstock x)

Prison Literacy and Montross and Montross both rely on theories of social cognitive deficits that emphasize interpersonal and moral development, theories that became especially popular in discussions of correctional education in the 1980s and 1990s and that I will explore in more detail later in this chapter. The weakness of the argument that illiteracy causes crime is evident in the necessity to define the sort of literacy required to address criminality. What is being taught, in the curricula presented by Montross and Montross and the authors of *Prison Literacy*, is not just the sort literacy defined and measured in the innumerable tests demonstrating the shocking level of illiteracy within prisons, but how not to think like criminals think.

I am not claiming that these writers, then, are advocates of offering educational opportunities for student-offenders limited to basic literacy instruction. Indeed, *Prison Literacy* openly asserts the value of postsecondary education. My point is that a reliance on an inferred causal link between a lack of education and criminality does not support an argument for broadly defined educational approaches. In the argument, a lack of education becomes measured in all sorts of ways, from a stark inability to read, to an ability to read at the fifth grade level, to a lack of proficiency at handling prose/document literacy. Making these measures evidence of a causal link between a lack of education and criminality supports education that teaches basic literacy skills, aims for proficiencies in literacy as measured by low grade levels or prose/document literacy, and nothing more than that. It supports arguments, such as those behind the amendment cited above, for mandatory literacy education, a compulsory vision that, as Austin MacCormick argued in 1931, from the perspective of an inmate, "makes education a thing to be avoided instead of a thing to be sought" (11). It supports the most basic approaches to literacy education, approaches that matter certainly, and should be available within prisons; inmates should have the opportunity to learn to read, to receive a GED, to develop math skills. However, by repeatedly positing causality on the basis of correlation between a lack of education and imprisonment, advocates of correctional education support funding approaches that actually limit the provision of education to the most basic and the least expensive sorts of education available. The correlation between a lack of education and incarceration proves too tempting to pass up as a justification for funding education within prisons, but it is a rhetorical gambit that ultimately limits the kinds of education apparently necessary within prisons. Using such logic, it becomes possible to require one kind of literacy education—that focused on the high school level—and effectively cut off another—that focused on receiving a college degree.

The correlation between imprisonment and a lack of education certainly has direct implications for educators, implications spelled out clearly by Austin MacCormick in *The Education of Adult Prisoners* over 70 years ago, a book that reads as remarkably undated (in its orientation, if not its language) and highly relevant up to the present. MacCormick immediately resists relying on a lack of education to understand criminality:

> To what extent lack of education is a cause of crime and to what extent merely an accompanying circumstance we do not know. How much effect education has on character we do not know: whether or not it has the power to create a moral desire or merely to stimulate a desire already existent and to give it something to feed on. We do know, however, that men and women in prison are as a rule undereducated and, however high or modest our hopes for the result, we should remove that deficiency as we should remove adenoids. If we believe in the beneficial effect of education on man in general we must believe in it for this particular group, which differs less than the layman thinks from the ordinary run of humanity. If on no other grounds than a general resolve to offer educational opportunities to undereducated persons wherever they may be found, we recognize that our penal population constitutes a proper field for educational effort. In brief, we are not ready to make its efficacy in turning men from crime the only criterion in judging the value of education for prisoners. (3)

As MacCormick argues, education should take place in prisons, not because it will reduce criminality, but because so many prisoners are uneducated and deserve, by virtue of their humanity, the same access to education that all others deserve. MacCormick, it should be noted, did not believe that the duty to provide educational opportunities ended with teaching a prisoner how to read: "If we are to compel or induce illiterates to take the first difficult step along the educational path, we are justified in doing so only because we are going to try to interest them in continuing their education beyond the mere rudiments . . . [The illiterate] should be encouraged to go as far along his educational path as his ability and the time at his disposal permit" (66).

When criminality becomes used as a justification for particular kinds of education, it makes sense that it will also be used as a justification for denying particular kinds of education. The principle of less eligibility suggests that educational provision in prison might be justified up to particular levels expected among the poorest and most uneducated populations outside the prison, but that to go beyond that is to make prison somehow appealing. As long as education can be understood in basic and sometimes punitive ways, it can be justified as addressing root causes of criminality; when, however, it exceeds a particular level, it can be asserted not as addressing root causes but perhaps even as an inducement to committing crimes and going to prison, to benefit from opportunities otherwise unavailable. That level seems to have been exceeded by the provision of Pell Grants for prisoners.

Denying Pell Grants for Prisoners

> Just because one blind hog may occasionally find an acorn does not mean many other blind hogs will. The same principle applies to giving Federal Pell grants to prisoners. Certainly there is an occasional success story, but when virtually every prisoner in America is eligible for Pell grants, national priorities and taxpayers lose. That is especially true since the education department has no way to track success or even know for sure if a recipient is a prisoner. (Gordon)

In 1994, Section 20411 of the Violent Crime Prevention and Law Enforcement Act prohibited prisoners from receiving Pell Grants, shutting down a program that had funded post-secondary education in prison for over twenty years. The debate preceding the vote in the House of Representatives, opening with Representative Gordon's telling metaphorical comparison of prisoners to visually impaired swine, captured the emotional resonance this amendment tapped. Although several representatives spoke against the amendment, offering statistics to the effect that the Pell Grants for prisoners accounted for one-half of one percent of the annual Pell Grant budget and noting that in no case did nonincarcerated recipients of Pell Grants lose funding because prisoners received it, its supporters nonetheless repeated claims that prisoners took away funding from law-abiding citizens, that rewarding criminals with government support for their education was ridiculous and perhaps even dangerous.

Opponents of Pell Grants for prisoners relied on several demonstrably effective rhetorical tactics, among them a version of the principle of less eligibility as well as blaming criminals for the economic hardships faced by ordinary decent citizens. These themes in particular are represented in a letter from a constituent read during the debate by Representative Holden from Pennsylvania, one of the sponsors of the amendment along with Gordon:

> Where is an average, hard-working student who wants to make something of herself and get somewhere in life supposed to turn for help? Over the years we have told our daughter, "Keep your nose clean, stay out of trouble. If you have a police record, you will never get into college." My daughter has listened but where has it gotten her? She reads about prisoners getting Pell grants and free college educations.
>
> What does this tell her?
>
> It tells her: If she was sitting in jail she would get a free education.
>
> Just where does a hard-working normal honor student involved in many extra curricular activities not only in school but also in the community go for help? The prisoner is rewarded with a free education.
>
> The average honor student is penalized because she tried to save money for college and she is penalized because she stayed out of trouble. Who can justify all of this?
>
> Do I tell her to put on a ski mask, go to the local bank, rob it, get a criminal record and then receive a free education?

In this scenario, Pell Grants for prisoners represent a ludicrous inversion of the social order, in which young adults like this woman's daughter receive no reward for their commitment to living a crime-free life at the same time that criminals receive a free education, simply because they are criminals. The availability of a free education for prisoners appears as an inducement to criminality, implying that prisons offer more than they should offer and thus become somehow desirable, a clear violation of the principle of less eligibility. The repetition of the word *free* also suggests a fundamental violation of the purpose of prisons, which are for confinement, not freedom.

The letter from Gordon's constituent also implies that criminals, because they receive easily that which "average, hard-working student[s]" must struggle for, are partly to blame for that struggle. As another sponsor of the amendment, Fields, R-TX, phrased it; "Every dollar in Pell grant funds obtained by prisoners means that fewer law-abiding students who need help in meeting their college costs are eligible for that assistance. It also means that law-abiding students who meet eligibility criteria receive smaller annual grants than they might otherwise obtain." (No one was denied Pell Grants because prisoners received them. Michele Welsh (157) cites a report estimating that each Pell Grant recipient received an extra $4.25 per semester as a result of making prisoners ineligible.) Crime thus becomes a way to take advantage of citizens who fulfill their lawful civic duty. As Katherine Beckett notes, "By attributing the very real economic plights of 'taxpayers' and 'working persons' to the behavior of the 'underclass,' conservatives diminish the likelihood that these grievances will give rise to policies aimed at redistributing opportunities and resources in a more egalitarian fashion" (87), policies, for example, such as providing Pell Grants for prisoners. (Blaming economic difficulties on an unskilled workforce operates similarly.)

An outgrowth of the Higher Education Act of 1965, Pell Grants (initially called Basic Educational Opportunity Grants and renamed, in 1980, after Senator Claiborne Pell of Rhode Island) became available in 1972, forming the largest student grant program administered by the Department of Education (Peramba 165). Along with other financially needy students, inmates qualified for the program if they were enrolled in an undergraduate program leading to a degree and making satisfactory progress. The availability of Pell Grants for prisoners was the major impetus for a massive jump in college prison programs. In 1965, only twelve postsecondary programs existed in the United States. By 1982, there were 350 programs offered in 90 percent of the states, with an estimated 27,000 inmates taking advantage of the opportunity, 37 percent of them receiving Pell Grants as their primary support, the most frequently named source of funding (Taylor 170). Pell Grants were not the only method of supporting students, but they were the primary reason that programs could be developed within prisons.

In the early 1990s, however, Pell Grants for prisoners started appearing as a kind of injustice. Senator Jesse Helms, introducing an amendment to the Higher Education Reauthorization Act to deny Pell Grants for prisoners in 1991, worried on the floor of the Senate that "American taxpayers are being forced to pay taxes to provide free college tuition to prisoners at a time when so many law-abiding, taxpaying citizens are struggling to find enough money to send their children to college" (qtd. in Taylor 169). Although the Helms Amendment, and its counterpart in the House, the Coleman-Gordon Amendment, were defeated as riders to the Higher Education Reauthorization Act, the same sentiments appeared in 1994, this time successfully.

Although exact numbers are hard to pin down, because there has not been a comprehensive study on the topic, any estimate of the impact of the prohibition of Pell Grants for prisoners is significant. Marks puts the level of college programs, one academic year after the Crime Bill passed, at 40 percent less than the previous year, with 44 percent fewer students enrolled; Mary Wright points out that the same period saw a 7 percent rise in the prison population. Welsh notes that, eight years later, correctional officials in charge of education around the country "perceived a significant decrease in access, quality, and success due to the elimination of Pell Grants for prisoners" and that they believed that the future of postsecondary education "will not be significantly different from the current deteriorated state" (157). Although other funds can be found to support postsecondary education, it is clear that the ability of inmates to receive a college education while in prison has been severely curtailed.

Jon M. Taylor, himself an inmate who received a college education and published extensively while incarcerated, pointed out numerous studies that demonstrated the effectiveness of postsecondary education within prison when measuring recidivist rates. Stephen Duguid (*Can Prisons Work?*) presents extensive data on the effect of twentieth years of postsecondary education within British Columbian prisons, arguing that even high-risk offenders demonstrated significantly reduced rates of recidivism. There are philosophical risks in using recidivism as a measure of educational success, as suggested by MacCormick's resistance to justify education on the basis of reducing criminality. Gehring ("Recidivism") notes that recidivism rates can just as easily justify the elimination of educational programming as they can support it and points out the often clumsy ways in which recidivism measures are utilized. Even so, extensive evidence supports postsecondary education on the philosophically narrow measure most commonly used to justify any programs within prisons. I will examine more closely the particulars of Duguid's argument in a later section, but here I simply note that whereas opponents of the amendment that eliminated Pell Grants for prisoners pointed out several measures that indicated the reduced recidivism of inmates who received a college education within prisons, proponents of the amendment more or less repeated versions of the arguments made earlier. Except in the disparaging metaphor of the blind hog finding an acorn, the rehabilitative ideal of prisons was simply not addressed by proponents of the amendment, who focused instead on a politically powerful paradigm of imprisonment as punishment and deprivation.

WHAT IS MOST IMPORTANT FOR THEM TO KNOW: PRISONERS AND THE PRISON IN CORRECTIONAL EDUCATION

> Show the convict the first letter in the Bible, that is, I. Let him find the same, wherever it occurs in the first verse. Having done this, show him the second letter of the Bible, that is, n. Let him find every n in the first verse. Having done this and being told what I-n spells, he has already learned to read the first word in the Bible, wherever it occurs in the first

> chapter. Having done this he will probably never forget it. This is his lesson. Let the second lesson be the second word in the Bible, the letters of which and their combination should be as before. Let him proceed in this manner through successive lessons, til he has learned to read the first verse in Genesis—"In the beginning God created the heavens and the earth." Having done this, he has got his reward. One of the most sublime ideas ever presented to the mind of man, he has obtained by diligent attention for a few hours learning to read. . . . If persons who know not a letter of the alphabet, can be taught in five or six weeks, as in the prison at Sing Sing, to read in their own language the sacred volume, which is to make them wise to salvation, and to unfold to them the unsearchable riches of Christ, then ignorant adults wherever they can be found, in the Christian or heathen lands, can much sooner than has generally been supposed, be so instructed as to read for themselves, what is most important for them to know. (Chaplain, Sing Sing Prison, 1828 [qtd. in Gehring "Characteristics" 52–53])

Teaching reading using the Bible as the primary text was by far the most common focus of correctional education in its early history, instruction that included, of course, preaching and ministering. An education shaped by Christianity, it was hoped, would provide the necessary spiritual foundation for the reform of prisoners' characters. As described by the Boston Prison Discipline Society in their reports from the early to mid-nineteenth century, "Here, or nowhere, these neglected and unfortunate youth must be instructed in the first principles of education, their minds elevated, and they thus prepared to become better sons, better husbands, better parents, better citizens" (qtd. in ibid. 52).

This almost relentless focus on betterment within correctional education highlights a distinction between literacy events and literacy practices. If we classify reading the Bible, for example, as a literacy event, in that it revolves around a written text, we still have little notion of what it means as a literacy practice. The literacy practices surrounding reading the Bible might privilege some combination of historical, literary, theological, spiritual, skeptical, or other readings, so that the potential meanings of this literacy event are highly variable. Likewise, the same educational literacy events potentially have an enormous variety of literacy practices behind them. Reading the Bible in an educational setting, for example, might involve making the students wise to salvation or better sons, better husbands, better parents, better citizens, but it might also teach a particular kind of exegesis, or methods and debates surrounding translation, or even a rejection of Biblical tenets. The practices encouraged by a particular literacy event, that is, are not determined by that literacy event.

In an educational setting, this observation reiterates my claim from Chapter 1 that educational literacy practices cannot be understood only by observation of local settings, in this case usually a classroom. In correctional education, educational literacy events recognizable to most literacy teachers often involve literacy practices that would be wholly unfamiliar to those same teachers, an unfamiliarity stemming from the goals toward which those educational literacy events work, the worlds that *ought to be* that justify them. That these justifications are necessarily rhetorical is one reason why an examination of pedagogic discourse becomes vital to understanding educational literacy practices, because within that discourse, as an intrinsic aspect of its regulative discourse, are claims and definitions about the world in which we need to live.

That world, in correctional education, is often pulled between individual and social goals, between changing criminals one at a time or changing social structures within prisons to foster an educational environment. I examine variations on these priorities in this section. Before I begin, however, some necessarily brief comments on the receding of the rehabilitative ideal of prisons will provide helpful context.

Stephen Duguid (*Can Prisons Work?*) argues that from roughly 1945–1975, the North American prison philosophy was dominated by what he calls the medical model of criminality. This approach embraced the idea that criminality can be, in effect, cured, the central debates revolving around the right kind of treatment to fix the criminal. The point of imprisonment, then, involved "a subtle de-centring from the 'act' of deviance—the crime—and onto the individual deviant" (35), the criminal. This follows Foucault's observation that prisons focus not on the crime but the person who committed it, emphasizing more of an identity than an action. The crime receded into the background and the criminal, defined as a delinquent, as deviant, became the focus, the delinquency itself subject to a cure through the right sort of treatment. Somewhere in a mix of "mental deficits, skewed patterns, or immaturely developed abilities" existed the roots of deviance "that the psychologically driven medical model was designed to correct in order that the prisoner could acquire sufficient insight into his or her actions to be trusted once again in society" (52). Correctional efforts during this period focused largely on finding the right treatment to effect this transformation.

A highly influential critique of this model appeared in 1974, when Robert Martinson's survey of prison programs emphasizing rehabilitation reverberated across the correctional landscape. Still cited today as the "nothing works" article, Martinson argued that there was no reliable evidence that any particular approach to rehabilitating prisoners worked. His survey presented several examples of exactly how various approaches sought the "cure." Martinson looked at group therapy designed to foster an "improvement in attitudes" (31) for juvenile offenders; "milieu therapy . . . designed to make every part of the inmates environment part of his treatment" (33), requiring, in effect, an institutional restructuring—surgery (successful only in Danish sex-offenders who had been castrated; "One hopes," Martinson commented, "that the policy implications of this study will be found to be distinctly limited" [36]); drug therapy; psychotherapy; and so forth. His assessment of all of these was that "*With few and isolated exceptions, the rehabilitative efforts that have been reported so far have had no appreciable effect on recidivism*" (25, emphasis in original). He noted that such "treatment programs are based on a theory of crime as a 'disease'—that is to say, as something foreign and abnormal in the individual which can presumably be cured . . . These treatments have on occasion become, and have the potential for becoming, so draconian as to offend the moral order of a democratic society" (49). Martinson, Duguid claims, was "the sociologist resurgent" (*Can Prisons Work?* 70), arguing for the "normality of crime in society and the personal normality of a very large proportion of offenders, criminals who are merely responding to the facts and conditions of society" (Martinson 49).

Martinson's critique did not, on its own, bring about an end to the medical model, but it is representative of the ways in which it lost sway in the 1970s. (Also influential in this regard was Foucault's *Discipline and Punish.*) As the medical model fell into disregard, prisons also stepped back from making their goal of rehabilitation primary. Prisons would no longer act primarily to rehabilitate but would instead emphasize punishment and deterrence and removal from society. If prisoners sought to change, Duguid notes, it became their own decision, not the systems': "The ball was tossed into the prisoners' court, placing the onus on them to choose to make changes and in the process of course, conveniently absolving the corrections' system of any responsibility for the fate of those prisoners who 'chose' not to attempt rehabilitation" (75). Although there seems little to grieve about in the demise of a model that wholly objectified prisoners in an attempt to cure crime, it was attended with a general retreat from the possibility of rehabilitation, a retreat which challenged the very assumptions grounding the field of correctional education.

At the same time that correctional institutions began absolving themselves from a rehabilitative mission, however, they also often turned those ideals over to outsiders willing to promote them inside prisons. The period from the late 1960s into the 1990s saw a flourishing of educational programs in prisons, often connected to universities. Although I do not have the space to explore these programs in detail, Duguid (*Can Prisons Work?*) defines the "sustaining core" of almost all these programs:

> In virtually all of the post-secondary programs operating in this period the curriculum was grounded in the classic liberal arts discipline, often with a strong focus on the humanities. There was an explicit assumption

> operating in all these prison education initiatives that 'knowledge' rather than, for instance, 'work' or even 'insight' can lead to freedom. There was an assumption of there being a link between learning and action in the world, and this assumption was central to the conviction that these programs could change peoples' lives in the sense of helping them remain free of crime and hence of further imprisonment. (*Can Prisons Work?* 129)

In short, these programs usually sought to define inmates primarily as students, *not* as criminals who either needed a cure or, in the increasingly dominant model, as menaces who needed to be removed from society, incapacitated and warehoused behind bars. The tensions such an approach evoked can be seen in the debate surrounding Pell Grants for prisoners, in which the perspective of inmate as social menace finally won the day. The conflicts between correctional institutions and the educators entering from outside becomes a generic feature of accounts and analyses by those outsiders. Karlene Faith, for example, one of the founders in 1974 of the Santa Cruz Women's Prison Project, the first university program in the history of women's prisons, notes that the project continually elicited the ire of institutional staff: ". . . the majority [of the prison guards] were disdainful of trying to educate 'stupid convicts' and outwardly resentful that 'inmates' would be able to get college credits, which they perceived as rewarding prisoners for committing crimes . . . [M]any members of [the] staff, especially male guards, were contemptuous of anyone who did not regard 'criminal women' as a breed apart" (175). Simply to regard inmates as students rather than criminals was to engender suspicion and disdain.[11]

Here, then, we see again the tensions produced by promoting an educational mission within a correctional setting. The tensions have everything to do with the ways in which the inmate—or the student, the distinction of course being crucial—becomes identified. If the inmate is primarily a criminal, defined not only by a particular act but by a sort of mental predilection toward crime, one increasingly understood as intransigent, the value of an educational program can only be institutional; education might serve, say, as a useful distraction for inmates, addressing the stultifying intellectual conditions of imprisonment and thus functioning to enhance the social control of the prison. To identify the inmate as anything else than a criminal—especially as a student, the identity itself implying a willingness to learn, to change—becomes a profound challenge to the prison itself because it is an implicit and sometimes explicit critique not only of the prison system but of the criminal justice system itself. The extremely punitive nature of contemporary imprisonment relies on constructions of inmates as people whose criminal identity is primary and fundamental. If an individual bias toward criminality no longer becomes the single thing that inmates have most in common, then prisons themselves lose a central construct that justifies the ways in which they operate, and when this happens, the entire criminal justice system—and the social and economic system within which it is embedded—becomes available for critique. The cannon ready to be fired into the classroom is present not only to protect teachers from students; it is there to assert students' primary identities as criminals, as dangerous and untrustworthy.

In this section, I explore a particular way in which this tension becomes played out in the discourse of correctional education. I first examine one of the most influential theories in the history of correctional education, which uses a conception of social cognitive deficits to explain how criminals think and understand morality. In turn, this provides an educational solution for a kind of criminal mentality. The theory seems to explain a good deal about how inmates think and act, and, thus, it has considerable commonsense appeal. However, I argue here that another profound aspect of its power lies in its ability to ignore the prison itself, something that is perhaps less an ability than a theoretical necessity. Educators such as those entering through the Santa Cruz Women's Prison Project or even those in the Douglas County Jail in Lawrence, Kansas, cannot help but notice the ways in which the particular institution functions to constrain meaningful education. Duguid argues, in fact, that the entire bureaucratic structure of the prison is at odds with any sort of rehabilitative ideal:

> Prison programs throughout the modern period made various claims to rehabilitative ideals, to teaching moral virtues and forming therapeutic communities, but at their base they are bureaucratic organizations whose primary concern is a management style that centers on the basic demands of order and discipline. Whatever reformative or humanistic ideals may be communicated from above or from outside the prison itself are in most cases muted or undermined in the name of administrative convenience or security considerations. (*Can Prisons Work?* 80)

Duguid notes that prison bureaucracies must focus closely on keeping their employees as satisfied as possible, especially given the notoriously low pay and the extraordinarily difficult working conditions for correctional officers. They must also maintain a strict separation, based on moral superiority, between employees and inmates, a separation fostered by "uniforms, numbers in place of names, strict if often nonsensical rules, and even sometimes the sanctioning of brutality," all adding "immeasurably . . . to the difficulties encountered by rehabilitation efforts that include the prison staff" (81). From the perspective of the institution, docile, predictable, and compliant behavior on the part of the inmate is required. The theory of social cognitive deficits emphasizes the inmate entirely; constraints regarding learning are recognized as individual, not institutional. From an institutional perspective, that orientation is obviously useful.

Arrested Development: The Problem with Offenders' Thinking

Perhaps the most influential response to this changing correctional context came in the emergence of social cognitive theory in discussions of criminality. Social cognitive theory offered a deficit model of thinking that accounted for certain types of criminal behavior and held out the promise that education could effectively and efficiently address those deficits. Based particularly in models of Piagetian cognitive development and cognitive moral development suggested by Kohlberg as an elaboration of Piaget, a cognitive skills methodology became prominent, first in Canadian prisons and then in the United States during the 1980s. The approach stemmed from arguments that prisoners, usually referred to in the literature as "offenders" and sometimes just "criminals," suffered from "developmental delays in the acquisition of a number of cognitive skills necessary for the development of one's interpersonal problem-solving ability and moral reasoning ability which are required for effective social adaptation" (Fabiano 101). As Montross and Montross summarize, following Piaget's stages of cognitive development, "it is evident that the offenders fall somewhere between the preoperational and concrete operational stages. That is, they have the cognitive development of an 11-year-old. Could it be coincidence that most offenders despite educational achievement still function at about the 5th grade level?" (182) Regarding Kohlberg's stages of moral development, they argue that the moral judgments of inmates "reflected stage two thinking—the stage often referred to as Instrumental Relativism . . . Since Kohlberg believed that most Americans operate at stage 3, it is inevitable that those operating at stage two will come into conflict with the acceptable behavior of the general public" (183). Elizabeth Fabiano, a central figure in the rise of this model to a level of prominence in the field, explains more particularly what that delayed development means:

> We found that many offenders lack self-control. They are action-oriented, impulsive and unable to consider the consequences of their actions. Advice, warnings or punishment often seem to have little impact on them because they fail to reflect back on their behavior and its effects. Many offenders have never acquired critical reasoning skills, and they show a host of thinking errors. The most common of these is externalizing the blame for their actions onto other people or circumstances "beyond their control." (102)

This is only the beginning of a long list of deficits found in "many offenders," including "exceptionally shallow and narrow . . . inflexible, uncreative and maladaptive" thinking, an inability "to distinguish between their own emotional states and thoughts and views and those of other people," an inability "to form acceptable relationships with people," and so forth. "These deficits," she emphasizes, "were not reflective of a low I.Q. Cognitive deficits are deficits in social or interpersonal reasoning, not deficits in intelligence as measured by I.Q." (102). Harder versions of this model exist as well, most significantly in the work of Stanton Samenow, a psychologist who makes a series of categorical statements about offenders: "Offenders do not perceive human beings as individuals"; "the offender perceives other people as instruments to fulfill or block his objectives"; "The offender lacks a concept of injury to other people" ("Correcting" 57) and so forth. For Samenow, criminals can be understood as lacking particular and universally identifiable social cognitive skills. There is, in other words, a sort of criminal mind. More common is the softer version that universalizes neither offenders nor the deficits, using them to suggest potential characteristics rather than universal features.

Once these deficits become identified, strategies for educational intervention gain clarity. The problem with many offenders, Fabiano notes, "was not that they have not been thinking, but rather that they have not acquired the skills of thinking" (102). A rehabilitative curriculum, then, would teach those skills primarily, following naturally from a detailed analysis of the range of cognitive deficits present in many offenders. Beginning in the mid-1980s, especially following the publication of Robert Ross and Fabiano's *Time to Think: A Cognitive Model of Delinquency Prevention and Offender Rehabilitation*, cognitive skills became a major theoretical underpinning for the discourse of correctional education. Rehabilitation—or as it was often rephrased, "habilitation," because "The criminal cannot be restored to something he never was" (Samenow *Straight Talk* 1998)—was possible after all, and the people best positioned to effect it were educators: "arrested development rather than skewed development was the problem, leading to an educational rather than a therapeutic solution" (Duguid *Can Prisons Work?* 186).

Curricula devised using the cognitive skills models provide compelling evidence for my claim that an understanding of educational literacy practices requires an examination of how they are invoked as mechanisms of change and transformation. The field's major publication, *The Journal of Correctional Education*, is replete with examples that tie literacy practices to cognitive development. Here, I will examine two articles, noting the ways in which educational literacy events familiar to literacy and English teachers, such as essay writing, journal writing, and literary analysis, become cast in correctional education as literacy practices that many of those same teachers would find unrecognizable.

In "Teaching Cognitive Skills to Effect Behavioral Change Through a Writing Program," Cynthia Blinn describes *Writing for Our Lives*, a program she developed in conjunction with the Massachusetts Department of Corrections. The program was mandatory for inmates who voluntarily entered the Correctional Recovery Academy at Northeastern Correctional Center. Using daily journal entries and classroom discussions of student writing and short stories, "the curriculum works to shift the offender's self-identity from procriminal to prosocial," promoting reading and writing "as prosocial leisure time activities" (147). Blinn used evaluations completed by fifty-four of the seventy-two students who completed the first six classes of *Writing for Our Lives* to assess the success of her original goals.

In their daily journal entries, students (usually referred to as "offenders") recorded at least one prosocial activity, one of which they shared with the class during their weekly meeting. "The principal goal here is to have offenders view themselves as prosocial beings" (147). Blinn notes that "inmates generally exhibited increasingly prosocial behaviors—both in complying with the specifics of the assignment and in sharing their entries as models their peers could emulate" (151). Journaling here, then, becomes an exercise in learning prosocial behavior, both by reflecting on one's personal decisions on a daily basis and by simply following the assignment. Weekly writing assignments emphasize reflection about "how [offenders] may succeed as productive members of a prosocial society" and not on the past (thus avoiding "the blaming characteristic of offenders who view themselves as victims of society or the criminal justice system" [147]). Assignments included "How It Feels to Be Prosocial Me," which required a prosocial ending and "How I Am Growing in the Correctional Recovery Academy" (154 n. 2). The written feedback given by the instructor focused "on healthy life choice statements, with the purpose of providing tangible positive reinforcement for prosocial statements" (147). Literary analysis, using short stories as the primary texts, is "intended to increase inmates' awareness of social perspectives other than their own" (148):

> Aspects of literature such as plot, character development, and point of view were addressed in relation to offenders' changing self-identities and their progress in recovery. For example, when discussing impulsive actions (related to antisocial behavior), Flannery O'Connor's short story, "A good [sic] Man is Hard to Find," wherein a grandmother's impulsivity lands her entire family in trouble, was used. Point of view, for the development of social perspective-taking skills, was discussed in terms of how a story would change were it told from another character's perspective. (152)

Blinn notes that this aspect of the curriculum was not as successful because the purpose of the exercise was never clarified for the students: "In future classes, the curriculum design will take account of the offender's need to have social perspective taking skills explained in conjunction with opportunities for participants to shift to another's perspective when discussing the stories" (152).

Although most literacy teachers at any level likely utilize some or all of these techniques in their own classroom, thus being familiar with them as literacy events, it is less likely that they use them to promote prosocial behavior. The educational literacy practices in *Writing for Our Lives* connect literacy to social perspective-taking and other forms of prosocial behavior, specifically addressing a future in which offenders will actively "begin (or continue) the process of changing their self-identities from procriminal to prosocial" (151). These literacy practices, then, are defined not locally but within the larger discourse of cognitive skills education, by the changes in offender self-identities they attempt to effect.

Clyde Ahmad Winters also ties essay writing to a model of social cognitive deficits in his essay "The Therapeutic Use of the Essay in Corrections." He argues that essay writing

> helps in the social education of inmates because it: 1) is a transforming experience; 2) helps develop discipline; 3) enhances the oral and thinking processes of inmates; and 4) encourages students to be challenged by their own words. When the offender takes the time to write an essay, it is a transforming experience because he must think critically about the topic at hand. This critical thinking should cause himself to put himself in the place of others or bring about self-disclosure and a full examination of inappropriate values. (59)

Winters' overt agenda in teaching essay writing—demonstrated in his list of sample topics, such as "How can you better yourself?" "What are some ways to earn respect?" "Is there anything wrong with gangs?" "Finish these sentences (and elaborate): 'The key to success is . . .'" (60)—is not to help students get a better job (as it is in some curricula) or to help students succeed in other areas of their education (as it is in other curricula) but to effect a moral change in how inmates think of themselves in the world: "Some students realized that their behavior was wrong, and that all of their problems were not the result of a conspiracy hatched by the 'MAN' or the 'SYSTEM.' These students through introspection discovered that they must change their own lives, if they wanted to be positive members of society" (60). Essay writing, then, "helps our students contribute to their own moral development" (60). Winters here uses the language and the concepts of the social cognitive approach, and his approach is clearly focused on individual rather than institutional change. As with *Writing for Our Lives,* essay writing as a literacy practice thus takes its meaning not only from the local setting, but from broader discursive considerations about education and its purposes. The significance of literacy in this case comes from somewhere else, is shaped by a wider and extremely vexing discursive context.

One reason social cognition became such a compelling model is that it just seems to make sense, to explain how a collective group of people could willfully and in a sustained manner reject accepted social mores. I suspect most people who have spent time working within prisons can present several examples that could be explained by this theory. I recall, for example, an early experience in my teaching at the jail when I was stunned to hear one of the students in my class mock a woman who clerked the convenience store he was convicted of robbing. He mimicked her testimony at his trial, ridiculing her claim that she needed extensive therapy after the robbery. How could she have been traumatized? he wondered; the money he stole wasn't hers. From the perspective of a cognitive skills approach, this is easily identifiable as a deficit in what Ross and Fabiano call "social perspective taking," "the ability to recognize and to understand the perspective of other people and the rules, conventions, attitudes and behavior of social groups" (53). Many students in my class had what seemed to me a bewildering conception of personal responsibility combined with an amazing ability to justify the actions that had put them in jail; many seemed impulsive, selfish, narrowly focused. Many of my students, I should note, seemed to have none of these "deficits," but my experience nonetheless suggested the undeniable explanatory power of the cognitive skills approach.

What that theory explains is how and why inmates end up in prison, and why they return. Duguid's labeling of social cognitive theory as "the medical model redux" (*Can Prisons Work* 178) highlights the terms of that explanation as individual, internal, and available for particular directed treatment. This relentless focus on the individual as the object of corrections necessarily, and I think deliberately, downplays not only the setting in which education takes place, the prison, but also the cultural and political contexts fostering the mass imprisonment of the last thirty years. The theory, itself in large part a function of the social conditions produced by imprisonment, must by its own terms resist including those conditions as part of its theory. The theory accounts for the overwhelming fact of the prison by ignoring it, by making moral and cognitive development wholly internal, a process that occurs regardless of social contexts. Given the emphasis in social cognition on the individual cognitive deficits of offenders, the prison itself, as an institution and as a social setting, recedes into the background. To accept that the prison influences the behavior of inmates—or even further, to suggest that it fundamentally shapes that behavior—is to avert the gaze from the prisoner to the prison, an aversion that fundamentally disturbs the theoretical foundations of cognitive theory as well as the institutional requisites of the prison itself.

Offenders out of Context: The Problem of the Prison in Correctional Education

Karlene Faith's account of the Santa Cruz Women's Prison Project gives several examples of how a curriculum that turns away from narrowly defined goals of individual rehabilitation becomes perceived as a threat from an institutional perspective. She describes a unit, in a women's health course, on nutrition and medication. One assignment—certainly a standard aspect of a course emphasizing nutrition—had students keeping a detailed record over the course of a week of food, drink, smoking, medication and vitamins, exercise, sleeping, and work environments. This questionnaire, Faith explains, "resulted in a month-long break in the program and our first major concern as to whether the program could continue at all" (183):

> The health officers did not want to risk having information on overdrugging (for the purpose of maintaining a placid population) recorded and made public, and so it was predictable that the authorities would censor questions about this aspect of the prison regimen. However, the administration also made it clear to us that we had overstepped our boundaries by inquiring about the food. Women routinely complained about their over-cooked, high-starch, low-protein diet and the lack of fresh fruit or vegetables. No one defended the diet, including the authorities, who blamed the problem on an inadequate budget. Thus, we were taken by surprise when this component of the questionnaire was treated as a major subversive action. After more than two months of negotiation, . . . the new warden canceled the health course. (183)

Even this limited turn outward made the educational literacy event of the health questionnaire become a threatening literacy practice that required curtailment. Educational literacy practices which emphasize change as entirely a matter of individual will and effort, such as those promoted by Blinn and Winters, support the institutional mandates of the prison, but a curriculum that turns even slightly toward the institution, even as an aspect of an individual's health, easily becomes perceived as dangerous to the institution.

An especially compelling example of how a focus on the prison might shake the foundations of social cognitive theory appears in "The Necessity of Moral Education in Prisons," in which Tricia Fox describes theories of morality and their applications in correctional education. Fox explores the challenges of a prison curriculum based on moral education, relying in part on a developmental model of morality, and she deals forthrightly with the ways in which the discourse must account for the institutional and cultural reality of the prison. She argues that an individual's morality can be explained in relation to cognitive development or to environmental influences. An explanation based on cognitive development argues that "stimulating cognitive growth allows a prisoner to change his/her moral reasoning which in turn facilitates changed behavior" (22), whereas one based on environmental factors argues "that moral development results from experience within one's environment and is ultimately due to an innate tendency to develop moral reasoning" (22). Fox claims quite clearly that the conditions of the modern prison dictate which choice the educator must make. Under the environmental model,

> [g]iven that the institution functions on a very strict, regimented timetable coupled with a sterile, restrictive environment, it appears that prisoners cannot realistically practice morality . . . At this time, because of the limitations associated with the prison environment and the dominance of the purpose of prisons being to incarcerate, the cognitive development perspective is more applicable to fostering moral education in prison. (22)

In other words, if you opt for an environmental theory of morality, moral education in prison becomes pointless, because everything about the institutional environment is anathema to moral development. An educator's only alternative, then, is to understand morality as a cognitive issue. From a cognitive perspective, criminals in a prison can be changed, one at a time; from an environmental perspective, criminals will take their morality from an institution that precludes moral development and rehabilitation, and "the central 'problem' shifts from the prisoner to the prison. The prison, whether by its very nature or via the criminal subculture imported by the inmates, thus is seen as overwhelming any attempt at change or rehabilitation" (Duguid "Confronting" 58).

The difficulty of reconciling the goals of individual rehabilitation with the conditions of the modern prison becomes especially vivid in the case of "locus of control," a central concept regarding social cognition. Locus of control refers to "the degree to which the individual perceives that the reward follows from, or is contingent upon, his own behavior or attributes versus the degree to which he feels the reward is controlled by forces outside of himself and may occur independently of his own actions" (Rotter qtd. in Love 36). One's locus of control runs along an internal/external continuum: "Internals perceive that what they get out of life is determined by factors within themselves, such as ability or hard work. In contrast, externals believe that what happens to them is determined not by their efforts or skills but by external factors" (Ross and Fabiano 47). In correctional education, the theory works like this:

> Correctional educators are familiar with inmates who externalize the blame for their offenses onto other people or to circumstances "beyond their control." They blame everyone from other family members to "bad company" to society in general, and especially all members of the criminal justice system who could have elected not to investigate, prosecute, and sentence them to incarceration. Offenders blame everything from alcohol or drugs to uncontrollable urges of passion. (Love 36)

When guided by a concept like the locus of control, the goal of correctional education becomes clear: Students need to develop an internal locus of control, a sense that they are something other than victims, that they actually have agency in their own lives. They must be taught to take responsibility for their actions.

Thus, a psychological model of criminality becomes recontextualized in certain approaches to correctional education, part of its regulative discourse. Little attention is given to the prison as an institution; rather, the discourse attends to the criminal. However, an emphasis on this sort of personal transformation risks neglecting the effect of where student/inmates live, and how, aside from the commission of a crime, they ended up living there. Developing a pedagogy based on the locus of control, for example, presents certain obvious challenges in correctional settings. One of the points of prisons, especially in the United States, from their architecture to their structuring of time, is to remove criminals from a world with actual choices. Prisons are what Erving Goffman has called "total institutions," which he describes in the following terms:

> First, all aspects of life are conducted in the same place and under the same single authority. Second, each phase of the member's daily activity is carried on in the immediate company of a large batch of others, all of whom are treated alike and required to do the same thing together. Third, all phases of the day's activities are tightly scheduled, with one activity leading at a pre-arranged time to the next, the whole sequence of activities being imposed from above by a system of explicit formal rulings and a body of officials. Finally, the various enforced activities are brought together into a single rational plan purportedly designed to fulfill the official aims of the institution. (6)

Roger Matthews argues that within prisons, inmates enter a world in which time is experienced in substantively different ways than outside prisons:

> For the prisoner . . . because the present is placed in suspension, the ability to link the past to the future is limited, since the meaning of 'time' itself is lost. For some long-term prisoners for whom the future is an unthinkable and terrifying prospect, time is reduced to a continuous

> present and therefore lacks any proper chronology. These prisoners are in danger of losing a sense of personal development or purpose. (40)

To teach for the development of an internal locus of control in a world in which control is constantly emphasized as external highlights one of the central contradictions in the discourse: How do you teach productive social skills in a place designed to limit individual agency?

It seems nearly impossible not to accept such extraordinary social conditions as profoundly affecting the identities of inmates experiencing them as their life context. Roger Matthews points out that one of Goffman's most valuable observations in his work on total institutions stems from his argument that the social setting of prisons fundamentally shapes a "newly-developed inmate 'self' . . . constructed through daily interaction with other people in prison and by engaging in the daily rituals which operate in these institutions" (63). That setting is "a unique world of the unfree, gendered, class bound, and ethnically unbalanced" (Duguid *Can Prisons Work?* 79). It is so radically different than the world the inmate will encounter again as a noninmate that whatever form the self takes within the prison cannot be understood as the same form it will take outside:

> on leaving the prison, ex-prisoners are likely to revert to their previous selves in as much as they engage in the same type of activities that occupied their time before they entered prison. These transformations of the 'self' may go some way to explain the apparent paradox that the behaviour and attitudes of people in prison is a poor predictor of their post-prison attitudes and activities. (Matthews *Doing Time* 63)

If the prison as a social setting has such a strong impact on the identity of an inmate, it follows that educators within prisons ought to care about that setting, ought to think about that setting as an integral aspect of the educational enterprise.

As Fox suggests, taking the prison into account as a concern of the correctional educator comes as a peril for the prison teacher, because it risks making the educational project appear impossible, especially insofar as that project emphasizes the implicit and explicit moral goals promoted by advocates of cognitive skills education. That is, the prison overtly operates against the goals of an educator who seeks to instill in inmates a certain kind of critical thinking, personal responsibility, personal agency, and an ability to negotiate through society (prison conditions, I should note, clearly encourage many of these attributes, but not the way they are defined within the social cognitive perspective). Although it is certainly not possible to argue that inmates' interior lives are completely under control of the institutions in which they live, it cannot be argued that the disciplinary regimen of the prison emphasizes a sense of self-control. Supporting a curriculum predicated on developing the self-control of inmates, then, requires a theory that downplays the particular context of the prison as affecting that development.

However, the disappearance of the prison from the discourse leaves out a great deal more than the inherent institutional constraints of imprisonment. It also ignores the extraordinary changes in imprisonment and criminal justice over the last thirty years, the most dramatic rise in incarceration in the history of the United States. Consider again the claim made by Montross and Montross, cited earlier, in which they argue that "the expanding prison population results at least in part from a lack of education" (179). Given recent correctional history, this is an astounding claim, one that completely ignores the political and cultural shift in attitudes toward imprisonment and criminality, which have resulted in a massive increase in the inmate population in three decades. To suggest that this increase is based on a lack of education is disingenuous at best, and completely sidesteps one of the most pressing civil rights issues facing the United States at the beginning of the twenty-first century.

The numbers themselves suggest the absolute absurdity of blaming prison growth on the poor education of prisoners. In 1972, the national inmate population, in state and federal prisons and jails, stood at about 330,000; in June of 2004, the latest available data, 2,131,180 were incarcerated, an almost 650 percent increase in 32 years. As of June 2004, there were 923 male, state or federal prisoners, with a sentence of one year or more, per 100,000 U.S. residents, a standard way of measuring inmate population (the number increases to 1,348 when jail populations are added) (Bureau of Justice Statistics). This already shocking number—by far the highest in the world among industrialized countries, Russia a distant second—becomes more outrageous when broken down by race and age: Among African American males in their late 20s, the number of inmates per 100,000 is 12,603, over 12 percent. For African Americans aged 20–39, the total is over 10 percent in each age group. In 2004, an African American male had more chance—roughly one in three—of going to prison than he has of attending college (Sentencing Project). The population of African Americans in state and federal prison or local jails is significantly higher than the population of White inmates, 843,500 to 695,800 (Bureau of Justice Statistics), making African Americans—roughly 13 percent of the population of the United States—incredibly overrepresented in prisons and jails.

When the prison disappears behind explanations of criminality that rely upon individual educational levels and social cognitive deficits, so too does this extraordinary growth and racial imbalance and any political or cultural causes for it. That is, focus on the cognitive deficits of criminals turns away from the idea that criminality is also a social construct, that, aside from any psychological considerations, what also makes a criminal is the political and legal system that provides the label and defines appropriate consequences for behavior defined as criminal. However, it is difficult to attribute the escalation in imprisonment to a corresponding growth in the number of individuals with social cognitive deficits, nor does it correspond to rising crime rates. A more likely answer comes in the changes in policies and attitudes toward criminality in the last thirty years.

I have already noted Martinson's 1974 "nothing works" essay, part of a pattern in the early 1970s that suggested the impossibility of rehabilitation. This pattern corresponded with the growing popularity of a tough-on-crime rhetoric coming out of the 1960s, which peaked (or perhaps plateaued) during the Reagan-Bush administrations. The two premises, that rehabilitation was not viable and that out-of-control criminals required swift and harsh punishment, fueled initiatives and policies promoting inevitable and lengthy imprisonment as the best retribution for intransigent offenders. Such reforms as mandatory sentencing removed any independence judges had regarding penalties at the same time that they increased the power of prosecutors to get plea bargains from the indicted. Truth-in-sentencing laws required those indicted to serve their full sentences without hope of early release. Three-strikes-and-you're-out laws required lengthy sentences after a third offense variously defined by the states enacting the legislation.[12] All these became central in the war on drugs, which drastically increased the time served for drug offenses. This in turn translated into a massive industrial growth in prison construction and security. The enormous and ongoing potential for profit is suggested in the $8 billion allocated for building prisons in the same law that eliminated Pell Grants for prisoners. In 2000 alone, state and local funding of prisons stood at approximately $51 billion. At this point, the power of the prison industry and the amount of high-tech and expensive prisons suggests the difficulty of redirecting criminal justice policies away from mass imprisonment.

Aside from the statistics I have already cited, the evidence is overwhelming that these policies affected African American and other minority males disproportionately, thus making them the "expanding resources" (Chambliss 314) of the crime control industry. From 1980–1995, African Americans accounted for 21 percent of all drug related arrests (reaching a peak in 1992 at 36 percent). During the same period (1980–1992), Mauer (1999) notes, the chances of being incarcerated on a drug-related offense rose 447 percent, largely as a result of mandatory sentencing. Such mandatory sentences were especially harsh with those arrested for involving crack cocaine, arrests much more likely among African-Americans. Mauer notes that a mandatory sentence of five years attached to selling 500 grams of cocaine powder, the same sentence for selling 5 grams of crack. Mauer argues that "the drug war has exacerbated racial disparities in incarceration while failing to have any sustained impact on the drug problem" (143). One could gloss this by saying that the drug war and its associated policies have done more to create new categories of criminals and less compassionate paradigms for retribution than they have done to deal adequately with crime.

Analyses of the prison industry, the massive growth in imprisonment over the last 30 years, and the extreme racial disparities throughout the criminal justice system are extensive and enormously complex, too much so to receive any adequate summary and discussion in this chapter.[13] My point here is simply to note that when the discourse of correctional education defines criminality as a result of individual deficits and predilections that can be addressed educationally, it avoids other extremely compelling factors surrounding criminality. As David Downes claims, "If individuals are entirely responsible for crime, structural and cultural theorizing is inadmissible" (55). Clearly, how one theorizes criminality has enormous implications for educational programs designed to correct criminality, a process that becomes vastly more complicated when the "correction" seems to require as least as much a social as an educational response.

The difficulty of using this as a critique of the field of correctional education should be apparent, though. How should teachers in prison take into account such policies, such growth and disparities? Also, although everything about prisons makes them a stark example, similar issues should resonate with teachers in almost any situation. The discourse of vocational education faces a similar conundrum as soon as it acknowledges that issues such as outsourcing, the increase of service-level jobs with few or no benefits, a very low minimum wage, global free-trade agreements, and so forth are certainly more important in explaining economic shifts than a presumed widespread inability of adults to work in the high-performance workplace. Vocational curricula that are focused on such social and cultural issues are very rare, but imagine the far less likely presence of institutionally sanctioned correctional curricula that deal with, say, racial disparities in arrests, sentencing, and imprisonment, with the political and economic implications of the growing power of the prison industry. In the rest of the chapter, I argue for approaches to correctional education that at least begin to address the need to change the structure of prisons, but these approaches are quite far from any meaningful realization in North American prisons. Caught in a unprecedented change in correctional policies, in a mania of prison construction and privatization, teachers in prisons—like teachers anywhere else—typically must justify their work according to the logics of the system that employs them.

Prisoners and Prisons: Expanding Objects of Reform in Correctional Education

Stephen Duguid argues that, because North American prisons inherently work against educational goals of increased independence and critical social analysis, educators in those prisons must be separate, and understood as separate by inmates, from the correctional system. Educators, in other words, must remain outsiders, a position Duguid argues is necessary in order to foster a legitimate educational environment even if it will, more than likely, put them at odds with the staff of the system.

To even consider such institutional constraints necessarily changes the role of an educator within a prison. As Fox suggests, particular tenets of a theory of moral education are no longer viable given the conditions existing within most prisons. From this perspective, an educator can no longer focus on addressing individual shortcomings and requirements of students. The goal of the profession becomes twofold, as Thom Gehring puts it, "to reform prisoners and prisons" ("A Change" 167). Noting that that when prisons function as "dungeons, factories, and warehouse[s]" they have been failures, Gehring claims that the only sensible alternative is to turn prisons into schools, so that inmates will "become more social" before they return to their (our) communities. Thus, the institutions as well as the prisoners become subjects of the discourse. This process of becoming "more social," however, is not simply a matter of putting in place a prosocial curriculum in prisons. Rather, it requires a fundamental change in understanding the role of the prison itself.

In a discussion of the Swedish correctional system, Svenolov Svennson asks, "Do we have *citizens in prison* or do we have *prisoners*?" (70) In a thinly veiled reference to United States prison policy, Svennson suggests the consequences of taking the latter perspective:

> To make the punishment reaction more clear, we tend to extend that reaction, in time and action. The rehabilitation is of course also wished for, but it's up to the individual to take that step and "to learn the lesson." Over time, however, this system seems to make it even more difficult for prisoners to take adequate steps in the right direction. They become caught in a negative spiral, receiving longer/harder sentences and making an increased reality of reintegration impossible. The effect is obvious. More people are imprisoned and the way back to society is harder and less probable. Some societies seem to have become immersed in this perspective, and they are "digging" deeper and deeper in an "impossible" process. (70)

For Duguid, understanding inmates as citizens requires a fundamental shift in attitude toward them, a belief that "citizenship is possible even with the most troubled of our peers if we appreciate their complexity, treat them with respect, and demand reciprocity—treat them, in other words, as subjects rather than objects" (*Can Prisons Work?* 18). Duguid's work is representative of a significant thread in the field that argues that the prison as it exists cannot sustain a meaningful educational experience. A major bureaucratic function of the prison, Duguid argues, is to objectify the prisoner, to define him or her as an object, as "the degenerate, the feeble-minded, the moral imbecile, the habitual offender, and, more recently, the psychopath" (ibid 28). Everything about the prison—uniforms, numbers, unceasing surveillance—emphasizes objectification, creating "a relationship of sterile dualism" (Duguid "Subjects and Objects" 241). The system then seeks to transform this objectified prisoner into the sort of subject valued by the prison: "The sense of character, dignity, and self-esteem that the prison regime attempts to impose on the prisoner is one that prepares the person for a life of submission to authority, rule following, and self-discipline, all qualities of functional value within the prison and, as perceived by some, in society" (231). But Duguid argues that the objectification of the prisoner simply masks the subjectivities that those prisoners enter with: "In the prison, . . . we are not offering a life of subjectness—the life of a citizen—to a mere object—a criminal. Instead we are trying to persuade a subject disguised to our eyes as an object to, in fact, switch subjectivities—a much more complicated task" (*Can Prisons Work?* 69).

Duguid argues that the programs that have had the most success encouraging inmates to reconceive their subjectivities are those that have come from outside, "incursions to the formerly closed world of the prison" (ibid. 230), particularly those that treated the prisoner as a subject, which "often centres on creating a democratic participatory environment" (230). He also stresses bonds with the "conventional world" and a sincere acknowledgement that "prisoner needs are many and varied and the intervener's skills and abilities both various and limited" (230). In such an environment, educational literacy practices must resist terms that emphasize a particular object turning into a particular subject (a criminal, for example, becoming prosocial). Rather, the educational literacy practices must allow for a subject to subject discourse.

Prefabricated curricula that advocate predetermined goals for inmate transformation are unlikely to meet such criteria, because they will not account for the actual students who attend classes and because they will not allow student voices in shaping and reshaping those goals. Duguid, who helped develop and run a postsecondary educational program in British Columbian prisons, describes an alternative educational space, one distinctly separate from operation of the rest of the prison, created so that inmates see themselves as being treated as subjects rather than objects:

> constructing an alternative community within the prison meant experimenting with democratic decision making within the program, offering classes that focused on controversial subjects, creating a fine arts and theater program with opportunities for performance and role-taking,

> and importing into the prison as many personalities as possible from the university community. Accomplishing this required from the prison a degree of autonomy that in many respects was unprecedented in its liberality and cooperativeness. (*Can Prisons Work?* 128)

The theater program, Duguid notes, was particularly successful, both in the sense that students who participated within it were active, eager, and capable and that "theater participants improved over their predicted rate of recidivism by an impressive 52 per cent" (245) in a study covering the 20 years of post-secondary education in British Columbian prisons. The theater program, he claims, created a public sphere for prisoners, a civic sphere requiring democratic decision making, and a private sphere allowing for self-reflection. Moreover, outside the theater program, the educational program as a whole often had considerable student input about administrative and pedagogical issues. Here, educational literacy practices become tied to the creation of separate social spaces that allow prisoner-students to practice democracy and decision making, which allow them to exercise choice and understand consequences.

Likewise, Kathy Boudin describes a basic literacy program she helped teach as an inmate at the Bedford Hills Correctional Facility, the women's maximum security prison in New York State. Noticing the extraordinary interest students had regarding a television show about AIDS, Boudin developed a curriculum around AIDS for the women. At the time, she notes, more than 20 percent of the women entering the prison were HIV positive, and the AIDS epidemic affected most prisoners' lives directly. Reading lessons, vocabulary lessons, and writing exercises all focused on AIDS. Finally, students wrote a play about AIDS, which involved studying other plays and understanding basic elements of drama, then writing and performing the play throughout the prison and for all the prison's counselors. Boudin claims that the play directly influenced the formation, by inmates, of "a program of peer counseling and education about AIDS" and that the women in the class had learned, through the process, "that their use of literacy ability—the reading and writing about AIDS and the writing of the play—had made a difference on a common crisis, AIDS" (142). She also described a class that wrote a handbook for new inmates "that would speak to their fears and questions" (142). After reflecting on their own experiences, including discussions about immigrants in prison and being pregnant in prison, the students created *Experiences of Life: Surviving at Bedford Hills*, learning in the process the elements of a book as well as editing skills and the existence of different language forms. Boudin's examples highlight educational literacy practices that treat the students as subjects and that emphasize immediate concerns at the same time that they allow for significant literacy learning.

To varying degrees, the program Duguid describes and the classes Boudin describes rely on carving out alternative spaces within prisons where voices can be heard and controversial issues examined and taken seriously. In these spaces, students can be something other than inmates, and the actual process of creating workable communities is a central meaning of the literacy practices. Duguid, a professional educator from the outside, and Boudin, an inmate, both operate separately from correctional officials, working in spaces that are not wholly determined by traditional correctional priorities. These are explicitly designed as different sorts of carceral spaces and they allow both for a recognition of student subjectivities and a community process suggesting potential subjectivities that go beyond some version of the "productive, tax-paying citizen" often advocated within the discourse of correctional education.

For some writers, setting aside separate places that can operate against the impulses of the prison system, whether in the form of a classroom or a program, is too narrow a goal. In this argument, the entire institution should operate according to democratic principles, the objective being "to transform the prison into a school, which can develop better citizens instead of better prisoners" (Eggleston and Gehring 307). Richard Arbenz, writing in 1994 as an inmate in the California Department of Corrections, argues that such a transformation in prisons requires seeing the entire enterprise through an educational rather than through a punitive framework:

> Every program, activity, and work assignment should be rooted in cognitive-democratic theory, and serve some purpose toward promoting the personal development of participating inmates. Comprehensive restructuring of this nature requires that correctional educators not only ascend to full authority over their traditional domain, but that these professionals assume authority over entire correctional agencies. (35)

In these scenarios, institutional literacy practices become educational literacy practices, and the prison becomes transformed into a school, one predicated on democracy and decision making. Although these suggestions still do not address the remarkable growth of imprisonment in the last thirty years, they suggest an understanding of the inmate that challenges a paradigm used to define inmates as superpredators or inherently deficient.

Perhaps the most sustained and remarkable vision of such a prison occurs in Austin MacCormick's 1931 *The Education of Adult Prisoners*. MacCormick traveled to nearly all the state and federal prisons in the country, focusing especially on their educational programs, and his assessment of those programs was beyond dismal: "Of all the fields in which the American penal institution gives evidence of futility, education very nearly heads the list" (38). MacCormick's solution involved a reconception of the prison itself, focusing on a system he called "inmate community organization":

> The institution is made as nearly like a normal community as possible. An opportunity is given for inmates to participate under careful guidance in the direction of its activities and, as a group, to assume responsibility for their proper functioning. The officials set up certain standards of work and conduct, differing little from those of free communities, but place on the inmate body as a whole the responsibility for seeing that these standards are lived up to. The individual prisoner feels that he is responsible primarily to his fellows and only secondarily to the institutional officials. He is taught to live as a citizen by practicing citizenship in a miniature community. (210)

MacCormick resists any overreaching definition of criminality, suggesting that prisoners are simply "a group of individuals who have one thing in common, that they have committed a crime, but in whom this common factor does not eradicate the other differences so that we can say 'This is the education the prisoner needs'"(37). In MacCormick's vision, inmates attend school fulltime, year round, in classes of no more than twenty students with a variety of offerings. A full contingent of teachers, administrators, and counselors run the educational programming, and a comprehensive and accessible library is available to all inmates. The educational programming ranges from literacy to basic mathematic courses to university offerings. Correctional education, by MacCormick's model, is not located within a prison—it is the prison. Educational literacy practices thus, by definition, emphasize the democratic operation of a functioning community; everything exists to promote a particular model of citizenship, and every aspect of institutional life emphasizes education.

Most startling in MacCormick's book, however, is his open and immediate announcement, made in the preface to his book, that none of the reforms he advocates are realizable in the penal system as it is constituted in 1931:

> It would be possible, within the compass of a brief volume, to record what is now being done in penal institutions, how existing educational work can be made more effective without any substantial increase in appropriations, and how the present low aim can be achieved a little more successfully. The writer does not believe this to be worth doing. He has consciously and deliberately set an aim higher than any penal institution can achieve with present appropriations and present personnel. The attempt has been made to formulate a complete and well-rounded program of education such as no penal institution can put in effect until it receives more substantial support from legislators and administrative officials. Without trained personnel this program can never be put in effect; in this respect it does not differ from all other educational work. (xi–xii)

MacCormick recommends, that is, what he frankly acknowledges cannot be accomplished. Likewise, Stephen Duguid argues for his vision of prison education after the Canadian government replaced the successful and innovative college degree program in a British Columbia prison in which he had taught and administered with a cognitive skills program that was cheaper and more rhetorically catchy. Both writers, that is, project a future that seems, given the political and cultural rhetoric and practices surrounding crime and imprisonment in the United States (and Canada), currently unrealizable. And yet this future remains at the center of their arguments.

Paraphrasing Duguid, when the central problem for correctional education moves beyond the prisoner, it almost by necessity focuses on the prison itself. No longer content with a theoretical model that emphasizes the transformation of criminal into noncriminal, these models of correctional education aim at the reform of the prison itself, advocating fundamental changes in their operation that will, arguably, enhance the development and positive education of those incarcerated within them. To theorize about educational literacy practices with this position toward prisons is to argue that teachers need to take overtly and carefully considered political stances about the institutions in which they teach, that they see themselves as advocates for students, even in those places outside the classroom where students become identified as something else. It suggests that such issues as racial injustice within sentencing and arrests, and the power of rhetorics of harsh punishment and relentless retribution, are central and pressing, not peripheral, concerns of correctional education. Even if the prison is not a central focus of one's educational theories and practices, however, those theories and practices remain fundamentally shaped by the prison. As Fox suggests, the fact of the prison itself potentially dictates the degree to which one gives credence to environmental or cognitive models of morality. No matter the theoretical orientation advocated, correctional education is largely determined, fundamentally shaped, by the institutions in which it operates. To claim this is not to suggest that teachers have no agency in likewise shaping that orientation; rather, it is simply to claim that no educational theory, no educational literacy practices, operate outside institutional locations that shape them directly. Thus, any theories about teaching and learning likewise need theories about the institutions within which teaching and learning take place.

CONCLUSION

At the heart of all these approaches, from social cognition to prisons becoming schools, are arguments about the world that is as well as the world in which we need to live, claims about the present and the future. In the world as it is, are inmates prisoners or citizens in prison? What position, if any, should the discourse take about the current functioning of the prison (always remembering, as with particular discussions of social cognitive theory, that a claim of no position is still a strong position)? How should educators take into account such criminal justice issues as mandatory sentencing and extraordinary growth in rates of imprisonment? How should they understand social conditions that lead to the vastly disproportionate incarceration of African Americans, especially African American men, and other non-White ethnic groups, as well as poorer members of society in general? If correctional educators do not consider these questions as central and vital, then they defer to the answers provided by the institutions and systems within which they work.

Likewise, correctional educators must have in mind a vision of the world in which we need to live. Does that entail the creation of better, more comprehensive cognitive theories of criminal behavior so that teachers can more adeptly address that behavior educationally? Is the future world one in which all the inmates can read at some particular basic level, or one in which all inmates have or are working toward their GEDs? Is the future world one with a broader perspective on the relationship of education to change? Should educators in prison have a position and response to the growth of the prison industry? How should the prison operate? What role should educators have in that operation? Just as broad questions about criminal justice and social equity matter in conceiving of the world as it is, so do they matter in the vision of the world in which we need to live. Again, when these questions are not considered seriously, answers will be supplied for them from the institutions and systems.

At the opening of this chapter, I used the cannon in the classroom as a metaphor for the way in which the prison, in whatever form, definitively asserts itself into the practice and theory of correctional education. To teach in a prison or jail is to know, always, where one is, if not exactly why one is there. Some sort of institutional reminder is always present, perhaps not in the shape of a cannon, but in the clothes students wear, the officer that might be in the back of the classroom, the clanging doors that punctuate class discussions, the intruding loudspeakers, the panic button I kept discretely tucked in my shirt pocket. A teacher in a prison is never apart from that prison, and never apart from the penal system and the criminal justice system either. The mandates and purposes of the institution and the systems shape that teacher fundamentally, regardless of the degree to which the teacher acknowledges it. In some form or another, the cannon is always there.

I claim in the introduction that there is always something at stake in arguments about educational literacy practices. In correctional education, what is at stake is the very purpose and role of imprisonment and punishment in the United States. What is at stake is the human possibility for change, the sorts of environments created by the state to house criminals, and the potential for education to play a primary and not merely subservient role in a profoundly vexing civil rights issue. To advocate particular educational literacy practices within the discourse of correctional education is to take a stance on these issues, implicitly or explicitly. Using Bernstein's terms, any instructional discourse is embedded within a regulative discourse, a discourse that implies a moral vision, a vision of the world as it *ought to be*. For correctional educators, who find themselves in overcrowded places rife with despair and hopelessness, with violence and wasted potential, a lucid and hopeful vision of the world as it is, as well as the one in which we need to live, has a particular urgency, for it is that vision that will sustain the practice in light of the contextual challenges.

In *Newjack: Guarding Sing Sing*, journalist Ted Conover describes the year he spent as a prison guard in New York's most infamous prison. He tells of a friendship he had with an inmate he calls Larson, who he identifies as Black, and describes a conversation in which Larson commented on the fact that the government was planning for prisons they will need in ten or twelve years. "What's wrong with planning ahead?" Conover asked him. Larson's reply highlights the tension between preparing for future criminals and educating an at-risk populace:

> Because, dig this. Anyone planning a prison they're not going to build for ten or fifteen years is planning for a child, planning prison for somebody who's a child right now. So you see? They've already given up on that child! They already *expect* that child to fail. You heard? Now why, if you could keep that from happening, if you could send that child to a good school and help his family stay together—if you could do that, why are you spending that money to put him in jail? (233)

Larson's question/lament about the futures we project for those most threatened by social inequities should matter to literacy educators at all levels. Educational literacy practices are about futures; they matter in the world in which we find ourselves, to be sure, but also for the world in which we hope to live. Kevin Warner notes that prison educators "must assert, in the penal context, those values consistent with good education, and, inevitably, that will entail challenging the misrepresentations and destructiveness inherent in many current policies and practices" (131). Regardless of whether a correctional educator accepts Warner's recommendations, she necessarily takes a political stance, one shaped if not determined by the institutions she finds herself embedded within; paraphrasing MacCormick, in this respect she does not differ from all other educators.

CHAPTER 3

Imagine That You Are

Literacy and Competencies for the High-Performance Workplace

At the beginning of the last chapter, I used the image of the cannon in the classroom to highlight the constant and necessary presence of the penal institution in the discourse and practice of correctional education. Metaphorically, I argued, the cannon always exists in correctional education, because theories about teaching and teaching itself are always shaped inherently by demands and realities of the prison and the criminal justice system. It is this relationship I extend in this chapter, arguing that the pedagogic discourse of vocational education cannot be understood apart from the economic interests it serves, apart, that is, from its various sponsors. Albeit typically in far less physically identifiable ways than in a prison, there is a kind of cannon in these classrooms as well, continuously asserting the expectations and assumptions that business leaders and politicians have about the role of education.

In her discussion of workplace literacy programs, Mary-Ellen Boyle notes that such classes serve an important symbolic role for businesses, demonstrating a commitment to their employees through a program ostensibly designed to make them more skilled, more employable and better workers in general. She notes that the employees subject to such classes are largely entry-level, often immigrants, and certainly for the most part of low-status both socially and in the workplace, and that the classes themselves do not operate to change that status, a change that would not be advantageous for employers who rely upon their labor. Thus, the classes serve the interests of businesses, which appear to be acting benevolently, while not meaningfully raising the literacy level of the student workers:

> by appearing to improve skills, employer-sponsored literacy education allows the firm to continue to employ inexpensive labor. And by documenting that workers are lacking in basic skills, the firm can justify paying them at low levels. The logic is circular, and could be worded as follows:
>
> > We cannot pay them more because they are illiterate, we want them to stay barely literate so that will not have to pay them more. But we will sponsor a minimal workplace education program, with a broad curriculum, because this will result in more loyal employees with the desired work attitudes, and will signal to other constituents that we are acting responsibly in the face of changing work demands and increased competition.
>
> This may explain why programs continue: employers cannot afford truly literate workers, and really don't need them. So they offer education for its symbolic value, ensuring that only incremental improvement occurs. (106)

Boyle argues that although workplace literacy programs might include a "modicum of basic skills enhancement," the primary goals are "attitudinal and cultural adjustments," which would develop more effective employees. Teaching workplace attitudes under the rubric of literacy instruction also aids, Boyle suggests, in the control of workers: "These attitudes are certainly positive from the employer's perspective, and might be understood as indicative of employee consent. Loyal, happy, learning focused workers appear to be in agreement with employers' goals. Consent is a subtle form of employer control, and the literacy program is a particularly ingenious way to bring about consent" (107). In addition, the provision of literacy programs has other potential effects, she notes, signaling the degree to which businesses value employees, differentiation from other organizations through their altruistic projects, and demonstrating the ethics of the company (50–51). This range of symbolic values, of course, relates directly to the institutions in which these literacy programs exist.

The idea that workplace literacy programs might primarily serve symbolic rather than educational purposes highlights their regulative purpose on several levels. At the same time that literacy programs aid in developing workers that can meet the economic needs of a company, they also foster its outside reputation: "Employers can remain profitable, while at the same time appearing benevolent and legitimate" (105). In part, such benefits accrue simply through the seeming transparency of the idea of literacy, which exists as a self-evident force of beneficial change, such that to provide workplace literacy programs appears as an inherent good. I highlight the symbolic nature of literacy education because it sustains many of the arguments I examine in this chapter. Politicians and businesses can claim concern for the employability and education of individual workers as their main impetus, while providing a curriculum designed to enhance profit and efficiency in the workplace, with little change in the status and power of individual workers.

The documents I explore in this chapter, the U.S. Department of Labor's Secretary of Labor's Commission for Achieving Necessary Skills (*Skills and Tasks, What Work Requires,* and *Learning a Living*) and Northwest Workplace Basics (NWB) *Assessment System*, present particular skills—what they call competencies—as necessary for learning to work in the high technology workplace of the twenty-first century. Although SCANS has had considerable influence, I examine these documents, not because of their individual effects, but (1) because they signify a particular change within the discourse of vocational education and (2) because they reflect particular rhetorical strategies prominent in official discourses of education. First, these documents are representative of what Diane Pullin has called "a movement unequalled since the founding of public vocational education in the early part of this century" (32), one which presents learning for work, not in terms of developing skills in a trade, but in terms of learning attributes such as critical thinking and teamwork. Such attributes are presented as transferable from job to job, allowing workers the flexibility necessary in an economy that does not favor employment in one job for life.[14] Second, these documents exhibit particular rhetorical strategies present in a range of official educational rhetoric. Centrally, they legitimate themselves by claims of neutrality and objectivity at the same time that they reaffirm a popular notion of education as functioning to do away with cultural hierarchies. This strategy props up the No Child Left Behind Act of 2001, for example, which asserts a primarily educational solution—one based on scientific research—to social inequality. This chapter, then, will explore the particular logic of competencies within the discourse of vocational education, arguing that such logic has become dominant within official educational discourse.

On one level, the competencies as they are outlined in these documents could be called definitions of literacy themselves, connected as they are to increased anxiety about the state of literacy, and especially illiteracy, in the United States. Note, for example, the fear of chaos and disintegration illiteracy invoked in this excerpt from *The Bottom Line: Basic Skills in the Workplace*, a 1988 precursor to the SCANS initiative released jointly by the U.S. Departments of Labor and Education:

> No issue is as crucial to the future of America as illiteracy in the workplace. We simply cannot allow this nation to enter the 21st century without a literate, skilled, flexible workforce. From individual businesses to entire industries, the effect of a workplace unprepared for an information based, service-oriented economy will be devastating. (19)

What does it mean, in these terms, to be illiterate? As the reference to an "information based, service-oriented economy" makes clear, illiteracy is being defined as an inability to function within a particular network of production, a network that demands flexibility and skills and one that is crucial to the economic well-being of the country. Literacy is here defined, naturally, as an economic tool in service of business, industry, and nationalism. Certainly, the intrinsic connection of the educational literacy practices advocated within this discourse to values associated with so-called high-performance workplaces highlight their regulative nature. Literacy practices within vocational education project a vision of workers, employers, and the workplace, emphasizing a particular version of control under the guise of empowered and flexible workers capable of a variety of employment and responsible for working in teams with management in a democratic spirit to maximize efficiency, quality, and profit for the good of all.

Developing my argument that all educational approaches advocate a vision of the world as it ought to be, I argue that the current discourse of vocational education has developed an especially compelling rhetoric, one that allows it to appear as neutral, simply helping students prepare for a workplace that already exists or is inevitable in the years to come. Thus, education appears to prepare students for a world that is. At the same time, the current discourse of vocational education teaches a particular approach to work that privileges changing and more sophisticated approaches to the control of workers. Thus, a seemingly transparent correspondence between the expectations of work and the curriculum provides a way to prepare students for a particular economic position.

I explore these arguments in this chapter, beginning with a discussion of the history and application of the idea of competency within education. A central claim of one approach to competency-based education—that particular generic skills can be taught and observed, so that one can be said to have the skill of, say, thinking critically—contributes to its discursive power. In effect, SCANS and NWB claim to promote objective and neutral skills that, once acquired on a wide scale, will be overwhelmingly transformative. The act of promoting competencies can be represented as outside an ideological framework at the same time that it serves everyone—workers, businesses, and the nation—in an equally positive manner. This representation of competencies as above ideology while inherently and wonderfully transformative has a good deal in common with early academic discussions of literacy. I argued in Chapter 1 that, notwithstanding literacy studies' two-decades-long project demonstrating the intrinsically ideological nature of literacy, the notion that literacy transcends ideology continues to have enormous appeal from a policy perspective. One purpose of this chapter is to apply that perspective to this discourse of vocational education. In the particular examples I study, I argue that the representation of competency-based education as above ideology masks its regulative focus on sophisticated methods of control in the workplace. I explore the competency of "learning to learn" especially, arguing that its focus on what Bernstein calls "trainability" becomes necessary in an economy emphasizing regular job changes for employees. I conclude the chapter by arguing that the influence of the current discourse of vocational education extends well beyond its traditional framework, suggesting that the rhetorical power of an education apparently connected via a one-to-one correspondence with the real world provides a model for pedagogic discourse that has considerable appeal and affects the work and professional position of teachers at all educational levels.

COMPETENCY, COMPETENCY-BASED EDUCATION, AND THE HIGH-PERFORMANCE WORKPLACE

> Words like "competence" and "standards" are good words, modern words; everybody is for standards and everyone is against incompetence. (Norris 1)

The two texts I examine closely in this chapter—SCANS and the Northwest Workplace Basics (NWB) *Assessment System*—rely heavily on the term *competencies* to support their educational agendas. The term, as Norris suggests in the preceding quotation, relies on an ideal of competent performance that itself is impossible to argue against. No one wants an incompetent teacher, or an incompetent doctor, or an incompetent employee, so an education that promises to base itself on ensuring competence in practitioners has a particular appeal. The idea of competence as an educational ideal, Bernstein argues, appeared in the 1960s as a recontextualization of popular social science theories, but its present day connotations have dramatically changed. The current meaning of competencies derives from a behavioristic approach to education that initially appeared as a reform for preparing teachers, and although it has been manifested in various ways within educational settings, the idea of competency-based education still focuses on controlling the work of teachers to ensure that they develop students competent to perform the work they are being trained to perform. That is, a system that initially started as a way to ensure that teachers leaving education programs were competent to teach became popular across a number of professions, but competency-based education still always acts as an educational fail-safe, eyeing teachers as its main subject of practical reform.

In a 1995 essay examining the competency-based education movement in England, Rob Moore and Lynn Jones note that the official power it had gained by that moment had nothing to do with the theoretical strength of its behaviorist approach, which they call "dated and simplistic to a remarkable degree," adding, "It is probably fair to say that it is only within the current competency movement that it retains any credibility" (80). Rather than point out, again, the theoretical shortcomings of the dominant view of education (a skill most critics of education have honed to a particular degree), their argument suggests that we should try to understand what makes such an outmoded approach to education so officially compelling; in fact, they go so far as to argue that the very features that open the competency-based model of education to critique make it valuable from a policy perspective:

> this model is well suited to fulfil a particular set of policy objectives. It is its appropriateness for policy rather than its intrinsic viability that has sustained it. Essentially, the problem is that it is precisely those features that constitute its virtues from a policy point of view (the clear and simple operationalisation of disaggregated 'skills' and measurable standards of performance) that condemn it theoretically and methodologically. Any attempt to strengthen the model by moving in an holistic or relational direction disables it as a policy instrument . . . The logic of competency is located within the politics of practice, not in social theory. (81, 84)

I mention this here as a reminder to me, and to any reader, that the project of critique does not necessarily amount to a significant response to dominant approaches to education. A sustained critique of competency-based education has been ongoing for several years, particularly in international journals of education, at the same time that models of competency-based education seem, if anything, to have gained more official currency. If the model has not been chosen for its theoretical viability but for its usefulness as a policy tool, it stands to reason that arguing against its theoretical viability will do nothing to decrease its power as a policy tool, because theoretical viability was never the point.

Thus, although this chapter does indeed join a long line of voices critiquing competency-based education, in this case focusing on two U.S. models from the 1990s in particular, the overall point of the chapter is not to highlight, once again, the theoretical shortcomings of this dominant approach. Rather, I follow Moore and Jones in asking what I see as the more compelling question: "In terms of which particular model of social order does the competency discourse make sense?" (83). In the terms of the argument I outlined in Chapter 1, that question could be rephrased as: What ideal of the world as it ought to be does the competency discourse project?

Moore and Jones turn to Bernstein's discussion of pedagogic discourse to further examine the competency movement, arguing that "Competency should be examined as a pedagogic discourse rather than as an educational theory" (84). Instead of examining the approach to competency as located within the field of production of educational theory (which would call for us to counter it with alternative theories and perspectives), we should understand models of competency as located within the field of recontextualization, having gained currency not for the theoretical viability of their instructional procedures but for the usefulness of the regulative discourses they promote. I use SCANS and NWB to explore this regulative discourse in this chapter.

Bernstein argues that the current idea of competence has been co-opted from an educational approach that signifies nearly its exact opposite. Initially, he claims, competence as an educational idea derived from approaches to social competence that gained particular currency in the 1950s and 1960s, appearing as linguistic competence (Chomsky), cognitive competence (Piaget), cultural competence (Levi-Strauss), members' competence (Garfinkel), and communicative competence (Hymes). In all these settings, "The concept refers to procedures for engaging with, and constructing, the world. Competences are intrinsically creative and tacitly acquired in informal interactions. They are practical accomplishments" (*Pedagogy, Symbolic Control* 42). Bernstein argues that "according to competence theories there is an in-built procedural democracy, an in-built creativity, an in-built virtuous self-regulation. And if it is not in-built, the procedures arise out of, and contribute to social practice, with a creative potential" (43). That is, individuals have the capacity, by nature of being human, of being creative and self-regulating and acting within a community, inherently learning language, social customs, acceptable ways of thinking and acting.

Recontextualized into educational settings, these became models of pedagogy that emphasized "the realisation of competences that acquirers already possess, or are thought to possess" (45). So, education becomes less a process of teaching and learning than of assisting students in reaching their full natural potential, and the process emphasizes "projects, themes, ranges of experience, a group base, in which the acquirers apparently have a great measure of control over selection, sequence and pace" (45). He contrasts the competence model to what he calls performance-based models of pedagogy, which place "the emphasis upon a specific output of the acquirer, upon a particular text the acquirer is expected to construct and upon the specialized skills necessary to the production of this specific output, text or product" (44). Thus, a competence model of education guides a student toward actualization of an inherent potential, whereas a performance models specifies (and assesses on the basis of) particular learning outcomes or texts.[15]

This realization of competence in education, then, focuses on creating membership within a community or group, a process, as Moore and Jones argue, that occurs in particular locations and is demonstrated by "contextually located social practices" (87). People in actual settings acquire competence tacitly, "realised in the routine exercise of tacit skills in the everyday world" (88). What this implies, they argue, is that "competence is only ever expressed through contextually defined social practices and is relative to the tacit rules and expectations of context" (88). Being competent, in this description, has everything to do with particular social, cultural, and institutional contexts. The idea of competence as manifested in the contemporary emphasis on competencies, however, has more to do with Bernstein's performance model than with a competence model, highlighting an inherent slipperiness of the term that is part of what Norris calls "the trouble with competence" (Norris 1). The noun has shifted from an inherent human capacity—competence—to a particular skill that one may or may not possess—a competency.

Most commentators link the emergence of competency-based education to reforms of teacher education in the United States in the late 1960s and early 1970s. In a 1976 article, Margaret Lindsay explored the roots and practices of competency-based teacher education in New York, arguing that the initial calls for reform stemmed from "widespread social unrest" (505) and that public education became an obvious focus of these calls:

> it is natural that education as carried on in the nation's schools comes in for reexamination. Generalizations are reached: For example, it costs too much; the program is too far removed from reality; it's geared to middle class values and aspirations; and does not meet the needs of all the children. Conclusion: Clearly those planning and operating the schools are inadequate and the materials supplied are biased and inappropriate. Something has to be done. (506)

Competency-based teacher education promised to address some of these problems by identifying what competent teachers do and making these behaviors central to teacher education. Student-teachers learned (and were evaluated on the basis of) competencies such as introducing lessons, appearing in their earliest forms as "checklists of teacher behavior, which are ticked off by an observer" (Whitty and Wilmott 309). Competence in this model thus becomes defined

> in terms of the discrete behaviors associated with the completion of atomised tasks. Its aim is the transparent specification of competencies such that there can be no disagreement about what constitutes satisfactory performance. In effect the task becomes the competency, so that if, for example, a mechanic can replace a fuel pump or a teacher introduce a lesson, s/he is said to possess the competency of lesson introduction or fuel pump replacement. (Gonczi)

Such an approach connects competence to observable behaviors and separates it from a holistic view of teaching (or car repair), making the pedagogy of particular actions central.

As defined by SCANS and NWB, however, competencies line up with what Gonczi defines as a second approach to competency based education, emphasizing

> the general attributes of the practitioner that are crucial to effective performance. Such an approach concentrates on the underlying attributes, e.g. knowledge or critical thinking capacity, which provide the basis for transferable or more specific attributes. Thus the general attribute thinking critically, it is assumed, can be applied to many or all situations. (Gonczi)

SCANS and NWB apply this approach to vocational education, emphasizing personal attributes instead of job-related behaviors. Rather than preparing students by teaching them vocation specific skills (like welding or tenkeying) or discrete behaviors associated with particular jobs, this approach to vocational education argues that the twenty-first century workplace (what SCANS repeatedly calls "the high-performance workplace") demands higher-level skills from its workers and that preparing students for such workplaces is a matter of deciding what sorts of generic skills are most necessary there. Success in acquiring these competencies will lead, the argument goes, to increased employability on the part of job-seekers, increased productivity on the part of industry and business, and support for national economic superiority. (These promises, as I shall note, are of course threats as well.)

In the early 1990s, the U.S. Department of Labor Secretary's Commission for Achieving Necessary Skills produced several documents detailing their skills, policies needed to successfully enact them, and theoretical issues surrounding their recommendations. The first, *What Work Requires of Schools*, introduces the skills, and subsequent ones detail their relevance to workplaces, as well as the legal and political challenges they must confront in enacting these skills as part of a national workplace related curriculum. Through these documents, SCANS seeks to present and elaborate on a set of competencies and foundation skills that they believe students should learn in schools and workplaces should emphasize in job creation.

Based on questions asked of hundreds of employers and thousands of employees, SCANS developed a highly ordered set of skills, divided into two areas, the competencies and the foundation (I will hereafter refer to both as SCANS competencies), for families, schools, and workplaces to embrace. The competencies include five categories, each with several subsets:

1. **Resources**: Allocates time; allocates money; allocates material and facility resources; allocates human resources.
2. **Interpersonal**: Participates as a member of a team; teaches others; serves clients/customers; exercises leadership; negotiates; works with cultural diversity.
3. **Information**: Acquires and evaluates information; organizes and maintains information; interprets and communicates information; uses computers to process information.
4. **Systems**: Understands systems; monitors and corrects performance; improves and designs systems.
5. **Technology**: Selects technology; applies technology to task; maintains and troubleshoots technology.

Likewise, the foundation skills come in three categories, with several more subsets:

1. **Basic Skills**: Reading; writing; arithmetic; mathematics; listening; speaking.
2. **Thinking Skills**: Creative thinking; decision making; problem solving; seeing things in the mind's eye; knowing how to learn; reasoning.
3. **Personal Qualities**: Responsibility; self-esteem; sociability; self-management; integrity/honesty. (U.S. Dept. of Labor *Skills and Tasks* xvii–xviii)

Each of these subsets includes elaborate explanation of how this skill operates in a job setting. "Seeing things in the mind's eye," for example, (a thinking skill) has to do with the ability of a worker to organize and process "symbols, pictures, graphs, objects, and other information: for example, [the worker] sees a building from a blueprint, a system's operation from schematics" (C-2), and so forth. These skills appear as the necessary characteristics of America's twenty-first century worker, if America hopes to maintain global economic superiority. In a phrase reminiscent of E.D. Hirsch's ambition, with his list of what all Americans should know, SCANS argues that these competencies will aid in "develop[ing] a better means of communication, a common vocabulary to guide the conversation between the business and school communities" (U.S. Dept. of Labor *What Work Requires* 5–6).

Like SCANS, the Northwest Workplace Basics *System*, developed as a pilot project by the Northwest Regional Educational Laboratories, relies on a set of competencies and skills focused on employer needs. Designed for use by adult basic education programs in Oregon and Washington, the NWB *System* closely adapted competencies developed in *Workplace Basics:*

The Essential Skills Employers Want (Carnavale, Gainer, and Meltzer). In its introduction to, and defense of, their *System*, the NWB designers excerpt a lengthy portion of that book, and then go on to present the following seven competencies "to reflect the needs of Northwest employers" (N. 1):[16]

> **Learning to Learn**: Personal; Interpersonal; Cognitive.
>
> **Basic Skills**: Reading; Writing; Computation.
>
> **Communication:** Listening; Speaking.
>
> **Thinking Skills**: Problem Solving Skills; Higher Order Thinking Skills; Creative Thinking Skills.
>
> **Personal Management for the Job**: Self Esteem; Goal Setting-Motivation; Personal Development; Career Planning and Development; Life Skills.
>
> **Group Effectiveness**: Interpersonal; Negotiation; Teamwork.
>
> **Influence**: Organizational Effectiveness; Career Growth Within an Organization; Leadership.

Within each skill under each competency are several subskills, totaling to 125 components defining what it is that employers want. The NWB *System*, however, goes one step further than SCANS by providing specialized curriculum and assessment tools for use in teaching and measuring the competencies, for a total of three weighty notebooks. I encountered this *System* in the fall and winter of 1992–1993 as one of 10 Washington State adult basic education instructors chosen to implement it as part of the Washington Integrated Curriculum for Achieving Necessary Skills (I-CANS).[17]

My point in using these texts as examples is not to indict particular manifestations of vocational education as insufficient or theoretically untenable. Rather, I use them to exemplify a particular pedagogic discourse, one that seeks to define what makes employees successful so that such attributes can become central to vocational education. I cannot claim the NWB *System* as having extensive influence. I use it as an example because I had extensive experience with it as a teacher. The SCANS documents were widely influential through the 1990s and continue to be referenced today, but I am not interested in exploring (or critiquing) the extent of that influence. Discussing these documents as manifestations of pedagogic discourses emphasizing employability, especially of so-called underskilled adults, and current conceptions of the workplace, allows me to explore the ways in which such discourses mask their regulative intent by claiming that they simply reflect real-world practices. I see this masking as an ongoing rhetorical strategy that presents officially sanctioned educational theories and methods as scientific and thus neutral, objective, real, uncontroversial. Likewise, the discourse of competencies, as with early arguments about literacy studies, explains social hierarchies through measures of individual ability, that is, unemployed and underemployed workers lack competencies, and when they get those competencies they will be equal members of the highly skilled and non-hierarchical high-performance workplace. Just as prevailing theories of correctional education rely on definitions of criminality that mask the prison, so do dominant theories of vocational education define unemployment as having individual, and almost never social or political, causes. More recent and influential reforms, such as No Child Left Behind, continue to proclaim individual educational achievement as the primary cause of and solution to economic and racial disparities in the United States.

For my purposes, then, the most important aspect of competencies is their reputed transparency, their ability to incorporate into the curriculum things that exist already outside that curriculum. In order to be successful, students need to learn how to perform well in the changing workplace, a workplace in which particular demands are made. Education can assist in this project by designing curricula (at all levels and in all subjects, according to SCANS) that emphasize what students will need to know and do in the world of work, focusing on what SCANS calls "real things for the real world." This claim of transparency, of direct correspondence to the "real world" of work, is a critical rhetorical claim for education and one commonly used in a variety of other settings. By basing their goals in a "real world" located outside the classroom, schools can maintain a necessary fiction of service to that outside world, a project that can be conveniently separated from having a moral or political, in Bernstein's terms, a regulative, function. Education should prepare students to exist in the world that already exists, or, in some cases, is inevitably on its way. The power of competency-based education, then, lies not in its theoretical strength or educational pedigree, but, at least in part, in its promise to teach students truly practical skills, skills that everyone can agree are necessary for success within, and for the development of, the high-performance workplace of the twenty-first century. Thus skilled, those students will achieve economic equality and security, and the nation will maintain its economic strength.

REAL THINGS IN THE REAL WORLD: THE RHETORIC OF LITERACY IN THE SCANS AND NWB COMPETENCIES

The idea of literacy that makes it such a potent symbol in workplace literacy programs, as Boyle suggests, is one in which literacy acts as an inherent good with intrinsic transformative powers. Relying on a representation of literacy as both context-free and inherently positive, as I argued in Chapter 1, allows for an understanding of teaching and promoting literacy in any context as a virtually nonideological act. It is simply for the better to promote literacy. Increased employee literacy being good for business occurs as an outgrowth of a more general notion that increased literacy, by definition, will be good for everything. There is seemingly nothing controversial about such a decontextualized literacy. It's all good. Likewise, if literacy is an inherent good that exists outside of particular contexts, then a concern about sponsors of literacy is also immaterial. To sponsor literacy can be represented as an act of altruism fostering general and positive social transformation. If a sponsor of literacy gains some sort of benefit from such a sponsorship, it is part of the general effect of promoting literacy. Everyone, not just the sponsor, benefits.

Although the lists of competencies in SCANS and the NWB *System* do not introduce themselves as definitions of literacy, I argue here that they provide their own broad definition of a literacy designed to ensure that workers meet the needs of national economic interests. As I argued in Chapter 1, thinking of literacy teaching in terms of teaching literacy practices means that we understand it as teaching ways of "utilizing written language" as well as the "values, attitudes, feelings, social relationships" (Barton and Hamilton 7) attached to those uses. The lists of competencies proposed by SCANS and NWB suggest a concern with particular literacy practices and the values attached to them. Along with, say, technological adeptness, the SCANS competencies teach self-esteem and responsibility, whereas the NWB *System* highlights the basic skills of reading, writing, and computation along with career growth within an organization and goal setting. These competencies, then, emphasize particular literacy practices, so while a traditional definition of literacy shows up as only one aspect in these lists (basic skills), the personal characteristics and cognitive qualities promoted are explicitly tied to what it means to be a literate American.

Both SCANS and NWB go to great lengths to present the development of this literate American worker as a nonideological act at the same time that they argue that it will have a dramatically transformative effect. As in the early theories of literacy I explored in Chapter 1, these competencies promote radical changes, outside of any politically charged context. Both SCANS and NWB give the competencies an independent and empirically verifiable existence; they don't create them but find them. The competencies, that is, exist in the world as it already is. That grounding means that any transformation their promotion might cause can be understood as simply maximizing the potential of an already objective reality. Therefore, promoting the competencies is not about creating a world that *ought to be*, in Horton's terms, but about making that world that *is* even better at what it's already doing.

In order to detach themselves from an act of creation, SCANS and NWB present their competencies as empirically derived, verifying their objective existence. By basing their list of competencies on thousands of interviews with employers and employees, SCANS asserts the competencies as pre-existing. The authors of the NWB *System* make a similar claim. After starting with the skills from *Workplace Basics* (Carnavale, Gainer, and Meltzer), themselves based on extensive employer surveys, "both Oregon and Washington validated the competencies statewide. The project received approximately 415 validation surveys across the two states. Of the 415, 268 were from employers. The remainder came from government employees, educators, job trainers, and others" (N. 1). From these surveys, the NWB authors claim, "two missing competencies" were "uncovered." Even the language suggests the pre-existence of competencies that must be meticulously discovered through surveys of experts, dug up like an archaeological find.

Likewise, the ability to assess and measure the competencies reliably suggests their objective existence. In *Learning a Living,* SCANS recommends that all students receive a document called the Certification for Initial Mastery (CIM) that would "contain information about courses taken, projects completed, and proficiency levels attained in each competency" (xix). The CIM, which they propose establishing at the eighth-grade level, would be the equivalent of a resume, but it would presumably give employers an accurate, and universally applicable, measure of the skill level of prospective employees: "The information would mean the same thing to everybody: this person has the SCANS workplace know-how noted here" (xix). The CIM thus promises to end ambiguities associated with assessment, providing a transparent demonstration of ability that requires no interpretation, that means the same thing to everybody, a claim of universality. Northwest Workplace Basics presents numerous assessment tools (diminutively referred to as "testlets")—from multiple choice questions to role-playing scenarios—designed to measure a student's competency level. By presenting several different measurement techniques to cover the range of competencies and subskills, NWB aspires to an objective measurement of a student's achievement. The testlets are divided up into appraisal, which determines the competencies a student needs to work on, pre- and posttests, which determine a student's understanding of a competency before and after instruction, and certification testing, "to verify what a learner has mastered" (NWB N. 2). Taken together, the testlets promise to provide a broad and objective picture of a student's readiness to work.

SCANS and NWB also present their competencies as universally applicable for all people in all places. In a document called *Skills and Tasks for Jobs*, SCANS details the ways that each skill is used in different ways, with differing levels of complexity, by workers as diverse as a high-level executive to an entry-level machine operator. Writing, for example, is utilized by an industry training specialist at the highest level of complexity, who does everything from researching the training topic to "giv[ing] photocopied pages to the clerical staff for the assembly and reproduction of the training manual" (2–56). At the lowest level of complexity, writing is utilized by the plastic molding machine operator, who in documenting the failure of a machine records pertinent data and writes down conclusions. This competency at writing can be learned, this suggests, without reference to particular contexts. In fact, reference to particular contexts—except insofar as they are on the job—must be avoided, because universality transcends any contexts. So, everyone equally needs to learn the skills; they apply wherever paychecks are distributed.

The claim of universality also operates as a rhetorical device to persuade teachers, employers, administrators, and the public of the importance of implementing the policies behind the lists. SCANS, for example, maintains that the competencies play a part in every service and industry in the country:

> The competencies span the chasm between the worlds of schools and the workplace. They are the basis of the modern workforce dedicated to excellence. They are the hallmark of today's expert worker. And they lie behind every product and service offered on today's market—putting food on tables, travelers in rooms, airplane passengers at their destinations, patients in the operating room, and automobiles on the street. (*Skills and Tasks* 11)

The competencies, in other words, reflect the universal needs of business at all levels, and by making this connection, as the preceding quotation indicates, SCANS can make a case that these competencies will strengthen the link between "the worlds of schools and the workplace."

If the competencies already exist, if they are universally necessary, then they are not controversial. As Ong put it, they are above the "arena where human beings struggle with one another" and exist in some way as part of our inherent human capacity. Promoting them is the only responsible action to take. This existence, seemingly independent of human agents, means that the transformation engendered by successfully teaching the competencies on a wide-scale is also, in some way, independent of human agents. People teach the competencies, and learn them, but the competencies themselves, taken on by individuals, effect the social transformation. To represent widespread social transformation as outside a political and ideological framework is a heady trick but one encouraged by a dominant understanding of literacy as a singular and objective ability. Like the transformations commonly associated with literacy, the increased acquisition of competencies benefits everyone and has no ill effects. (It's helpful here to remember Horton's suggestion that literacy education has no intrinsic value, that it matters and can be understood only in terms of the purposes for which it is used.)

In a world where the competencies organize educational agendas, businesses will become high-performance workplaces, and schools will become more relevant and connected institutions of learning, and citizen workers will become life-long learners. For example, in SCANS' vision of schools in the year 2000, schools have taken the skills as the driving force behind their curricula, and the difference SCANS imagines this making demonstrates the alleged transformative power of their skills. Speaking from the vantage point of the year 2000, SCANS pictures institutions where

> [a]ll teachers, in all disciplines, are expected to incorporate [the SCANS skills] into their classwork. . . . Students will find the content more relevant and challenging. Teachers will find their classes more attentive and interested. Employers and college officials will be delighted with the results because the curriculum will be tied to real things in the real world. (*Skills and Tasks* 21–22)

Embrace the skills, the commission suggests, and we will be safe: In their utopian vision of the year 2000, "students of all ages learn more per hour in schools of all sorts and workers earn more per hour on the job . . . our children are internationally competitive in math and science and, partly as a result, so are American goods and services" (*Skills and Tasks* 20).[18] Literacy, in the form of successful application of their model, transforms the learning and earning potential of individuals and the competitiveness of the United States.

Failure to teach, apply, and learn the skills, though, comes with the most severe of consequences. In an open letter to parents, employers, and educators that prefaces *What Work Requires of Schools*, the commission outlines the dire results of ignoring their recommendations. Parents must emphasize SCANS at home by posting the competencies and talking about them with their children: "Unless you do," the commission warns, "your children are unlikely to earn a decent living" (vii). Employers ignore SCANS at their own risk: "If you do not develop a world class workforce, your business will inevitably be at risk" (viii). And educators have the greatest burden of potential failure on them: "If you do not [instill in students the perspectives on results that the SCANS skills demand], you will be failing your students and your community as they try to adjust to the next century" (viii). All this adds up to the following premise (promise):

> A strong back, the willingness to work, and a high school diploma were once all that was needed to make a start in America. They are no longer. A well-developed mind, a passion to learn, and the ability to put knowl-

> edge to work are the new keys to the future of our young people, the success of our businesses, and the economic well-being of our nation. (*Skills and Tasks* 1)

Turn these around and the recommendations become threats, threats that parents and teachers will fail America's children, threats that businesses will go bankrupt, threats that the United States will lose economic superiority because its workers are not well-prepared for "high-performance work-places."

As Glynda Hull has noted, workplace and vocational literacy programs "regularly take as a given that literacy is a requirement for everything and anticipates benefits from a literacy program, both for the worker and the company, that are numerous and wide-ranging, such as productivity, promotions, accuracy, on-time delivery, self-esteem, and job retention. There are almost no attempts at qualifying this rhetoric" (36–37). This rhetoric is fueled by the classic literacy narrative, in which transformation is the standard result of becoming literate. In vocational education, the transformation brought on by literacy is far ranging. Individuals become more capable of finding and preserving jobs, they become more productive workers, companies are able to compete on the world stage, and the United States is able to maintain international economic superiority. The persuasive nature of this story means, as Hull points out, that the rhetoric of vocational education appeals not simply to "died-in-the-wool conservatives or right-wingers," but also to "concerned teachers, committed literacy specialists, well-meaning business people, eager students, interested academics, progressive politicians, worried parents, and a host of others as well" (22). That appeal is directly tied to the transformational powers attached to literacy.[19]

Finally, in ways I argue are intimately connected with control, these competencies naturalize the institutional and power separation between workers and management. Richard Ohmann (1985) has argued that since the term *literacy* appeared in common usage in the late nineteenth century (as opposed to *illiterate*, which had been in use much longer), it always operated as a way for the educated elite to maintain their cultural superiority in a seemingly objective manner:

> [The discourse of literacy] was a top-down discourse from the start, and its participants almost invariably took the underlying question to be: How can we keep the lower orders docile? . . . Once the lower orders came to be seen as masses and classes, the term "literacy" offered a handy way to conceptualize an attribute of theirs, which might be manipulated in one direction or the other for the stability of the social order and the prosperity and security of the people who counted. (677)

As a descriptive term, literacy is useful in distinguishing between classes; the competencies represent a particularly sophisticated method of promoting this separation at the same time that they disguise the very existence of hierarchical and power relations. One of the ways this occurs in the literature of competencies and skills, I have already noted, appears in the discussion of the high-performance workplace, which itself appears as an institution unfettered from bothersome hierarchies. This erasure of hierarchies occurs most subtly in the ways that the curricular and assessment documents, and the competencies themselves, include references to evolving forms of control over in the workplace. As I will argue in the following section, the goals of the SCANS competencies and the testlets NWB attaches to them can be read as preparing workers to take their proper position in workplaces directed by simple, technical and bureaucratic control. In addition, these competencies promote a new method of control, one suggested by the calls for nonhierarchical, high-performance workplaces, in which workers take on for themselves the goals and successes of the company.

CONTROL IN THE COMPETENCIES AND THE TESTLETS

In his history of workplace control in the United States, Richard Edwards (1979) describes a move from overt control—embodied in the relationship between worker and boss—to more covert forms of control—work dictated by technological forces or bureaucratic norms. Control becomes harder to link directly to the structure of business, shifting to technology and to the worker herself. The current trend in vocational education, I argue, works to evade notions of control through complicated descriptions of the high-performance workplace and the lists of competencies workers need to be successful within them. Control seemingly disappears as an issue on the job, as employees are handed more responsibility for decision making and provided more apparent autonomy.

Edwards presents the need to maximize productivity as central to understanding the organization of the workplace in its many historical manifestations. Business and industry, he argues, must exercise adequate control over the labor force to ensure that they produce sufficient labor power to maximize profits, a process that Edwards claims "remains to be carried out in the workplace itself" (13). I read much of the current concern over vocational education—in the workplace, in community colleges, and in secondary schools—as a move to engage the dynamics of control beyond the workplace itself, to enlist schools and educators, as well as industry, in the process of workplace control. In describing the formations this control has taken in the last 150 years, Edwards traces a movement from simple to structural control, the latter having both a technical and a bureaucratic aspect. The current discourse of vocational education displays a concern with each level of control, but the language of high-performance workplaces and highly skilled workers present in the discourse, like the technical and bureaucratic control described by Edwards, seems to eliminate control as a job issue at all.

Edwards argues that simple control stems from the hierarchical nature of small, entrepreneurial enterprises, where one boss directs everyone. As businesses grew larger, this method of control remained in place with foremen and supervisors directing the work at each level, themselves directed from the top. Such a system, however, became unwieldy as the size of corporations grew. Workers rebelled against it, and as more and more layers appeared within corporations, efficiently exercising control through such structures became ineffective. Such a method of power became especially difficult to operate as workers began organizing in resistance to the growth of monopoly capitalism. As Roy Jacques points out, "unlike the foreman, the overseer, the 'gang boss,' the office in the new industrial army had to become proficient in coaxing and persuading. . . . [I]t was clear that the traditional system of physical punishment and coercion was out of place in the new order" (88).

The insufficiencies of simple control, Edwards argues, were addressed by technical and bureaucratic control, which he claims tend to make power "invisible in the structure of work" (110). These two forms of control, I want to suggest, particularly bureaucratic, exist implicitly in many of the NWB and SCANS competencies. Technical control operates by basing production on technologies that control the labor process. Pacing and direction are determined by technology, shifting the conflict from boss (as under simple control) to machine. Technical control operates through the machine, which manages, monitors, and measures output, production, skill, and so forth. This coincides with what Jacques argues was a shift from an organization centered on workers to one centered on numbers and statistics: "Quantification implied a shift of knowledge (and thus authority) from the worker to the expert. It resulted in exteriorization of knowledge; it no longer resided in the worker, but in tables and slide rules which could be controlled differently" (106). This in turn facilitates a bureaucratic control, which "establishes the impersonal force of 'company rules' or 'company policy' as the basis for control" (Edwards 131). Workers receive intricate job descriptions and must learn the corporation's complicated sets of rules, thus making explicit "what the worker is supposed to do while at work" (136). Bureaucratic control makes the behavior of workers more predictable and offers a useful way to define the qualities of a good employee. Edwards cites three behaviors that bureaucratic control rewards: rules orientation, "an awareness of the rules and a sustained propensity to follow them" (149), dependability and reliability ("one who works diligently within the rules of a normal situation . . . and who carries on in the spirit of the job description in situation where the rules do not quite apply" (150)), and the "internalization of the enterprise's goals and values" (150). Like technical control, bureaucratic control distances power from a supervisor, who acts only to enforce already existing rules; "power appear[s] to emanate from the formal organization itself" (145).

Edwards never addresses the notion that such efforts at control might not succeed in achieving the desired invisibility. As Linda Valli notes, attention to the culture of work suggests that bureaucratic control easily fails to make power invisible in the workplace. Although one insurance firm she studied "seemed to employ the most rigid form of bureaucratic control of any of the organizations I observed," workers there blamed not the company policies, but the supervisors, "for the strain, pressure, and demands under which they worked" (164). However, Edwards's analysis helps highlight the ways that modes of control have become increasingly more covert. In fact, a seeming lack of control operates as one of the hallmarks of the so-called high-performance workplace. SCANS describes these new workplaces as "a model for a successful future. In this new environment, work is problem-oriented, flexible, and organized in teams; labor is not a cost but an investment" (*Skills and Tasks* 3). Carnavale, Gainer and Meltzer in *Workplace Basics: The Essential Skills Employers Want* describe the high-performance work system as one with the following characteristics:

> employees are involved, not passive . . . [E]mployees work face-to-face . . . spending most of the time interacting with co-workers or customers . . . [W]orkers are more autonomous in order to exploit more flexible work structures and technologies . . . [W]ork is more social, organized into teams and general community of practice . . . Everyone understands his or her role in the broader context of the entire work process from product design to customer, as well as the organization's strategy and vision. Everyone is responsible for the quality of the final product or service. (195, 240–42)

In such a vision, control is nonexistent; employees take responsibility for everything in a near utopia of autonomy and teamwork and employers seem altogether absent, perhaps just more team players. On the surface, this could be a description of a worker-owned cooperative, in which workers are motivated in part by being direct beneficiaries of the profit. SCANS and Carnevale et al., however, are not describing worker-owned cooperatives. They are more likely describing firms that Richard Lakes describes as "hierarchical and privatized, run by corporate elites as self-defined oligarchies."

In firms like these, Lakes argues, "high-performance workplaces are top-down management strategies used solely to enhance efficiency and productivity of the firm" (110).

Still, the ideal of the high-performance workplace becomes the basis for a new definition of a good worker, a definition that includes reference to earlier forms of control—simple, technical, and bureaucratic—but which extends one step beyond bureaucratic control by universalizing this ideal worker's characteristics. As part of this trend, the extensive list of skills is not specific for one job in one industry, like a job description under bureaucratic control, but interchangeable from job to job and workplace to workplace. As I shall examine later, the skill "learning to learn" in the NWB system becomes shorthand for measuring the adaptability of employees to shifts in job requirements or jobs. As befits an economy in which workers will presumably move from job to job several times over a life, these skills are meant to prepare workers for successful adaptation to a variety of work settings. At the same time, the outlining of these skills allows business to take a more directive role in shaping educational curricula; that is, instead of focusing on the individual skills of a single trade in direct vocational training, schools can now concentrate—indeed, have the obligation to concentrate—on a wide range of skills that will prepare students to take their proper role in the new high-performance workplaces. Setting educational agendas, then, becomes one way of addressing what Gee, Hull, and Lankshear call "the *core dilemma* of the new capitalism": how to "control 'empowered partners' in the absence of visible, overt top-down power" (60). As they argue, texts promoting the "high-performance workplace" typically include "a strong emphasis on bringing about a change in schools and thereby changing the values and attitudes of tomorrow's workers" (31).

The need for business to directly influence the goals of schooling is of course nothing new. Harvey Graff identifies one of early industrialization's principal problems as "the organization and indoctrination of the workforce" (*Labyrinths* 66). Literacy, Graff argues, was not a necessary condition for industrial development (in a commonly perceived causal relationship); rather, industrial development required a particular kind of literate worker. Industry creates new demands for education, calling for the development of workers in its own image:

> Literacy, then, constitutes a training in being trained. A person who in childhood has submitted to some process of disciplined and conscious learning is more likely to respond to further training, whether in an army, a factory, or in participatory activities. This training is the critical job preparation and the problem for industrial development; simultaneously it has been the first task of school and one critical use of literacy. (67)

In their history of schooling, SCANS presents a deterministic model of schooling that reinforces the notion that the proper role of education is to prepare students for the workplace. In the past, SCANS reports in *Learning a Living*, "[t]he schools did a magnificent job of turning out just the kind of product required. Workers needed enough education to read, write, and comprehend instructions. Above all they needed to follow instructions faithfully and show up for work reliably" (12). Now, however, "[t]he enemy is rigid insistence on a factory model of schooling" (xviii), in which students are viewed not as "workers in the learning enterprise" but "as buckets to be filled" (12–13). Crucially, this model of schooling is vilified not because it prepares students for the models of control on the workplace, but because the models of control it teaches are outdated. SCANS argues for a change in education reflecting a dissolution of three old rules of American work, themselves connected to simple and technical forms of control: "Rule one was that the boss was always right. Rule two was that the employees did what they were told. And rule three was that companies should standardize production because profitability depended on producing more and selling it cheaply" (11). SCANS seems to claim that the "factory model of schooling" was appropriate under former and less subtle methods of control, because it prepared students for their proper position. This is the only place in which they directly link the purpose of education to forms of control, but their call for schools to reflect changing conditions of work implies that a primary purpose of schooling is preparing students for the modes of control in the workplaces of the day.

The competencies themselves are full of direct parallels to methods of control in the workplace. Not surprisingly, they do not contain many references to simple control (the NWB system includes some). Though simple control, according to SCANS, is outdated in a high-performance workplace, technical and bureaucratic controls remain a cornerstone, and the competencies reflect that. Technical control, as I noted earlier, has the effect of making the machine, rather than the supervisor, the determiner of work, from pacing to technical responsibility; instead of being told to do something, a worker is guided by the demands of technology. SCANS provides technology as a distinct competency, in which the worker is meant to achieve proficiency in the selection, application, and maintenance of technology. SCANS defines the skill *selects technology* as "Judges which set of procedures, tools, or machines, including computers and their programs, will produce the desired results" (*What Work Requires* B-2). In both the SCANS and NWB competencies, the reasoning for including basic skills includes frequent reference to an employee's ability to understand technology. Quoting from Carnevale, Gainer and Metzer's *Workplace Basics*, the NWB authors report that workers need basic skills for operating and relating to machinery. A lack of skills, they claim, will make employees liabilities to a company in ways primarily, though not exclusively, related to technical control: "Deficiencies in such basic workplace skills create barriers that impair an employer's ability to meet strategic goals and to be competitive. They are reflected in productivity decline, increased accident rates, costly production errors, and the inability to effect critical job retraining" (NWB N. 1). Learning to use technologies competently, then, is important insofar as it enhances the goals and competitiveness of business.

But the competencies are most clearly related to bureaucratic control. As Edwards described it, bureaucratic control distances control even farther from the employers and management by making work contingent on policies and rules. Instead of the supervisor, the job description spells out details, and critical here is the worker's internalization of what it means to be a good worker. Edwards describes the hallmark of a good employee as rules orientation, dependability and reliability, and the internalization of a company's goals and policies. The competencies stress this most strongly, these skills presumably being (along with learning to learn, which I will describe later) the most transferable from workplace to workplace.

"Personal Qualities" in SCANS and "Personal Management" in the NWB *System* are the competencies that most promote this vision of the good worker. In the NWB *System*, personal management is by far the most comprehensive competency, with four subskills and forty-three categories, including, under the subskill of personal development, the ability to "Identify appropriate behaviors and attitudes for keeping a job, e.g. punctuality, respect for others, good grooming, self-control." In the SCANS list, a person demonstrating competency in the subskill of responsibility is one who

> Exerts a high level of effort and perseverance towards goal attainment. Works hard to become excellent at doing tasks by setting high standards, paying attention to detail, working well, and displaying a high level of concentration even when assigned an unpleasant task. Displays high levels of attendance, punctuality, enthusiasm, vitality, and optimism in approaching and completing tasks. (*Skills and Tasks* C-2) [20]

Certainly, a student or worker who displays mastery in personal qualities or personal management is one who, among other attributes, is well-prepared to meet the demands of bureaucratic control, in which an employee has fully internalized the goals of the company. This ideal worker will need almost no supervision, happily completing the most onerous tasks in a timely manner and with "enthusiasm, vitality, and optimism." In these circumstances, management is almost completely effaced as a reality, and this is the naturalizing of cultural hierarchies at its most insidious. Employees do not produce because they have to, or because they are told to, or because they are paid to; they produce because they want to.

Likewise, the repeated emphasis on group effectiveness and team skills reorients control away from management. Work is done in teams, with equals, committed fully to the company's nearly socialistic vision. Susan Robertson notes that this emphasis on teamwork promotes a sort of self-regulation that elides control as an institutional concern:

> Group or team-oriented strategies overcome the problems of alienation inherent in Taylorist forms of labour organization. . . . Of particular interest to researchers has been the way in which workers in teams become self-regulating. That is, the group becomes a means for the regulation of worker behaviour and performance, as opposed to regulation through hierarchical forms of supervision. . . . Because these new organisational principles are only adjustments in the technical relations of work—or in other words, choices about which technique might be used to enhance worker productivity—they are little more than sophisticated means of worker control. (127–28)

Indeed, the high-performance workplace can be seen as the logical extension of bureaucratic control, a place where workers are motivated by personal commitment to their work and to the quality of their company's product or services.

The preparation for control is even more explicit in the NWB *system* testlets. Here, students seem to be assessed most closely about to bureaucratic control. In the testlet focusing on Group Effectiveness: Negotiation (N. 2), for example, the following question is notable for its complete focus on rules:

> Read the following question and select the best answer:
>
> 2. Ann has been working for the State Forest Service for one year, and there are some things that she would like to change about her job. Which of the things is Ann **most likely** to change through negotiation with her supervisor?
>   a. Changing the week she will take vacation this year.
>   b. Being excused from wearing her Forest Service uniform on days that she is not working with the public.
>   c. Reporting directly to the head of the State Forest Service, instead of to her regular supervisor.
>   d. Selecting the crews that go out to put out fires.
>
> **Question 2:** The correct responses for the test items are as follows:
>
> The job requirement to wear a uniform and the organizational structure of the Forest Service are elements of the job that an employee of one year is not likely to change. The correct response is:
>
> a. Changing the week she will take vacation this year. (NWB N. 2)

Here, rules, unattached to any person, direct Ann's conduct, which is the hallmark of bureaucratic control. The role of the worker, and the conditions that guide her job, are completely separated from employee hierarchies within the workplace (except insofar as spelling out whom Ann should report to [c] and whom she has authority over [d]). This is a focus not on negotiation, as the curriculum claims, but on recognition of rules.

In the assessments for critical thinking, which NWB borrows from the Comprehensive Adult Student Assessment System (CASAS), students are asked to read the following policy in a test of their ability to "[i]dentify appropriate behavior, attitudes, and social interaction for keeping a job and getting a promotion."[21]

> If an employee is going to miss work due to sickness, the following procedure should be followed:
>
> 1. Notify your supervisor that you will absent.
> 2. Immediately upon your return to work, complete a sick leave form and return it to your supervisor for signature. Please note the number of hours missed and the reason.
> 3. Observance of this procedure is mandatory for insurance purposes.

Students are then asked to consider the case of John, who was sick today and did not notify his supervisor: "If you were John's supervisor, what would you do?" CASAS provides sample responses for four different levels. In the highest, a 4 response, the respondent asks John why he didn't notify the supervisor, "because procedure should be followed and is mandatory for insurance purposes" (9). CASAS provides this 2 response, suggesting that what they are really testing for is not understanding of workplace requirements, but English proficiency: "I think I should tell John, next time you didn't notify, you are got a big problem with the boss. That's not the way to do" (9). (The 1 response likewise parodies the speech of a speaker with limited English proficiency.) Though the focus in the question is on understanding company policy, and the correct answer involves the student commenting on the necessity of following procedure, the sample answers reveal a system that marks difficulties speaking English as failures to demonstrate competency, the implication being that deficiencies in language skills signal deficiencies in other areas as well. Moreover, the relationship of this question to anything resembling critical thinking is tenuous at best. Here, critical thinking is defined simply as an ability to interpret rules (as well as an ability to speak standard English in the first place). Crucially, in no case does critical thinking ask students to question conditions on the job, relationships between workers and between labor and management, or conditions of employment and power relationships in the United States.

William Covino notes that SCANS "is remarkable for its encouragement of conformity and cooperation, identification of the individual with automatistic functions, abbreviation of complex processes into simple directives, and inattention to critical thinking" (112). One of the beguiling features of both sets of competencies, which Covino calls "official magic ritual formulas," is their relationship to seemingly natural forms of control on the workplace. My intention is not to argue a conspiracy of capitalists set out to turn entry-level workers into brainwashed robots; as I have noted, these competencies, in conjunction with workplace literacy programs, have a wide appeal that crosses political, economic, and social differences. Instead, I want to argue that the very appeal of these competencies is the commonsense aspect of equity they portray. They seem to represent an attempt to help, to make students employable, and I am not questioning the sincerity of the authors or the teachers or the business leaders who seek to implement these competencies. My goal here is to highlight the ways that these competencies, like sophisticated forms of control, reinforce hierarchies by seeming to do away with them all together, and the ways that these competencies train students to enter a workplace prepared to take their appropriate position in that increasingly murky hierarchy.

"IMAGINE THAT YOU ARE": LEARNING TO LEARN AND THE TOTALLY PEDAGOGIZED SOCIETY

In *Workplace Basics*, the source of NWB's list of competencies, Carnevale et al. wax at great length to define learning to learn as the sine qua non of the competencies, the foundation skill that prepares students and workers for a productive life. The key to success in this competency is making the process explicit: "Individuals begin to develop informal learning-to-learn strategies in infancy and may subconsciously continue to make marginal improvement in the skill throughout their lives. It is probable, however, that in the absence of explicit training in this fundamental skill, many will reach a learning process plateau" (37). But what is learning to learn? Carnevale et al. quote various apparent tautologies in their attempts to pin down the concepts. One author states that "[l]earning how to learn involves possessing, or acquiring, the knowledge and skills to learn effectively in whatever learning situation one encounters" (Smith qtd. 37). Another author calls it "the crucial difference between what we call normal thought and creative thought" (Minsky qtd. 40).[22] Carnevale et al. claim historical lineage with Socrates, Benjamin Franklin, Arnold Toynbee, and John Dewey, but the application of the concept (in this acknowledged paraphrase of *Workplace Basics* appearing in the NWB *System*) limits the concept rather severely by squeezing learning to learn into a palatable format for employers:

> From the employer's perspective, an employee who knows how to learn is more cost-effective because time and resources spent on training can be reduced. Employers recognize that long-term relationships with employees are the most cost-effective; therefore, employee ability to adapt to company needs through retraining programs becomes crucial as technology creates shifts in job market demand and job content. Employers see the skill of knowing how to learn as the key to retraining efforts. But most important, the employees who know how to learn can greatly assist an employer in meeting its strategic goals and competitive challenges, by more efficiently applying new knowledge to job duties and tasks. (N. 1)

A brief analysis of this passage makes clear the role NWB sees for adult learners. Of the five independent clauses, three have the employee in some role as the agent of the sentence, but the actual agency is qualified in every case. In the first sentence, agency has a role only "from the employer's perspective." Calling an employee "cost-effective" likewise orients the concern to the employer. In the other situations, employees have agency only as they are able to "adapt to company needs" or "can greatly assist an employer." Employers, though, "see" and "understand"; they are granted vision and insight and perspective. As such, they do not need to learn how to learn. Instead, they need students who have learned that learning involves the subordination of their goals to an employer's needs. The learning to learn testlets, divided into personal, interpersonal and cognitive, constantly ask students to visualize their future role in these terms:

> Imagine that you are a food server in a restaurant. You arrive at work for your shift just as the manager of the last shift of the day is leaving. This manager says to you on the way out the door, "Make sure to refill all the sugar containers for tomorrow." You say goodbye to the manager and then walk into the kitchen to get the sugar. You discover that there is no sugar anywhere to be found. What would you do next? (N. 2)

Other questions ask students to "Imagine that you are a secretary for three different middle managers" or "Imagine that you are a worker who pumps gas at a gas station." These questions, designed to test cognitive learning-to-learn skills, implicitly define learning to learn as the ability to solve a problem without causing a loss of business profit and image and without bothering the employer. More importantly, though, these questions ask students to explicitly imagine themselves in terms of their relation to authority. In each question, the student must deal with an incapacity to adhere to the orders of a boss; the cognitive challenge and demonstration of her learning-to-learn ability is handling the situation in such a way that minimizes impact on the business and employer, and maximizes her reputation as a hard-working and loyal employee (supposedly increasing her job security). Students have successfully answered this question when they accept as natural their responsibility to refill the sugar container, because they were ordered to do so by a manager, even though there is "no sugar anywhere."[23]

Thus stated, "learning to learn" sounds remarkably like Graff's "training in being trained." Students need to know how to work out a problem in the workplace to suit the employer's bottom line. Knowing how to do that will ensure students a secure position with a regular income. In fact, Graff challenges the notion that this type of training has anything to do with cognitive goals: "it is precisely the non-cognitive functions of schooling which most directly relate to the creation of a workforce acceptable to modern industrial capitalism" (*Labyrinths* 178). Though Graff's study applies here to nineteenth-century Canada, I want to argue that it is these noncognitive functions that are emphasized in NWB's learning to learn. Students here are trained to imagine themselves in a subservient position; as Ohmann argues, that is a fundamental purpose of such literacy education. In the NWB *System*, this takes shape as lessons in which docility is the only reasonable alternative, in which the prosperity and security of employers and the United States economy becomes the natural goal of learners and teachers.

This emphasis on trainability, of course, fits well into an economic context highlighted by job instability and frequent employment transitions. For workers to flourish in such an environment, they will need an ability to be quickly trained, to quickly and accurately imagine their role in a new workplace; likewise, such employees would serve the needs of businesses by reducing the costs of the inevitable employee turnover. The important issue is not the theoretical viability of learning to learn or the practical possibility of teaching that to someone who doesn't know how to learn; what matters, rather, is its value from a policy perspective. Learning to learn seems an impossible-to-argue-with educational ideal, a categorical good, the sort of thing, just as literacy itself often appears to be, that acts simply for a general and equal benefit of all concerned. To know how to learn, one can assume, is to open oneself to the world, to desire to take in new information and ideas and grow intellectually all the time. Certainly, this desire and capacity for intellectual development is something any teacher hopes her students will develop. However, an emphasis on the concept allows for the ability to center lived experience around an ongoing series of official pedagogic interventions. That is, the promotion of learning to learn emphasizes the necessity of learning from an economic perspective, providing, at the same time, not only a justification for, but an obligation to provide, a particular kind of educational opportunity that can be heartily (and, I think, sincerely) represented as serving the interests of all. People need to learn to learn because they will continuously face the necessity of being trained.

In one of his last pieces, Basil Bernstein ("Video Conference") claimed that Britain was entering what he called a "totally pedagogised society" (T.P.S.), "in which the state is moving to ensure that there's no time or space which is not pedagogised" (377). A central concept in this formation, he argues, is life-long learning, New Labour's name for what NWB calls "learning to learn":

> The world of work translates pedagogically into Life Long Learning and this is both the key and the legitimator of T.P.S. It is not difficult to see how the management of short-termism, that is, where a skill, task, area of work, or the like undergoes change, disappearance, or replacement, where life experiences cannot be based on stable expectations of the future and one's location in it, translates paradoxically into socialisation into T.P.S. via life long learning. (365)

One can see evidence of the totally pedagogized society at all levels: mothers learning how to read correctly to their children (Williams); companies marketing "educational" magazines, based on children's programming, to parents (Buckingham and Scanlon); newspapers selling themselves as educational tools for schools; companies producing curricular packages based on their products. For Bernstein, the concept of life-long learning is central to the totally pedagogized society. At its heart is the notion of

> trainability, that is, the ability to profit from continuous pedagogic reformations and so cope with the new requirements of "work" and "life." The concept of trainability places the emphasis upon "something" the actor must possess in order for the actor to be appropriately formed and reformed according to technological, organisational, and market contingencies. This "something," the key to trainability, which is now crucial to the survival of the actor, crucial for the economy, and crucial for society, is the ability to be taught, the ability to respond effectively to concurrent, subsequent, or intermittent pedagogies. Cognitive and social processes are to be especially developed in the actor for such a pedagogised future. (365–66)

In effect, Bernstein argues, establishing the necessity of continual training is the centerpiece of the totally pedagogised society.

Lost in this concept, Bernstein suggests, is a sense of meaningful identity. For the process of formation and reformation to have meaning for an actor requires that actor to have a "specialised identity," one that is "not purely a psychological construction by a solitary worker as he/she undergoes the transition which she/he is expected to perform on the basis of trainability" (366). Rather, a meaningful identity "arises out of a particular social order, through relations which the identity enters into with other identities of reciprocal recognition, support, and legitimation, and finally through a negotiated *collective* purpose" (366). I read Bernstein here as arguing that identity must be understood not purely psychologically, but as derived in particular contexts, and that for learning to have meaning for actors (rather than having instrumental value for them or society), it must have an intrinsic relationship to that socially realized identity. "The concept of trainability, the key to life long learning and life long learning itself, the mode of socialisation into the Totally Pedagogised Society, erodes commitment, dedications, and coherent time, and is therefore socially empty." Likewise, "the identity produced by trainability is socially empty" (366). Who actors are, their pasts and their histories, their relationships to others, becomes subsumed by their ability to be trained, their skill in learning to learn. Min-Zhan Lu suggests a version of this socially empty identity in her description of "the standardized template of selfhood" available in "the discourse of fast capitalism":

> someone willing to (1) see the world in terms of either a pre-existing market to be passively registered and adjusted to or something waiting to be aggressively customized; (2) see one's self as a "portfolio"—as embodying itemized discursive skills that can be flexibly arranged and rearranged as one moves from "project" to "project"; (3) relate to co-workers as just another flexible portfolio and to others' outside paid work as a Market (Consumers or Providers of raw material, labor, or services). (43)

For an entry-level worker in a global economy (the sort of worker, that is, that most calls for vocational education address) taking on a new identity as a worker is as simple as imagining that you "pump gas at a gas station" or "are a food server at a restaurant" or work as a "secretary for three different middle managers." The particular job doesn't really matter; what matters is the ability to figure out and be trained into that job, whatever it is. Considering context becomes untenable from a policy perspective, since context shifts so rapidly in an unstable job market.

In fact, if context is seriously considered, after the fashion of actual ethnographies and observations of particular workplaces, the argument that the competencies exist and shape the identity of productive workers becomes severely compromised by portraits of actual people and their practices. To do this, of course, requires that the discussions move from the official to the cultural, from abstractions about "what employers want" to details about particular workplace practices. Charles Darrah remarks that this movement from the official to the cultural is notably absent in discussions of skills that future workers will need: "Expert interviews, survey instruments, and various round table discussions are the methods used to elicit this information. Largely missing are observational studies that incorporate the understandings of the people who actually perform the work" (264). It's easy to see why commissions like SCANS and NWB would resist turning to observational studies, since most of the ones that exist tend to demonstrate shortcomings and gaps in their utopian vision. Moving definitions of literacy into actual cultural realms almost invariably challenges broad generalizations about its form and consequences.

In an ethnography of a wire-and-cable shop floor, for example, Darrah challenges the idea that general skills can be claimed as applicable in specific job settings. He notes that each machine operator handled such tasks as troubleshooting and machine adjustment in a unique way, suggesting that there is not one skill that can cover the process: "most operators lack numerous 'required' skills, yet they develop into valued and competent operators" (267). Sheryl Gowen argues that in the work sites she studied, workers, regardless of the claims of management,

> did not believe reading and writing text were necessary for completing tasks or for training new workers. They considered the best ways to learn to be through observation and practice, and they valued knowledge that was learned through action more highly than knowledge obtained from print. Writing text was a bother rather than a help in communicating. And they believed the text that management generated was often unnecessary, inaccurate, and politically loaded. (39–40)

These writers argue that the only way to understand the skills required in workplaces is to go to specific workplaces, where generalizations simply do not apply.

Ethnographies are also valuable in detailing what Francis Kazemek calls "the false promise of job literacy," that studying and demonstrating a set of skills will lead to better work. (Myles Horton once noted, about the practice of "telling people that if they learn to read and write they'll get a job," that "Anybody that's dumb enough to believe that is too dumb to learn to read" [Horton and Freire 92]). Glynda Hull (*Hearing Other Voices*), for example, details a vocational program at a Bay Area community college that feeds students directly into part-time bank work with low wages, no benefits, and minimal job security, jobs where few of the skills they studied in school are applicable. Gowen notes of this false promise that it glosses over more pertinent social and economic issues involved in employment challenges:

> Young people in this country will not enjoy better employment opportunities until there are better jobs organized more equitably. Moreover, they will not seek or continue in these jobs unless they believe that they have the rights and opportunities to give them economic, social, and

> personal success of some measure. To assume that enhancing their literacy skills will accomplish these ends is to embrace a literacy myth that has long outlived its usefulness, even as a method of social control. (47)

The best foil for the list of competencies comes from cultural and contextual investigations, investigations that always suggest that the issues are far more complicated than list makers would like them to be.

FREE MARKET, CONTEXT, AND NO CHILD LEFT BEHIND

Like Moore and Jones, Emery J. Hyslop-Margison and Benjamin H. Welsh wonder why a demonstrably unfounded approach to education and work continues to hold such official sway: "Why, . . . given a lack of empirical data supporting the existence of any actual connection between supposedly high levels of technical knowledge and skill, and actual labour market conditions do governments continue to support employability skills education reform?" (13) They explore several answers. One, because "many of the jobs eliminated by technology are industrial, manufacturing, assembly-line, and production-type positions," government policy makers assume that "only high-tech employment opportunities will remain" (13), opportunities only available to workers with the requisite skills. However,

> Workplace technology is intended to enhance profits by reducing production costs rather than augment the number of high-tech employment opportunities available to workers. The belief that technology will ultimately lead to fuller employment, then, ignores the primary motivation for its implementation within market economy culture. Full employment is neither possible nor desirable in a high-tech economy valuing technology for its capacity to create a competitive business advantage by eliminating jobs to reduce production costs. (14)

Another reason behind the promotion of increased skills education has to do with the belief "that a highly skilled labour market protects national competitiveness, attracts international corporate investment, and generates job opportunities" (14). Hyslop-Margison and Welsh note, though, that more enticing than a highly skilled workforce are "other production advantages such as low wages, an absence of labour legislation and limited environmental regulations," for which "the manufacturing sector increasingly looks toward developing countries" (14). Although there is little apparent benefit for the workforce, however,

> there is an obvious advantage to corporations. A highly skilled labour market creates a supply side advantage to employers by ensuring intense competition between workers for available jobs. Competition between workers for available jobs reduces employee benefits, forces wages to be lowered, and encourages students to increase their human capital through additional education and training. (15)

Thus, although skills education might enhance economic conditions for corporations and businesses, there is little to suggest that it will enhance economic conditions for either individual workers or for the countries they live in.

Finally, Hyslop-Margison and Welsh argue that the "skills gap myth" addresses particular economic anxieties generated over the past two decades, anxieties having to do with growing income divisions, a decline in real wages, and a lack of meaningful employment opportunities (16). Suggesting that education assume "the goals of the market" means that "[m]arket economy principles and practices such as supply and demand, unfettered competition and routine occupational displacement are naturalized by career education programs as either inevitable or beyond reasonable dispute" (17). In the same vein, Susan Robertson argues that while new principles of workplace organization recognize that simple forms of control led to worker alienation, they also avoid any sense "that this alienation stems from the structural relations embedded within capitalism itself" (128). So an education designed to enhance worker empowerment by increasing their skills

> is conceived of by those in political circles (including unions) as offering greater opportunities for workers to have a say over the technical problems encountered in the workplace and in being able to choose more flexible types of work arrangements (such as flexi-time). . . . The existing social relations of the workplace are not contested. Rather, the division of labor is viewed as an immutable 'social fact.' (128)

This orientation, as Hyslop-Margison and Welsh argue, makes schools, rather than structures foundational to a capitalist economy, responsible for social inequities. Career education, they note

> diverts public attention from the structural causes of class stratification and other serious social problems by implying that public schools and worker skill deficits are responsible for deep-rooted structural difficulties. . . . The responsibility for unmanageable economic difficulties is conveniently shifted from corporate and political interests onto education. (18)

Thus, the promotion of education to redress a perceived skills gap has considerable power, which "may produce a subdued and ideologically compliant workforce" but "will have virtually no impact on alleviating the social and labour market problems it professes to address" (18).

The shift of responsibility onto the schools, of course, means that they need to be carefully supervised and managed. I have noted that competency-based education began as a reform aimed at teachers in training who would learn the competencies necessary for good teaching. In general, however, the official promotion of competency-based education for work, as well as the instantiation of officially defined educational standards, can be understood to focus as much on teachers as on the students whose future it ostensibly will secure. That is, although the competencies have gone well beyond those needed for good teaching, competency-based education and other recent reforms have as a central concern the ability of teachers to provide for their students the education deemed officially necessary. As Gemma Moss notes about the current official preoccupation with various forms of performance pedagogies,

> there is a double act of regulation going on: assessment of trainees and trainers/teachers and pupils is being elided, at every level of the system. Evidence of the achievements of the one stand for evidence of compliance by the other. Both are equally subject to external validation, judged by the texts they are expected to produce, rather than the inner process in which they are engaged. ("Literacy and Pedagogy" 555)

The economic and cultural urgency with which SCANS and NWB promote their competencies means that teachers, above all, fail in their social duty if students leave school unprepared for the demands of the high-performance workplace. This opens the door for arguments suggesting that schools operate more like profit-oriented businesses, with an eye to maximizing efficiency and productivity. In order for schools to aid in making states competitive within a global economy, they must take on business goals and business methods. Susan Robertson argues that for teachers, work expectations have been re-oriented along the lines of what she calls "the Eight Es for Successful Teachers,"

> a largely rhetorical though emblematic formula for conceptualising teachers' work in "fast schools."[24] That is, *empowered* teachers in the 1990s successful schools are ones who are *efficient* and *effective* with the resources at hand, *entrepreneurial*, oriented to the *economic*, committed to *excellence*, and ones who embrace the values and visions of *enterprise*, including a recasting of *equity* as equal opportunity to pursue self-interest rather than equity of social outcomes for collective actors. With this

> as the new formula, teachers' work has been extended and intensified in new ways in schools: greater involvement in school-level administration, more accountability to regulatory bodies such as school audit agencies and their definitions of excellence, and prioritising the development and teaching of workplace competencies. (168)

Representing schools as "small production sites" also "redefines the scope of teachers' work: they now work as direct agents of corporate capital or as site managers of business ventures" (172). In short, the sorts of reifications of the market economy that support competency-based educational reforms also justify increased supervision and control of teachers' work, so that they will support, and operate according to, the market and its inherent principles.

Thus, from an official perspective, the arguments supporting competency-based education are enormous. They provide a way to represent an economy marked by a loss of manufacturing and industrial careers as changing into a high-tech economy dominated by quasi-democratic and extremely efficient workplaces. They help create the conditions necessary for more sophisticated and effective forms of workplace control. They shift responsibility for addressing social inequities and injustice onto schools and teachers. They provide a justification for drastic reorganization of education and the work of teachers. In other words, as I have claimed, these arguments supporting competency-based education have everything to do with the creation of a world that ought to be. However, a central condition for the rhetorical effectiveness of these arguments is that they be justified not by a vision of the world in which we need to live, but by the world that already exists. Basing the argument for competency-based vocational education on things that can be argued as "real" and already existing—from the high-performance workplace to the force of the free market—means that the model and its social benefits can be represented as nonideological, as simply helping students live better in "the circle of the is" (Horton "Myles Horton's Talk" n.p.)

It's worth a brief discussion of the No Child Left Behind Act of 2001 (NCLB) (U.S. Dept of Ed.) to explore the ways such rhetorical strategies remain enormously compelling and powerful in official discussions of education. As I have argued, NCLB can be said to rely on an objective portrait of the world as it is through its repeated sanctioning only of approaches to teaching validated by scientifically based research. However, more critically for my purposes here, NCLB manifestly relies on the language of free market proponents to describe effective schooling. The reference guide to the Act, published by the Department of Education, puts it like this:

> Since the *Nation at Risk* report was issued nearly 20 years ago, there has been a vigorous national debate over how to improve our nation's

> schools and our children's achievement. Out of these years of debate, a general consensus has emerged that schools and districts work best when they have greater control and flexibility, when scientifically proven teaching methods are employed, and when schools are held accountable for results. (9)

This passage is interesting in many ways. First, it references *A Nation at Risk* (National Commission on Excellence in Education), a 1983 report commissioned by Reagan's secretary of education that memorably raised the prospect of imminent national economic collapse due to poor public education. In many ways, *A Nation at Risk* laid the groundwork for the sorts of educational initiatives I examine in this chapter. The "vigorous national debate" implicitly engendered by *A Nation at Risk*, then, reaffirms the validity of its premise that a decline in educational standards and expectations can be understood as the root of economic instability and a threat to the United States' power internationally. (The other "vigorous national debate" engendered by *A Nation at Risk*, focused on the viability of this premise in the first place, seems to me not to be the one referenced in this mention.) Also, the phrase *general consensus* points to a kind of accord simply not present in educational circles around the proposed solutions, and it also suggests that anyone questioning these solutions is somehow out of the educational mainstream (again not the case). So neither the premise of the debate nor the proposed solution can be accepted in the terms provided here.

Furthermore, terms like *flexibility* and *accountability* play into rhetoric reaffirming the viability of a free-market metaphor as the most effectual model for schooling. As in the rhetoric of the high-performance workplace, flexibility suggests that schools quickly and creatively respond to demands with the most up-to-date solutions. Flexible in this context means fast and unfettered by bureaucracy and hierarchy. (That curricular decisions must be made on the basis of "scientifically proven teaching methods" determined by a distant panel of experts suggests that flexibility is valued in name only.[25]) Likewise, accountability focuses on a "more bang for the buck" approach to educational funding. If schools want to receive money, then they need to show the results; as President Bush said in defense of the law, "When the federal government spends tax dollars, we must insist on results" (qtd. in Shannon 23). Schools must be, in other words, as productive as possible, producing the highest profits as efficiently as possible. All of this, as the reference to *A Nation at Risk* makes clear, in service of making sure that education lives up to its economic responsibility.

The results Bush insists on are scores on standardized tests deemed acceptable by the federal government, and accountability under NCLB entails severe sanctions. Schools defined as "in need of improvement" on the basis of these test scores face at least two explicitly market-based sanctions:

First, parents are to be provided funds, by the school, to pay "supplemental services" such as professional tutors and second, parents are to have the option, again at the expense of the school "in need of improvement," of bussing their children to an alternative and successful school. The law is inherently weighted against schools in poorer districts—the ones most likely not to meet the annual proficiency requirements, with the sort of students the law trumpets as its primary focus—and explicitly puts them in competition with private educational services and other public schools. Accountability, then, becomes a thinly veiled argument that schools, like businesses, will become more efficient, productive, and successful when they are forced to compete with other schools. Targeted explicitly in this Act as well are individual teachers, whose curricular choices are severely limited by expert panels defining scientifically based methods and by an accountability to standardized test skills that enforce what must be taught.

Those limits, not surprisingly, are most fully defined in the teaching of literacy practices, in which "scientifically based reading research" becomes the only acceptable basis for instructional methods. Under the Act, the "essential components of reading instruction" identified by that research are "phonemic awareness, phonics, vocabulary, fluency, and reading comprehension" (23). To teach according to these approved methods, "School districts and schools will select instructional programs and materials that support the essential components of reading" (24). Of course commercial publishers have risen to the occasion, producing such curricula as Open Court and Distar, programs literally scripted to ensure teachers go about teaching phonics—reading—properly and scientifically.[26] The scientific basis of these methods have been noted as rather limited, but, following Moore and Jones, their theoretical viability should not be understood as the point of requiring them. Ken Goodman, noting that these phonics programs have no clear record of success, argues that the intention of emphasizing reading in NCLB is not about improving reading; it is, rather, "a device for attacking public education. For the purposes of the campaign then, it actually serves [supporters] well if the programs they promote are not likely to be successful" (61). Here is how one teacher describes the literacy practices in her scientifically based kindergarten:

> How many phonemes (sounds) can [students] segment in one minute? OK, when I say "man" you say /m/ /a/ /n/. Easy! Just make sure that if I say "trick," you don't say /tr/ /ick/—that's too many sounds all mushed up together . . .
>
> And then there's the best indicator of future reading success, the nonsense word test. How many nonsense words can kindergartners read in one minute? . . . We go through the list: vaj, ov, sim, lut, and my personal favorite, fek. (Houk-Cerna 130)

The teaching of literacy practices becomes at the same time a power play by a federal bureaucracy intent on limiting teacher agency and, one could argue, pleasure in teaching and learning reading.

It is no wonder, then, that many commentators read the No Child Left Behind Act as a direct assault on public education designed, ultimately, to privatize education (see, for example, Goodman, Shannon, Goodman, and Rapoport; and Meier and Wood) Such an assault is the predictable result of defining education as relevant primarily in relation to the changing requirements of business and as responsible for all economic outcomes. Although a sustained critique of No Child Left Behind is necessary, it is also fairly clear, whatever the claims of general consensus, that the provisions of the Act have not been chosen because they support current theories of education and pedagogy; rather, NCLB is useful policy, allowing for the increased assertion of federal control over schools that will certainly be widely unable to meet the demands of the act, a control that includes increasing constraints on how and what will be taught and on what, in general, should be the goals of education. As the Department of Education claims, NCLB can be understood, as can SCANS and NWB, as an outcome of an increasingly unquestioned discourse that simply accepts the economic priority of schooling and its responsibility for productivity and profit in American businesses. The logic of competencies, then, is not a passing fad in official educational discourse; it is the groundwork for the most sweeping federal educational legislation of the twenty-first century and for a conception of education and its responsibility that directly affects the work of any of us who teach, especially those of us who teach literacy practices.

CONCLUSION

Most of the SCANS materials open with a disclaimer meant to put readers like me at ease. SCANS, they assure us, recognizes that education is more than just about learning to make a living: "A solid education is its own reward," they claim, and this attends to the development of the whole human being. Their focus is on only one aspect of education: "We do not want to be misinterpreted. We are not calling for a narrow work-focused education. Our future demands more" (*Skills and Tasks* v). At the same time, they urge that teachers in all subjects strive to incorporate SCANS skills consciously into their curricula, and they advocate a nationally standardized assessment form to measure students' achievement of the skills, which can be used as a kind of resume for future employment. Combined with the fact that the government is not putting together high level commissions directed at other functions of education (producing an active and engaged citizenry, for example), their disclaimer seems somewhat disingenuous. However, the sincerity of the authors is not the question, really; as I have noted, I assume that creators of SCANS, and other projects like it, actively promote a reform they believe to be in the best interests of students, workers and businesses. Instead, I see such a disclaimer as in part relying on another traditional equation in discussions of literacy, one that places the economic functions of literacy training as a prerequisite to, and thus a priority over, other uses.

Kenneth Levine's (1986) history of the term *functional literacy*, which examines ways in which the term became primarily associated with work, highlights the prioritizing of economic issues in defining literacy. According to Levine, *functional literacy* first appeared during World War II, when the United States government became alarmed at the inability of soldiers to carry out military tasks and functions. In 1947, the U.S. Bureau of the Census used the term in reference to people with a fifth-grade education or less. UNESCO then took on the term as part of its international project for literacy, claiming that the "skills of reading and writing are not, however, an end in themselves. Rather they are the essential means to the achievement of a fuller and more creative life" (UNESCO 1949 qtd. in Levine 27). Literacy was linked to increased productivity and development, but the definition itself remained apart from work as late as 1956, when W.S. Gray defined a functionally literate person as one who could "engage in all those activities in which literacy is normally assumed in his culture or group" (qtd. in Levine 28). By 1964, however, Levine indicates that UNESCO had begun defining functional literacy in ways that highlighted its relation to work and employability. According to the final report of the 1965 Tehran World Conference of Ministers of Education on the Eradication of Illiteracy, "reading and writing should not only lead to elementary general knowledge but to training for work, increased productivity, a greater participation in civil life and a better understanding of the surrounding world, and should ultimately open the way to basic human culture" (UNESCO 1976 qtd. in Levine 31–32). In other words, functional literacy operated to enhance individuals and cultures by first focusing on employment. In the United States, functional literacy became directly attached to the skills needed to get and hold a job. Kenneth Levine summarizes this as such:

> functional literacy was at an early stage adopted by parties in a series of political arenas, military, educational, and diplomatic, who needed a label for their convictions regarding the economic potential of, and justification for, mass training for adults in basic literacy skills. In the course of the extended battle for resources, 'How basic?' was converted into an economic rather than an educational issue, while the original idealism underpinning the quest for universal literacy was itself transformed into an ideology about the bases of cultural modernity and the contemporary prerequisites of citizenship and employability. (35)

In a hierarchy of sorts, work skills became a necessary prerequisite for literacy that would lead to general individual and cultural improvement. In such a relationship, work skills become a link in the connection of literacy to the improvement of the individual.

A functional literacy, as Levine describes it, then, creates citizens by way of creating qualified and capable workers, that identity a prerequisite to meaningful citizenship in the first place. Educational literacy practices under such a model, in the twenty-first century global economy, function to define citizenship through the sort of self that Lu highlights as an identity template under fast capitalism. To prepare students as citizens is to prepare them as workers, which means that the primary civic responsibility of schools in a global market economy is to create citizens by developing a skilled and efficient workforce. This begins to suggest the persuasiveness and force of the logic of competencies, because it creates conditions by which the proper work and practices of schooling can be increasingly defined, and so assessed and judged sufficient or insufficient, by official powers outside the schools. (Fortunately, as I argue in my last chapter, the application of this power is manifestly inefficient and incapable of asserting itself to the degree to which it attempts.)

The sorts of competency-based educational reforms I investigate here rely on a pedagogic discourse that, in Moss's phrase, "looks outside the confines of schooling, only to find replication of what it already is" ("Informal Literacies" 51). That is, these pedagogic discourses argue that the literacy practices and competencies advocated within the classroom are simply borrowed from an already existing economic structure. The classroom, then, rather than being a separate area of activity, promotes "real things in the real world." This correspondence with reality carries extraordinary rhetorical power: What "actually" happens outside the classroom justifies practices within the classroom. The classroom, then, can be represented as having a kind of practical value that it would otherwise not have. Students will "use" what they learn in another setting where their skills have empirically demonstrable value.

I have noted Bernstein's crucial claim that within pedagogic discourse, an instructional discourse is always embedded within a regulative discourse, and that the regulative discourse is always primary. To accept this means recognizing that any act of pedagogy serves to promote some vision of a social order, that in fact the primary purpose of any act of pedagogy is not to teach particular skills but to create "order, relations, and identity" (Bernstein *Pedagogy, Symbolic Control* 32). This means, of course, that any act of pedagogy promotes a certain ideological point of view, that schooling is never a neutral act. As I have argued in Chapter 1, pedagogy always sets about to promote some sort of world that *ought to be*. The world that ought to be in the discourses of competencies that I examine here is one in which businesses run efficiently and at great profit with little need to worry about control, because control disappears when everyone is self-evidently working for their own interests. The unlikeliness of the realization of this goal is not the point; what matters is that this world, free of economic conflict, dominated by employees socially empowered by competencies that simultaneously serve the employers who hire them, appears as such a compelling prospect. This world is the logical extension of one in which inequality and income disparity can be understood quite clearly as the result of a lack of skills, in which workers' inabilities to meet social standards fully account for poverty and the lack of success. If the problem can be understood as workers unprepared to meet the increasingly complex demands of work, and if businesses and the government ensure that schools fulfill their social responsibility to produce students capable of meeting the demands of the high-tech workplace, then SCANS and NWB and other educational/economic initiatives are evidence that the problem has been taken seriously. Critically, pedagogy can be represented not as centering around a highly controversial regulative discourse, but simply as, through an instructional discourse based on empirically verifiable and independently existing objectives, pointing to the world that already exists.

These discourses have direct implications for the teaching of literacy and literacy practices, because approaches to literacy, and arguments about why literacy matters, get co-opted by it. If a functional literacy is one that allows an individual to find work, then a functional schooling assumes that economic priority. I have noted Myles Horton's insistence that literacy by itself has no intrinsic value; in Highlander's Citizenship Schools, basic literacy skills were taught because without those skills adults could not vote, and voting was a necessary (but not at all sufficient) requisite for exercising a full and active citizenship. In any pedagogic discourse, literacy never matters intrinsically. Rather, it always matters in terms of a future world. When we teach about literacy, we also teach a model of that future world, whatever it is. We teach not only a way to use literacy, but a vision of the sort of place and time in which that literacy matters. Central to pedagogic discourse, that is, is a construction of the world in which, according to someone or some group of people, we need to live.

Within the approaches to vocational education I examine here, that world centers on identities and relationships within work. Profit, efficiency, productivity, and quality assurance are the hallmarks of this world, and the workers within that world share these not only as primary and natural goals within the organizations that employ them, but as primary and natural goals for themselves. Workers move from job to job with a sense of personal accomplishment, recognizing that businesses share and thus enhance their ability to realize their personal goals and with the assurance that their creative and team-grounded contributions will be appreciated by each employer. In this world, when students have all the competencies, when they become literate American workers prepared to work in a high-performance workplace, they will find work in such a workplace. The more skilled workers that schools produce, the stronger the economy will be, because more high-performance workplaces will become enabled. Work becomes intrinsically satisfying, so that power at work no longer needs to be an issue. Endowed with competencies, workers gain a sort of general social equality and value, and in this world, everyone who attends school at any age learns the competencies necessary for work as their central achievement.

That vision of the future world is everywhere in official educational discourse, which even in its titles (the subtitle for *What Work Requires of Schools* invokes "America 2000") projects a future (U.S. Dept. of Labor, SCANS). This world, however, appears as inevitable, shaped by free market and global forces that will require very particular identities for those employed within it. Critical pieces of that world, including important manifestations of the high-performance workplace, already exist in the present; what educators and policy-makers must do is help realize that inevitable future with commitment and focus, because if that future is not realized in one nation, it will be realized in others, and competitive advantage and global strength will be squandered due to a lack of resolve and foresight and, finally, because workers did not become skilled enough.

That I find this vision not only unappealing but unrealizable is not my primary point. (I agree with Myles Horton that any goal worth working toward should be understood as unachievable.) Instead, I am interested in the ways in which these discourses, both in their structure and their goals, affect teachers of literacy practices at any level. In their structure, the discourses rely on a construction of the world that appears not to be a construction. The world constructed is represented naturally as both the world that already is and the world that will inevitably be. This removes human agency nicely from the action of education, because the point in the discourses is, not to create a future world, but just to make that future world, already largely determined, a better and more effective place. Thus, teachers can understand what they do not as ideologically grounded but as historically and culturally necessary, the only acceptable choice they could make. Likewise, the goals of the discourses define the value of literacy practices in primarily, indeed almost exclusively, economic terms; educational literacy practices matter insofar as they provide students with more resources to work successfully in the high-performance workplaces of the future. Thus, education can be naturally understood as a primary tool in the economy, and the effectiveness of the teaching of literacy practices can be assessed by how much they correspond with the present and future needs of business. A focus on issues of democratic citizenship, of course, has several problems under these models. That concept is not quantifiable and so not testable, and it has no demonstrable economic potential. However, perhaps more than this, the idea of democracy, mired in, as Ong put it, "the arena where human beings struggle with one another" (43) interferes with the efficient operation of an unregulated free market:

> if the market is making the big decisions about the direction of education, then the community is not. It is one thing to make production and investment decisions in education on the basis of economic development; it is quite another to bring people together to discuss those decisions collectively and make choices based on consensus or majority rule. If we emphasize the former, we move away from the latter and thus preclude any kind of democratic decision making for the schools. Ultimately, the institutionalization of market ideology eliminates democratic alternatives from the ideological competition in the politics of education. (Engel 30)

If education matters primarily economically, any other priorities have value only insofar as they do not distract from economic concerns.

To rage against this model, to critique it and point out its shortcomings and theoretical and political insufficiencies, is not, then, enough. This rhetorical structure, which defines education and educational literacy practices as (ideally) above the world in which human beings struggle with each other, affects anyone who has ever had to defend their teaching or their pedagogical theories against, or with recourse to, a construction of the "real world" in which those practices should have value. Likewise, few teachers of literacy practices can ignore the pressures to construct those practices as meaningful primarily in economic terms. Perhaps some teachers can claim to resist those pressures, to keep them at bay in individual classrooms, but even this act of resistance concedes the cultural power of this model. As I argued about correctional education, when we teach literacy practices, whatever acts of resistance we foster and whatever stances we advocate to our students, we teach in institutions whose goals we necessarily project as much, and perhaps more than, we project our own.[27] To only critique the structures and goals that fundamentally shape the work that teachers do is to leave teachers without the critical and theoretical tools they need to understand, and think with and through, the contradictions. More important, I think, is that we understand as teachers the goals and structures, the rhetorics, not necessarily our own, that so fundamentally shape the work that we do; only then, I argue, are we in a position to shape them and our work, in turn.

CHAPTER 4

The Boldest and Most Insulting Thing

Officially Threatening Literacy Practices at the Highlander Folk School

The first available document in the long file on the Highlander Folk School,[28] kept sporadically by the United States Federal Bureau of Investigation, dated January 29, 1940, introduces notes from a presentation by James Dombrowski ("which name in itself," A. Citizen intoned later in the files, "sounds suspicious" [FBI 61-7511-5 July 30, 1940 01 n.p.]), delivered at churches in Nashville, Tennessee, on November 19th and November 20th, 1939. The report, titled "HIGHLAND [sic] FOLK SCHOOL, Monteagle, Grundy County, Tennessee," listed the "Character of Case" as "SUBVERSIVE ACTIVITIES (COMMUNIST ACTIVITIES)," its writer, name inked over, noting that the school "is alleged to be communistic" (FBI 61-7511-2 Jan. 29, 1940 01 n.p.) The mimeographed notes of Dombrowski's speech, "The Philosophy and Program of the Highlander Folk School," came to the FBI from someone "who manifested a keen dislike for persons engaged in subversive activities" (ibid.). This someone's name is also inked out, part of the policy of protecting the identity of people named in documents released under the Freedom of Information Act, but certainly there was no shortage of people with such a dislike in Monteagle, Grundy County, Tennessee, and many of them directed their ire at Highlander, which, since its founding in 1932 had been repeatedly accused of communism and general subversion of American ideals.

In his talk, Dombrowski, a history teacher and the chairman of the school, outlined one of the motivations behind the founding of the school: "to relate religious idealism to the social problems of to-day, particularly to relate the social aspirations of religion and of the labor movement." Such a program rested on a school of theology called The Social Gospel, promoted by people such as Walter Rauschenbusch and Reinhold Neibuhr, which held as a primary tenet, Dombrowski claimed, that "The salvation of the individual . . . is impossible apart from the salvation of the whole of society." Under the heading "The Problem for Christian Sociology," Dombrowski attempted a general definition of religion, following the ideas of John Benton, Vanderbilt University's dean of the school of theology, probably overstating the sort of consensus it would generate: ". . . it is generally agreed that religion is present whenever we confront the brute facts of reality with an ideal . . . whenever we are aware of *the tension between what is and what ought to be*" (ibid.).

Dombrowski sketched a dismal picture of *what was* in the South in 1939: abysmally low incomes, terrible living conditions, inadequate funding for education, and restriction of political participation and workers' rights. *What ought to be* was based on the claim that:

> *Poverty is now entirely voluntary.* This fact should haunt every Christian concerned with establishing a just society, every citizen interested in a rational society, and all of us seeking to safeguard democracy. Democracy means freedom, and we are not free until we liberate all of the potential material and spiritual resources of our nation.

Labor could foster this vision of democracy by advocating for better wages, higher living standards, and progressive legislation, by "Giving dignity to workers," by bringing democracy to the workplace in the form of collective bargaining, by improving education, and by "Giving concrete expression to the religious ideals of service and brotherhood which otherwise find but little practical outlet in the hurly-burly competitive world" (ibid.).

Highlander's role, as Dombrowski put it, was to "provide a cultural and education center for the training of a native leadership for the southern labor movement." Students were selected by unions or co-operatives and required only to be able to read and write. College students were accepted on a limited basis and only if they planned to do labor or social work. His description of the course work privileged a pragmatic attention to running a union knowledgeably:

> *The courses* are grouped in two categories: first, the practical 'tool' courses in the work of the union, e.g. public speaking, and parliamentary law, trade union problems, journalism, mimeographing, poster making; and secondly, the background and cultural courses such as dramatics, economics, folk dancing and group singing, history and recreational programs.

> *The methods* are a combination of lectures, discussion and workshop. The material as far as possible is based on the experience of the students. Classes are informal. In the work-shop classes students experiment with visual materials, reducing materials from their classes and experience to graphic form in charts, posters, etc. . . . There is an attempt to relate the material from the various classes, for example, the dramatics group wrote published and produced five plays this summer. The dramatic material was drawn from the students' experience and from their discussions in union problems, economics and work-shop classes. (ibid)

Dombrowski also outlined a community program designed to "preserve and enrich the indigenous cultural traditions of the southern mountains; through democratic and co-operative procedure to seek actively the solution of basic community problems." The community program included recreational and cultural activities and attempts to develop cooperatives, an example of which was the nursery school run at Highlander by community members. They also ran a community discussion group, Dombrowski said, with the intent to link their local concerns to "the larger problems of the nation" (ibid.). Finally, the extension programs run by Highlander brought the labor education to particular sites around the South. He concluded by describing the staff, the advisory committee, and the finances of the school.

The FBI presents this text with little commentary, other than to take from it a list of names of advisors of the school (which included Neibuhr, George Counts, Sherwood Eddy, and several others) and the names of two people mentioned by Dombrowski as officers of the alumni association, "on whom," the agent noted, "Nationalistic Tendency cards have not been previously prepared" (ibid.). Three years later, the FBI concluded that Highlander was not connected to the Communist Party, that they were not subversive, but they announced this conclusion only to themselves, and Highlander remained a constant target throughout the South, first of anti-union forces and later, with even more viciousness, of segregationists. However, there are few clues from the FBI about how they read Dombrowski's notes, about what they made of his endorsement of a social gospel that sought to eliminate poverty, of the liberation of "all of the potential material and spiritual resources of our nation." The only clue, in fact, to the way they interpreted this artifact is their misreading of *Highlander* as *Highland*, just as agents continually referred to a "Miles" Horton in later documents, a casual inaccuracy that belied the Bureau's vaunted attention to detail. As I shall argue, the attempt to link Highlander to a Communist authority was also a fundamental misreading of the school. Apparently, however, in combination with the regular attacks in the media on Highlander and the letters sent to the FBI warning, among other things, that Highlander was "a starting nest of Communists" (FBI 61-7511-5 July 30,

1940 n.p.) the notes warranted opening an investigation on Highlander, the fuller reports of which began appearing in early 1941.

Dombrowski's speech, embedded as it is in FBI "Form No. 1," is an appropriate opening to the FBI files on Highlander. Dombrowski outlines a philosophy which seeks dramatic social change through increased democratic participation. It forthrightly sets out the methods and direction that by 1941 had made Highlander one of the most important labor schools in the South, and the school's belief that the labor movement "is the backbone of the progressive movement seeking to change the present order and to establish a more just and ethical society" put Highlander in obvious conflict with the southern and national political establishments. There is nothing in Dombrowski's speech hinting at a sympathy with communism, but such evidence was never necessary; Highlander's stated mission proved they opposed the present order, and opposing the present order rarely garners official political endorsement.

Attackers of the school almost always interpreted, or at least claimed, communism as the ideology lurking behind Highlander's practices. Communism was the name attached to Highlander's threat against the present order, and calling Highlander Communist meant defining the staff as firebrands who hated America and American freedom, traitors who supported Russia, trouble makers who promoted miscegenation, agitators who just wanted to disrupt a society functioning perfectly well. Of course pedagogical theories and practices of any stripe are always embedded in something, part of what Basil Bernstein calls the regulative discourse, and the struggle to define that regulative discourse was the centerpiece of Highlander's constant harassment and the eventual loss of everything—everything but the idea and the will to continue—that the school owned.

The controversy over Highlander centers less on what Bernstein calls the field of reproduction, which emphasizes what teachers do in the classroom, than on the field of recontextualization. Controversy centered on defining the pedagogic discourse that structured the school's practice, which meant, primarily, defining the regulative discourse, the vision of the social order, that drove the school. The regulative discourse is always central, whether to attackers of the school or its staff and supporters. Although Highlander's methods were sophisticated and ground-breaking in terms of its instruction, the staff refining and always changing practices depending on who the students were, where the classes were held, and what the students wanted to gain from the process of learning, what happened in the classroom only mattered in terms of its potential social effect.

How to define that potential social effect, the regulative discourse that guided Highlander, became the nexus of conflicts around the school for most of its early history. For supporters of the school, the social effect was a more democratic society, one in which full citizens worked together to create more just and equitable social systems. Notably, Highlander's praxis rejected the notion that conditions stemming from poverty and racism could be blamed on the poor and African Americans. Inequity, the school steadfastly maintained, existed as a result of a lack of democracy. At the same time, however, Highlander taught that responsibility for changing the conditions stemming from poverty and racism lay on those most negatively affected by them, if only because no one else was likely to promote those changes. Unlike dominant discourses within correctional and vocational education, that is, Highlander consistently turned to social explanations for inequity, rather than relying on explanations positing individual deficiencies. For opponents of the school, the social effect most commonly represented as Highlander's goal was a totalitarian Communist society, in which races were mixed beyond distinction and all accepted social norms were overthrown. Explicitly tied to this agenda, in the claims of Highlander's opponents, was its covert but emphatic sponsorship by the Communist Party. The battles surrounding Highlander's regulative discourse, then, provide a fascinating case study of the tensions and the anxiety about defining and limiting the possibilities engendered by pedagogic discourse. Highlander, in its educational literacy practices, rejected limits on pedagogic discourse that required a stance of apparent political neutrality, and in so doing became a threat that required containment.

By labeling themselves a school that promoted an overt social and political agenda, the Highlander staff embraced what was to others a seeming contradiction. Schools taught neutral skills and objective knowledge through official, accredited institutions, and finishing school meant students demonstrated a particular skill level or subject mastery. The association of schooling with a direct political agenda already called into question Highlander's status as educational, making it at best an instrument of propaganda (even, in many cases, for those who supported the politics of the school). Highlander worked to persuade students to become community leaders, and most typically throughout its history billed its work as leadership training. Highlander emphasized, in other words, what pedagogical discourse most typically tries to cover and resist: that education is an act of persuasion, that to learn something is also to be convinced of the value of what is being taught, and that this value always has a moral and political dimension. Staff at the school saw themselves as educating toward a broad and democratic social movement, teaching individuals what they needed to know in order to foster assertive and democratic communities capable of addressing official and cultural injustice and inequity. The educational literacy practices emphasized at the school—from learning to read and write to public speaking and journalism (the list could go on)—mattered only in this broader context, and Highlander's main objective was to persuade students to play a role in a movement emphasizing true democracy. No wonder, then, that a school guided by these principles would come under constant attack: It openly touted its desire to convince as many people as possible to act on principles that overtly sought to undermine an undemocratic social order.

So, Highlander helps to highlight one aspect that distinguishes educational literacy practices from the sorts of vernacular literacies that have been a regular subject of literacy ethnographies—ethnographies that have typically focused on the use of literacy in particular local contexts. Literacy practices within education are focused, of course, on use, but they are also focused on persuasion. Educational literacy practices seek as well to persuade students to use literacy in particular ways, they are part of a pedagogical process of persuasion, and the best students, typically, are the most readily persuaded, the ones who come, most easily, to accept the practices being taught them as valuable and productive.

This is an uncomfortable dynamic for many teachers to accept, because it highlights the rhetorical dimension of their work as teachers, the fact that teachers in any setting are always trying to persuade their students about something and that teaching and persuasion, pedagogy and rhetoric, can never be separated. In openly touting the social goals that it hopes students will embrace, Highlander simply acknowledges what already exists in any educational program. Dombrowski sought to distinguish Highlander by emphasizing that it focused on what ought to be rather than on what is (a regular emphasis in discourse from the school, as indicated in my discussion of Horton in Chapter 1). This is a rhetorically effective representation but not wholly accurate. Educational programs *always* have in mind a world that ought to be, but to acknowledge that risks emphasizing a regulative discourse, so more typically that desired world becomes constructed not as what ought to be but as what already is (see, for example, my discussion of the high-performance workplace in Chapter 3). Teaching toward a world that presumably already exists appears a neutral and wholly practical act. This is, I argue, a central way in which educational rhetoric masks its moral agenda.

In this chapter, I examine the Highlander Folk School as one example of what can happen when educational literacy practices become defined as an official threat. The repeated, often ridiculous, and finally extremely effective attacks on the school always sought to prove that those literacy practices were sponsored, not by labor unions, not by civil rights organizations, but by Communists, most typically with a direct and insidious connection to Russia. The attacks attempted to stain Highlander with a vision of the social order that overturned freedom and democracy and the ill-defined but always rhetorically compelling Americanism. At the heart of both the practice of the school and the attacks on Highlander, then, is a discussion about regulative discourse, about the meaning and purpose of educational literacy practices, about the possibility of teaching toward a goal of radical social change.

After briefly discussing the history of the folk school, I discuss its philosophy and practices, focusing on a variety of programs but especially on the Citizenship Schools, one of the most significant programs developed by Highlander. Highlander's uniqueness lies not in working toward an idealized future; as I have argued throughout, educational discourse relies on a rhetorical construction of a world that justifies the discourse, and educational literacy practices matter primarily in relation to that constructed world. What distinguishes Highlander and makes it threatening is its acknowledgement first that its goals are ideals and not reality, and second, that those are, by any social definition, revolutionary. Highlander's disavowal of neutrality in education gave it particular strength but also opened it to constant attack. I examine those attacks, with close attention to the FBI files on Highlander, arguing that the representation of Highlander as a Communist tool reveals anxiety about regulative discourse within education, in this case presented as a concern over sponsorship. The FBI investigation, in particular, studies educational literacy practices, attempting to discern the extent to which those practices reveal a Communist sponsor. Highlander's threat, of course, lay not in its sponsoring organizations, but in its interest in developing democratic leaders who could organize people to demand increased political, social, and economic rights. As Horton argued, "We've always been after something more radical than communism. What we've been after from the beginning is democracy" (qtd. in Egerton 89).

THE HIGHLANDER FOLK SCHOOL: A BRIEF HISTORY

In 1932, Myles Horton founded the Highlander Folk School with Don West on a donated property in the Cumberland Mountains of Tennessee. For several years, Horton had been preparing himself to do such work, studying first theology at the Union Theological Seminary in New York (under Reinhold Neibuhr), and then sociology at the University of Chicago. He then traveled for several months throughout Denmark, learning Danish and visiting the Danish Folk Schools. He returned to his native Tennessee in 1932, met the similarly inclined West, and Highlander opened its doors.

Horton's original vision for the school included a focus on local issues and community organization in Grundy County. Most dramatically, Highlander helped organize Grundy County Work Progress Administrator workers in the 1930s, who briefly enjoyed some success in negotiations with state and federal WPA officials, but this union and its local political influence fell apart in the face of concerted opposition. For several years, Highlander ran a nursery school for locals, but this ended in 1943 after a loss of funding. Highlander staff decided, finally, that they were unlikely to change local conditions, and aside from Saturday night square dances their subsequent community involvement was limited. Instead, they focused on labor education for the broader region.

Over the next 18 years, Highlander's primary emphasis remained union education, work they primarily accomplished in two ways. Residential classes at the school, lasting up to six weeks, brought labor leaders and potential labor leaders together to learn the skills and information they would need to run a union successfully. Extension programs sent teachers throughout the South for local labor education. Highlander developed a national reputation for their ability to train workers who then developed programs throughout the region, endorsed by the Committee for Industrial Organization (CIO) and other powerful unions. They also had the support of educators such as John Dewey, Eduard Lindemann, and George Counts, who praised Highlander for its unconventional educational techniques. Of a less salutary nature, Highlander became a regular focus of attack in the region, with community members, regional newspapers, and politicians launching constant charges that Highlander was a Communist organ, charges that needed no evidence other than persistent repetition, and Highlander's avowedly radical social mission, to gain credence.

I do not have the space, of course, to fully detail Highlander's accomplishments in labor education, but Highlander's influence in Southern labor was extensive and significant.[29] Highlander's students founded other unions, developed educational programs, and helped create a stronger labor presence throughout the South, and in the 1940s, Highlander was the school of choice for the CIO. Horton and his staff traveled throughout the South, using labor education to promote their vision of a more truly democratic society. Glen estimates that between 1932 and 1947 Highlander taught almost 20,000 students, over 6,800 attending residential sessions and institutes on the school's Monteagle grounds, and over 12,000 in their extension classes (Glen 125). Although the school always struggled financially and politically, Horton's vision, though by nature never wholly realizable, was nonetheless reaching a productive fruition.

A number of factors, however, shifted Highlander away from labor education in the late 1940s and early 1950s. Significantly, as the Cold War developed following World War II, unions began distancing themselves from organizations with such an openly radical agenda, and the untrue but constant Communism brandings had made Highlander vulnerable to criticism. Refusing to cede its independence to any union (or any other outside institution), Highlander officially began focusing its attention in other directions, and by 1953 differences both political and pedagogical conspired to sever official ties from labor organizations. In August of that year, the CIO removed Highlander from its list of approved schools, because of its supposedly Communist tendencies. By that point, the executive board and the staff had already begun to focus their programs more openly toward integration in the South, and in the 1950s the school became a central educational arm of the Civil Rights movement.

From its opening, the Highlander staff had always argued that improvement of race relations was critical to unions operating at their full potential, and, adding to its often negative official reputation, the school pushed the boundaries of racial separation first by inviting Black speakers to the school, and finally, by the mid-1940s, realizing their long-term goal of openly integrated classes. As their involvement with the unions dwindled, Highlander began to focus more on racism and integration, and in the summer of 1953 they held two workshops on school desegregation, which they believed would become legally mandated in *Brown v. Board of Education of Topeka, Kansas*. Students at Highlander's workshops during the 1950s and 1960s included Septima Clark, who became a staff member, Rosa Parks, who went on to spark the Montgomery Bus Boycott, John Lewis, later chairman of the Student Nonviolence Coordinating Committee (SNCC), and Marion Barry, future Washington D.C. mayor. Over the course of the 1950s, Highlander moved beyond school desegregation to advocate racial equality in other areas. They were especially involved in voting rights, and in 1960 and 1961 the school ran workshops for students throughout the South who began sit-ins at lunch counters and other public facilities.

During a workshop on the United Nations in 1954, Esau Jenkins, an African American from the Sea Islands off the South Carolina coast, noted that adults on Johns Islands needed to learn to read so that they could pass the literacy test designed specifically to disenfranchise African Americans. Voting ostensibly required an ability to read and understand South Carolina's constitution, and Jenkins, a community leader on the island, had run informal sessions on a bus he drove between Johns Island and Charleston, helping at least one woman pass the test. His comment during the workshop inspired a series of research trips to Johns Island by staff members in order to foster voter registration, and after various unsuccessful attempts to register significant numbers of African Americans, Highlander decided to try a direct program of literacy education.

Bernice Robinson, a beautician and the first teacher of what would become known as the Citizenship Schools, was a reluctant recruit, agreeing to teach the class only after being convinced by Horton that she could do it. She declared to her first group of students in January 1957 that she was not a teacher, that she would learn with the students, and then she asked them what they wanted to learn. Their answers spawned her curriculum, many of them remaining as centerpieces in the Southern Christian Leadership Conference's (SCLC) *Citizenship Workbook* almost ten years later: They wanted to learn to write their names, read well enough to understand the newspaper and Bible and pass the voter registration test; they wanted to learn how to fill out money orders and mail-order catalogue forms; and they wanted to learn basic arithmetic. Robinson hung up a copy of the United Nations Declaration of Human Rights as a reading goal for students at the end of the term (Glen 194). By all accounts a masterful and driven teacher, Robinson stayed with the Citizenship School program for several more years.

Students who attended the classes not only learned to read, but all of the students who attended the five months of classes passed the literacy test in 1958 and became registered voters. The success on Johns Island inspired classes on other islands and in Charleston, which Septima Clark played the leading role in developing. Classes run throughout South Carolina in the 1950s enabled hundreds of Blacks to secure voting rights, and by 1960 Blacks on Johns Island and Charleston became an important political constituency.

Bolstered by such enthusiasm and progress, Highlander developed classes throughout the South, in Georgia, Tennessee, and Alabama. Like its predecessors, classes in these places were tremendously successful, and Highlander began training teachers to start classes in more locations. From 1959 to 1962 Highlander trained 220 Citizenship School teachers, and the classes helped to register over 42,000 Blacks. In 1961, the Southern Christian Leadership Conference (SCLC), under the leadership of Martin Luther King, Jr., took over the Citizenship Schools, taking Clark and Robinson with them. Although Highlander continued to train teachers, the size of the project had grown too large for Highlander, especially because they faced the most determined legal struggle of their thirty-year history.

On July 31, 1959, Tennessee and Grundy County law officers raided the school grounds, arresting Septima Clark, who did not drink, on charges of possessing whiskey. Others were arrested for public drunkenness and interfering with officers, and the discovery of open bottles of rum and gin in Horton's house provided Tennessee district attorney Albert Sloan, who led the raid, material that he hoped would revoke Highlander's charter. Highlander's offense, clearly, was its commitment to integration; the charges that stuck were convenient fabrications. Hearings instigated by Sloan commenced in September, fueled by rumors of interracial sex and drunkenness. Horton acknowledged making beer available to students, who paid an extra fee to defray the cost, and his testimony along with other evidence prompted the state to padlock the school, pending a hearing on a permanent injunction. Likewise, Horton was charged, ridiculously, with running the nonprofit for his own personal gain. Over the next two years, Highlander's charter was revoked, an appeal denied by the Tennessee Supreme Court and the United States Supreme Court, and Highlander's property confiscated. In December 1961, the state began selling Highlander's assets. The Highlander Folk School had been shut down.

My focus is on aspects of the school from 1932–1961, but Highlander continues, now under the name of the Highlander Research and Education Center, chartered in 1961 when it became clear that the original school would shut down. This center was headquartered in Knoxville until 1972, when it moved to a farm twenty-five miles east near New Market, Tennessee, where it still operates today. Nearing its seventy-fifth anniversary, the school maintains a commitment to fostering a more democratic society, addressing issues such as globalization and community development, among others. As Horton told Bill Moyers in 1984, in a phrase he had often repeated, "Highlander is an idea—you can't padlock an idea" (Moyers 250).

DEMANDING DISSENT: CRISIS EDUCATION AND THE WORLD BEYOND THE SCHOOL

In April of 1960, in a rapid response to a dramatic shift in the Civil Rights movement, Highlander assembled the first large gathering of student sit-in leaders for the school's annual college workshop. In February of that year, four Black students remained seated at a Woolworth's lunch counter in Greensboro, North Carolina, setting off a wave of sit-in protests throughout the South in which at least 50,000 Blacks and Whites had participated by the following April (Glen 173). The change represented more than a shift in tactics, for the sit-in leaders also expressed impatience with the mainstream movement's focus on constitutional rights and emphasis on recourse to legal means of addressing problems. These student-led protesters sought a quicker means to address economic and racial injustice and were willing to break the law and go to jail to defend their ideals.

Immediately following a worship service on the Sunday morning of the three-day workshop, Horton ran a discussion demanding that students articulate an ethical stance to justify breaking the law. The worship service included Biblical and poetry readings that emphasized working for justice, acting on principle, and not becoming deterred by obstacles. Horton entered at the end "to ask some questions and some answers on some things he has to say" (Highlander "College Workshop" 3). The group of integrated students he addressed, most of them already active protesters in the new sit-in movement, were called upon by Horton to defend tactics and ideas that were anathema, in his representation, to mainstream civil rights leaders.

Horton ("College Workshop") takes on the role of a White or Black supporter of the Civil Rights movement who believes that "all progress comes through orderly development, and that law, not spiritual law, not natural law but civil criminal law as we think of law on our law books, and our courts, that law is a part of that, through which change is made" (6). In a discussion that takes up nearly twenty transcribed pages, before it fades out, still continuing heatedly, Horton persists in his character, challenging these students to defend both their tactics and their philosophies of law and justice. "We are governed by law, not by people, I'm sorry" (9). Horton's character maintains against student claims that the people of the United States run the country. Thus, he tells them, if the law says something is wrong, it's wrong. The proper recourse is legal, to take a law to courts and wait, even if it takes several years:

> Now, I am a law-abiding citizen, you see. I think that you have to follow the law. And I don't like people who think they are going to violate the law. Even if they do it for the right purpose, because how do you decide what is right and what is wrong? . . . If I decide that there is a law that says that I can't beat you over the head because I don't like Negroes is un just [sic], I beat you over the head. Why can't I decide that? (ibid. 11,12)

Asking first for responses from those students who have demonstrated and been arrested, Horton steadfastly maintains an attitude supportive of change through legal process, even if it takes years, and he repeatedly demands that the students articulate their reasons for opposing those methods:

> You believe in the law when it serves your end, but you don't believe in laws when they don't. Now, what kind of philosophy do you have that enables you to stand here and talk to me as you are doing? . . . By what kind of accusation, what philosophy, do you say that this country, the United States is governed by law, if you yourself can decide what is right and what is wrong. (ibid. 17)

The evidence of the heatedness of this discussion appears in the transcription's regularly being drowned out, sometimes several times in one page, by a "MIXTURE OF VOICES" (ibid. 19) trying to answer Horton's most challenging questions and to respond to the claims made by various students. The transcript captures the passion engendered by Horton asking complex questions of students who had been jailed for breaking laws they perceived as unjust. Horton never lets them rest, and never breaks character, in the portion transcribed, and there is no moment of resolution; at the fade-out, Horton still prods the students about the tension between breaking the law and respecting it, a tension his character is unable to reconcile. It's an exhilarating transcript: The exuberance and thinking expressed in the interchange, the combination of obvious engagement and challenging intellectual development represent a sort of ideal for many teachers who run discussions in their own classrooms.

This session demonstrates the power of what Horton called "crisis education leadership development." For Horton, the most effective moment to provide wholly educational experiences was at the moment when specific social problems demanded a response:

> The best results in leadership training are obtained when people want help with solving their own problems or in carrying out an urgently needed program, because they are challenged to do something which involves them in a leadership role. Such results are often obtained when there is a 'crisis' situation, in which interest is heightened and learning [is] faster. Therefore the place to attack a problem is at the point at which the people concerned are aware of it. . . . Crisis education involves making a choice and taking action which will remove the cause of the crisis. . . . Objectivity is essential in analyzing a problem, but personal value judgments and moral decisions determine what is to be done. Resolving a crisis demands dissent; crisis education is always controversial. There is no place for historical romanticism. In crisis education, theory and practice are often merged, as are means and ends. (Horton "Statement" 2–3)

For students who had been arrested, who believed in actively breaking the laws that supported an unjust racial order, nothing could be more relevant than the set of questions Horton posed; they were central to their developing activist identity, and it's clear that Horton, who himself firmly believed in challenging such laws by breaking them, wants to assist the students in defending their position, in developing and articulating an argument that supports their more confrontational approach. The passion and energy of the transcript comes from the crisis these students find themselves within, the crisis they find themselves addressing. If Highlander had a method (a notion Horton always resisted) it revolved around an ability to respond quickly to political and social crises by providing a forum in which adults could develop skills and knowledge in service of democratic leadership and action.

Although no one in the room was learning to read and write, Horton was teaching literacy practices as he led this discussion. Students argued about the meaning of the Constitution, about the appropriate stance they should take toward the law and court rulings. If we understand the teaching of literacy broadly, as teaching not just reading and writing, but "general cultural ways of utilizing written language which people draw upon in their lives," as well as the "values, attitudes, feelings, social relationships" (Barton and Hamilton 7) that attend that utilization, then Horton is involved here in literacy instruction, in helping students develop an intellectual relationship to written texts that play an increasingly significant, almost determining, role in their lives. Understanding Highlander's work as "crisis education" is essential to understanding the ways in which educational literacy practices assumed definition and value at the school. Literacy practices mattered educationally at Highlander when they were useful in addressing specific problems, when they assisted students at the school in dealing with the crises, whether within a labor conflict or a civil rights protest, that they faced in their day-to-day lives. One of the remarkable aspects of the Highlander Folk School was its ability to react quickly to developing crisis situations, such as the shift in the Civil Rights movement represented by the sweeping student sit-ins.

Crisis education addressed particular issues, but for Highlander, those issues never wholly defined what the school could do. As the shift from a labor school to a civil rights school indicates, Highlander's commitment was not to particular causes, but to larger, and by definition unachievable, goals. Horton notes in his autobiography that "Goals are unattainable in the sense that they always grow. . . . In any situation there will always be something that's worse, and there will always be something that's better, so you continually strive to make it better. That will always be so, and that's good, because there ought to be growth" (*Long Haul* 228). In working toward their goals, Highlander always sought to enhance the effectiveness of community projects and the work of activists around particular issues, but that was not how the school saw its primary value. Rather, Highlander explicitly sought to expand outward the practices of the communities they worked within. They specifically sought to link communities with other communities, to note that particular struggles in geographically and culturally disparate places were in fact connected. The point, then, wasn't to provide individuals with more agency in their own lives, or to help individuals control the ways they used literacy in their own spheres. It wasn't even to integrate lunch counters or create a more powerful minority voting bloc. Rather, the point was to create communities that understood that they could be part of a process of social change, that they could change, not just their local context, but other local, regional, and national contexts, by a determined creation of alliances that would invoke a more democratic nation and world. So, in the case of the labor movement, Highlander sought to instill a sense that workers were connected to a larger social struggle, and that their work was meaningful not only, not even primarily, in the context of enhancing their own local working circumstances, but in the context of a larger social movement seeking a more equitable way of understanding the relationship between employers and employees, itself important only as a critical aspect of a more democratic society. The "crisis moment" was an educational tool that provided motivation and direction, but it did not provide the ends of the educational process, ends which were always fluid, always growing.

According to Horton, the distinction between making a particular goal the priority and developing potential leaders who could advocate for community change was a distinction between organizing and education. Horton discusses a hypothetical example of this in regard to a neighborhood wanting to tear down or restore a run-down building in order to improve the community, "something small but very important to the people in a neighborhood." For Horton, if that is your primary goal, then it doesn't matter what you do to succeed:

> An organizer . . . might very well have said to the people, "Don't say anything, just get a little committee and go to the ward heeler here and help him, get him interested and promise him your support, and get him to do it quietly. If you go out and demonstrate and start yelling, you'll interfere, so keep your mouths shut." And the ward heeler would take care of the building, and it would help the community because that building shouldn't be there. The goal would be a worthwhile social one, but no learning would take place. In a situation like that I'd think, "This is a good opportunity to educate people, for people to become educated as to what they can do with their power, and how they can do things using people power." I'd try to create a crisis, using it as another part of the education, in which people would learn to deal with opposition and to work through it. When I was done. if I had succeeded, the people would have both a good building and a lot of strength. If I have to make a choice, I'd let the building go and develop the people. (Horton *Long Haul* 182–83)

Individual agency, even community agency, matters here only in service of a broader social agenda, otherwise it remains "something small," however important it may be locally. And education had to occur from the bottom up, not from the top-down: "You don't just tell people something; you find a way to use situations to educate them so that they can learn to figure things out themselves" (122). Highlander sought to instill that same goal in those local leaders, whose work would help others "learn to figure things out themselves." Such a process remains both committed to and distrustful of a reliance on individual agency, committed because the point was to get individuals to take action, to see themselves as part of a process of social change, but distrustful because individuals must work with others to accomplish the sorts of goals Highlander worked toward, which meant that individuals could not see their own individual agency, or even the agency of a local community, as the ultimate goal. Rather, the educational philosophy of Highlander always looked outward, into broader social frameworks.

For example, the Highlander Folk School Report to William Roy Smith Memorial Fund describes the activities of residential students in the 1939 summer term at Highlander, outlining the activities of classes in dramatics, visual aids, and journalism. The day-to-day work of the visual-aids workshop demonstrates Highlander's concern with an education that linked itself to action in a larger community, effectively publicizing the union and representing the ways in which union work was linked to national social and economic concerns. Students learned how to mimeograph, how to design various sorts of charts, how to create an appealing layout on posters, blocking, sketching, lettering, and other activities. The July 11 description of the class reads:

> The posters were continued.
>
> We had been on the lookout for the best means of tying in the work of the class with the needs of the southern labor movement. And in the last portion of this period we discussed how we might help in a textile strike at Dalton, Ga. Among the students was Brandeau Huston, member of the Dalton local of TWUA. He told the class the situation and the group decided to make picket signs for the strikers. The dramatics class had already decided to take a play to Dalton and said they would be able to use the signs in the play. With this in mind, Brandeau mentioned the most important points which he thought should be stressed in the signs. ("Highlander Folk School Report" n.p.)

Students, then, learned these techniques and then put them to work in the service of an actual strike. The point of the visual aids workshop was not simply to teach particulars of effective design; rather, it was to put those particulars to work in the service of winning a strike. In another part of the class, students learned about charts and graphs, emphasizing first how to read them and then how to produce them, connecting work with the economics class in particular to charts and graphs covering such issues as "The potential productive capacity of the country," "the relation of the cycle of depressions to the growth of the AFofL," "the number and size of clothing plants," "the number of workers in various industries," "numbers employed in average industrial plants for the year 1935" (ibid. n.p.) and so forth, students using their own experiences in connection with concepts and statistics from their economics classes. The Highlander curriculum centered on such connections, not only among classes but among communities and regions, because those connections, and not an increased sense of layout or skill in chart development, were the goal of the school.

As with any class in which literacy practices are the central object of learning, understanding those literacy practices—in this case making posters and charts—demands movement beyond the classroom. Students are of course learning to make posters and charts and other graphics, but the point isn't only, or even primarily, the teaching of skills of letters and graphic design to students. The point, in the early years of Highlander's history, was to teach students how to attract others, how to foster the development of unions, how to educate workers so that they understood both the necessity and the power of uniting to create more just and equitable working conditions, itself only part of a much larger struggle for a more democratic society. Postermaking and creating charts have meaning only as they are embedded within those purposes. As I argue throughout this book, although the agenda and practice were distinctive, this sort of relationship between a classroom and a larger purpose is not unique to Highlander. The literacy practices within any classroom necessarily point to a place beyond that classroom, are necessarily embedded within a larger framework.

When Highlander developed programs to teach adults how to read and write, it did so in alignment with the sorts of goals that drove their union education and their work with student leaders. The literacy education addressed immediately the need to increase voting among African Americans, but this remained "something small," if "very important." Highlander's larger goals, as always, looked well beyond the immediate situation to a more democratic world continually shaped by active and engaged citizens. Teaching adults to read and write so that they could vote was a necessary goal, but it was always important only in the context of a much larger ambition.

THE CITIZENSHIP CLASSES

> What is too big for one person to handle can be figured out by all of us together. We will have a new kind of school—not for teaching reading, writing and arithmetic, but a school for problems. (Horton, qtd. in Highlander Folk School "My Reading Booklet")

In 1895, South Carolina called a constitutional convention with the primary intent of developing ways to limit the enfranchisement of Blacks and to circumvent the Fifteenth Amendment of the U.S. Constitution, which guaranteed the right to vote. United States Senator Ben Tillman, the state's former governor and a long-time opponent of Reconstruction, chaired the committee on the suffrage, which openly worked toward ways to keep Blacks from exercising their supposedly federally protected rights. The plan finally ratified, and still largely in place (with women added) when Bernice Robinson met her first class on Johns Island off the coast of Charleston, limited registration "to adult men who paid taxes on at least $300 worth of property or could read and write any section of the constitution to the satisfaction of a registration official" (Kantrowitz 225). Based on the success of similar literacy laws throughout the South, this law replaced an earlier attempt to limit the Black vote, the so-called "eight-box law" which stipulated a number of ballots for each election, each of which needed to be placed in the proper box (so-labeled) or the ballot would be nullified, a law designed to be administered differently for Whites and Blacks. The new law included an "understanding clause" in place until 1898 as a protection for poor Whites who might be caught by a law designed for Blacks: The literacy requirement would be waived if the registration official determined that the applicant demonstrated a sufficient understanding of the South Carolina constitution. The purpose of this law was straightforward and often openly recognized. As one delegate to the convention quipped, "My 'understanding' is that this will disenfranchise every negro" (qtd. in Kantrowitz 226). Although Tillman bristled at such brash acknowledgement, that certainly reflected the political ambitions he had in mind for the new law. Not without resistance, including the claim that the law amounted to a legal sanction of election fraud, this became the law of South Carolina until it was overturned by the U.S. Supreme Court in 1965. So, when Esau Jenkins suggested, during the 1954 United Nations Workshop at Highlander, that what adults needed most on his native Johns Island was to learn to read and write, the need was expressed not because reading and writing would help these students find better work or increase their self-esteem, but because the inability to read and write was a legal validation of a racist policy of disenfranchisement.

In an essay about students at the literacy center where I taught for several years (Branch "In the Hallways"), I argued that the power of literacy can be used as a kind of bureaucratic bludgeon. Using oral histories of students at the center, I pointed out stories about land being stolen from people who signed a bill of sale instead of a lease, about students describing being beaten because they couldn't pass a spelling test in school, about feeling bilked when they shopped because they couldn't check the prices or follow sales. Nonreaders often experience and describe literacy as a power that works against them, that threatens them physically, economically, and emotionally. Thus, I claimed, one of the educational functions of literacy is to stave off such threats, to keep the power of literacy from acting negatively and sometimes violently against oneself. Although such a goal is critical for literacy educators, it is also constrained as well, positing the value of literacy education primarily as reactionary rather than creative.

On one level, the Citizenship Schools existed precisely for this reason. Designed to thwart the legal justification that kept them from voting, the classes taught reading and writing to nonliterate adults in order to get them to register. Variations of "My Reading Booklet," appearing first in mimeographed form and then in a professionally produced format under the Southern Christian Leadership Conference (then titled *Citizenship*

Workbook) emphasize first the right to vote.[30] The opening section from "My Citizenship Booklet" (and the later *Citizenship Workbook)* produced for classes from 1961–1962 and titled "The Purpose of the Citizenship School" announces achievement of the vote as the initial goal: "The citizenship schools are for adults. The immediate program is literacy. It enables students to pass literacy tests for voting" (Highlander Folk School "My Citizenship Booklet"). The right to vote, a constant centerpiece in the struggle for civil rights, holds the prominent position in the curriculum of the Citizenship Schools. So the Citizenship Schools can be understood as a response to a power of literacy that prevented nonliterate African-Americans from voting.

However, central to Highlander's philosophy of education was the notion that education could not only be about reaction and resistance, but that it must also be creative and productive. Immediately after the announcement of the franchise as the initial goal, the introduction goes on to broaden the agenda:

> But there is involved in the mechanics of learning to read and write an all-round education in community development which includes housing, recreation, health and improved home life. Specific subjects are emphasized as safe driving, social security, cooperatives, the income tax, and an understanding of tax supported resources such as water testing for wells and aid for handicapped children.
>
> The citizenship schools provide a service to the people which is not available through any other private or public program at the present time.
>
> It is open to all people of a community who face problems related to first-class citizenship and want to do something about them. (Highlander Folk School "My Citizenship Booklet," 3)

The "problems related to first-class citizenship" only began with the right to vote, which was simply the means and not the end of a process focused on "all-round education in community development."

Even ending segregation appeared as an important but not a final goal. In "A Plan for Furthering the Citizenship Potential of the Southern Negro," undated but written after the formal cooperation with SCLC had begun in 1961, true integration gets defined as something more productive than equal rights and equal access:

> integration must offer more than equality with the Southern white man, with all the inherent sicknesses of a decaying way of life. Integration much be a creative process to which the Negro brings as much as he gets, making all parties stronger because of it. This is the work that must be begun

> now and carried on simultaneous to the struggle for dignity. Indeed the struggle for dignity itself is in danger of becoming only a protest movement if the Negro cannot begin to contribute more than a judgement on the present situation. (Highlander Folk School "A Plan" n.p.)

This concern about the struggle for integration becoming "only a protest movement" suggests that the long-term goals of the Citizenship School, and a fuller definition of the concept of a first-class citizenship, is an even more broad social change than the already sweeping change involved in the integration of public and private facilities and schools. This is an approach to literacy education that moves considerably beyond a struggle against restrictions on voting and toward literacy education as a creative and productive practice that involves community development and ongoing social change.

I have already noted the success of the first class, after which all the fully attending students successfully registered to vote. The classes grew considerably after that, moving throughout the Sea Islands and into Charleston. Horton attributed the success to Highlander's larger social mission, claiming in a recorded conversation with Clark and one other person that classes without that larger purpose would not have been popular. He described sitting next to "an elderly Negro lady" while he was visiting a class on Edisto Island. She told him that she was there out of curiosity, to figure out why the classes worked, because a literacy program she had tried to develop for more or less the same people, more than twenty years earlier, had fallen apart quickly. Why were these classes successful? she wondered aloud to Horton:

> I replied that the only thing I could say that might throw light on the answer—and I think it's important—is that we treat these people as adults and give them very challenging responsibilities. We say, "It is your responsibility to be a citizen, in the fullest sense of the word, even though you don't read or write, even through you're a Negro on an isolated island, you have, as a human being and a citizen of the United States, this responsibility." And then they say, "How can we exercise these responsibilities when we're not allowed to vote, we're segregated, and uneducated." And then we say, "You'll have to find a way to become citizens, so you can work for integration, so you can be a citizen of South Carolina and of the world, and we'll help you." And then we start right back at the beginning and say, "To be able to do the things that you want to do, that you should do, you have to be able to vote. First thing you have to do to vote is to learn to read the state constitution. So you learn to read to vote so you can assume your responsibilities as a citizen." This, I explained, is a pretty challenging thing, an adult challenge that we give people, and they respond because they are adults, and have been talked to as grown men and women. We challenge something that's basic in people. (Highlander Folk School "Conversation" 8–9)

This is worth quoting at length because it emphasizes Highlander's belief that learning mattered only in the context of a more democratic participation. To analyze the Citizenship Schools, then, only for what occurred in the classes, or to evaluate them simply on the literacy skills that the students learned, is to mistake those skills for the point of the class. Literacy mattered, not because it was an inherent good, but because, without being literate, these adults could not vote, a necessary but only a preliminary step toward a more democratic society. This restates an emphasis I have had throughout this book: An understanding of educational literacy practices cannot be based primarily on the study of classroom practices, because the work of that classroom always points somewhere else.

The workbooks themselves used in various locations and times for the Citizenship School always emphasize Highlander's ideal for a more democratic society, for educating a "first-class citizenship." The booklet produced for classes on the Sea Islands, "My Reading Booklet", first introduces Highlander and its mission, and then follows with an essay titled "Our America." The essay celebrates the United States, calling it a "great nation" that "holds opportunities for our children and grandchildren," sounding at the outset like a typical patriotic primer. However, it continues with a metaphor, perhaps inspired by the island setting:

> Day by day we pour the concrete of love into the furious violent ocean of hate. Some day that concrete will build a foundation that will support a bridge to span the channel and open lines of communication to all peoples.
>
> Our hearts are filled with that spirit of brotherhood and our hands move forward defying all acts of violence. (Highlander Folk School "My Reading Booklet" 4)

The booklet also includes excerpts from and details about the South Carolina election laws, including the form for registration that students would have to fill out, information about Social Security and taxes, mail order forms, and money order blanks, as well as information about how to contact and address politicians ("Your task is not done once you have gone to the polls. You must also watch the officials in action" [13]).

The later workbooks, "My Citizenship Booklet" and "Citizenship Workshop", included an alphabet with words connected to government and the Civil Rights movement ("J judicial–jurors–judge–judgement–justice"; "V valid–vital–voucher–vouch–voter–votes–voting"), and more readings that emphasized the linkage between reading and writing, voting, and first-class citizenship, always emphasizing that the point was not individual but community and national betterment. In "Citizenship Workshop", a reading near the opening of the workbook, "The Bible and the Ballot," opened with an excerpt from Luke and argued that the Citizenship Schools have taken on "Jesus' work": "We are to release the captives of this segregated society, and bring liberty to those who are oppressed. We must preach the good news of equality and brotherhood to the poor" (Southern Christian Leadership Conference "Citizenship Workshop" 4). The reading, which links voting as an opportunity to act for the "good of all mankind," includes leading questions for discussion, such as "If you are not registered to vote, do you think you are doing justice to yourself and your fellow man?" (4) Other readings in the workbook, such as "The Power of Non-Violence" and an introduction to Black history, "Heroes of the Past," also direct the readers toward the larger goals of the program. Crispus Attucks, "one of our first freedom fighters," helps emphasize the power of individual action: "The Negro has yet to win his freedom. As Crispus Attucks helped by giving his life we can help by giving our vote" (24). A discussion question about the American Revolution asks: "How was the problem of taxes like Negroes problem of voting?" (25) The final worksheets in the booklet outline for students how to plan a voter registration campaign, using a block party and a neighborhood canvass: "A good citizen must be a registered voter. But the job does not stop there. We cannot rest until **every** citizen is a registered voter. You have been helped to register through this citizenship course. It is now your time to help your neighbors" (29).

These workbooks, in Bernstein's terms a form of instructional discourse, openly declare their larger purpose as well as implicitly warn against believing that the immediate purpose—access to the vote—is satisfactory. By reiterating the ways in which the responsibilities of individual students go far beyond voting to helping neighbors vote and, by association, become capable in turn of helping their neighbors, the Citizenship Schools hold literacy as valuable only because of its role in developing an engaged citizenry who will mobilize to teach and recruit others whose limited literacy has been overtly used as a tool of their own oppression. The discourse surrounding the Citizenship Schools, then, continually emphasizes and celebrates its regulative nature. In this way, Highlander defines educational literacy practices primarily in the terms of the social order they will help engender. Highlander never represents itself as helping students live better lives in a present-tense society; the focus is always on Highlander's vision of "the world, *in which we need to live*" ("Myles Horton's Talk" n.p.)

In the case of the Citizenship schools, then, as with Highlander's program in general, the practice is continuously tied to the vision of "where we ought to be," in Horton's words addressing teachers training for the expanded SCLC schools. In an undated outline of the workshop on "Training Leaders for Citizenship Schools," the week-long session opens on Sunday night with an emphasis on this aspect of the Citizenship Schools, calling them

> a new kind of school, where adults learn how to help themselves and their neighbors to become first class citizens, and to use their voting power effectively for realizing the opportunities of citizenship. The process of "citizenship" is learned and practiced with the learning of reading and writing, which is the first step in making citizenship possible. *Learning and purpose for learning go hand in hand.* (Highlander Folk School "Training Leaders" 1, my emphasis)

Or, as it is stated in "Highlander's Concept of Education for Social Action" written by Anne Lockwood, "Traditional education is concerned with learning a skill, regardless of what use may be made of the skill in the future. Highlander is concerned only with how the skill will be used" (n.p.) From such a perspective, literacy itself can never be inherently valuable. It only matters in terms of its usefulness in helping to realize particular goals.

Certainly for the purposes of emphasis, the sort of dichotomy between Highlander and traditional education outlined by Lockwood in the preceding quotation, and repeated over the years by Highlander literature and staff has great rhetorical potential. Traditional education, as I note in Chapter 1, is regularly placed in an inferior position in relation to adult education of any kind primarily because adult education supposedly demands a greater relevance in students' lives. However, calling the Citizenship Schools new because they connect learning and the purpose for learning, or because they are concerned only with how the skill will be used, masks a real difference with an apparent one. As I argue throughout, all models of education concern themselves, like Highlander, with where we ought to be, with some vision of a world in which we need to live. The difference is that some—I would argue most—models *pretend* to do otherwise, pretend to justify what they do based not on an ideal but on a representation of what actually is. Highlander's disruption, its uniqueness, is not only that it openly acknowledges the inherent biases of its educational literacy practices, but that it celebrates those biases. In Basil Bernstein's terms, Highlander always embraced the primacy of the regulative discourse into which all the educational work they did was embedded.

This open acknowledgement of its social mission makes Highlander a rich topic for several reasons. First, staff at the school consistently maintained that the success of the Citizenship School classes stemmed from their ability to harness motivations that led to conditions the school saw as imperative in learning for social action: "We have learned from four years' experience with Citizenship Schools that both speed and effective action depend upon motivation, and that when the motivation is desire for first-class citizenship, both learning and effective action are accelerated to a degree beyond the individual's normal capacity" (Southern Christian Leadership Conference "Citizenship School Training Program" 2). Thus, when "Ordinarily it would take years to learn to read well enough to pass this test, deliberately made difficult to prevent Negroes from voting," Highlander's approach provides such impetus for learning that "some classes are ready within a month's time for the reading lesson on voting" (Highlander Folk School "Training Leaders" 3). Throughout Highlander's history, educational practices have always relied on the power of motivations students have for creating a better society, a process enabled in large part, Glen claims, by the talents of Horton: "Horton seemed to have a genius for anticipating the emergence of major reform movements in the region and for using Highlander's educational methods to contribute effectively to them" (280). Tying education to such dramatic social and political situations, arguably creates the conditions for effective learning.

Second, Highlander's model challenges the nature and mission of education at all levels. Horton and staff at the school never accepted any sort of claim to neutrality on the part of education, and once they had rejected that notion, the obvious step became working toward a particular social vision. "As soon as I started looking at that word *neutral* and what it meant," Horton claimed in discussion with Paulo Freire in 1990, "it became very obvious to me that there can be no such thing as neutrality. It's a code word for the existing system. It has nothing to do with anything but agreeing to what is and will always be—that's what neutrality is. *Neutrality is just following the crowd.* Neutrality is just being what the system asks us to be. Neutrality, in other words, was an immoral act" (*We Make the Road* 102). Of course Highlander took sides, but also important to Horton was the ability to defend its positions: "You need to know why you take sides; you should be able to justify it" (102). Highlander's decades-long justification of its project presents a compelling model for an education that takes sides.

Finally, that refusal to represent its practices as neutral made Highlander both socially threatening and vulnerable to attack, and part of the compelling aspect of Highlander is the fact that it faced down what to my knowledge are the most persistent, extensive, and longest-running officially sanctioned attempts to thwart an educational institution in the history of the United States. That a school run by activists in a rural county of Tennessee could be a focal point of over thirty years of vitriol and venom suggests the extent of the threat they represented. How educational practices become so threatening officially that the considerable resources of local, state, regional, and federal powers are garnered against them raises a simple but extremely provocative question: How is it that education can be seen as such a threat? Of course an inverse to that question is: Why is it so unusual for education to be officially threatening? In that regard, Highlander becomes an exception proving the rule that education supports official social and political goals and ambitions.

The Citizenship School workbooks, with their emphasis on American history and democracy, continue Highlander's longstanding self-representation as actors in the struggle to realize American ideals that have been systematically and historically denied, whether to workers or to minorities. By its own standards, then, Highlander's project could not be more American. However, the very notion of what it meant to be an American also focused the attacks on the school. The rallying cry of the Grundy County Crusaders—"No *ism* but Americanism"—recoils from the *-isms* they argue as associated with Highlander, most insidiously, of course, communism. Opposing communism in this case becomes the primary definition of what it means to be American, so that the particular—if on occasion laughable—representations of communism controlling Highlander mark the school, by definition, as anti-American. Highlander's own discourse inverts this, repeatedly invoking democracy as their goal and suggesting that the powers who seek to limit democracy, legally sanctioning inequalities between employers and employees, or between Whites and Blacks, are themselves anti-American. To be fully engaged in the struggle to develop democratic access is, then, the very definition of what an American is. Critical to these competing representations, however, is a concern with sponsorship and a regulative discourse. For opponents of the school, marking it as Communist driven discredited completely its entire educational project—if such a project could even be considered educational instead of deliberately subversive. Highlander's openness about the revolutionary aspect of its educational goals became the focal point of both its considerable successes and the forces attempting to weaken and destroy it. The depth and constancy of those attacks demonstrates that Highlander's threat was powerfully felt by official interests for decades.

"THE BOLDEST AND MOST INSULTING THING": HIGHLANDER AS A COMMUNIST MENACE

> Mrs. Roosevelt asked her about being at Highlander, and what she'd done in Montgomery, and then she asked, "Have you been called a Communist yet, Mrs. Parks?" When Rosa answered yes, Mrs. Roosevelt said, "I suppose Myles told you when you were at Highlander that you'd be called a Communist." Rosa told her I hadn't warned her, and Mrs. Roosevelt criticized me for not telling her. I said, "If I'd known what she was going to do, I'd have told her. But when she was at Highlander, she said she wasn't going to do anything. She said that she came from the cradle of the Confederacy, and the white people wouldn't let the black people do anything, and besides, the black people hadn't been willing to stick together, so she didn't think she'd do anything. I didn't see a reason to tell a person who wasn't going to do anything that she'd be branded as a Communist because I knew she'd never be

> called a Communist if she didn't do anything. If I'd known she was going to start the civil rights movement, I'd have told her." (Horton *The Long Haul* 190)

By 1934, only two years after the founding of the Highlander Folk School, the charges started, each charge becoming evidence for subsequent ones. In June of that year, the Tennessee Manufacturers Association singled out Highlander for its union activities, denouncing them on a broadsheet that opened with the headline "STOP! LOOK! LISTEN!" Written by its president, John Edgerton, the broadsheet included a "startling fact . . . which I feel every manufacturer in our state should know":

> Yesterday, I received a letter from Mr. Myles Horton, one of the promoters of the so-called HIGHLANDER FOLK SCHOOL at Monteagle, Tennessee, inviting me to have a representative of the Tennessee Manufacturers Association to appear before the student body and present our views. Let it be known that this school . . . has on its advisory committee such men as the following: Norman Thomas, Arthur Swift, Reinholt Neibuhr [sic], W.W. Alexander, Sherwood Eddy, Alva Taylor, Joseph K. Hart, William Spofford, and Kirby Page. Assisting Mr. Horton in operating the school is a M. Dombrowski, who is armed with Russian posters collected during a recent visit, Miss Hawes, organizer for the Amalgamated Clothing Workers in East Tennessee, and two or three others.
>
> The purposes set out for this great educational institution are as follows:
>
> "To train rural and industrial workers for the new social order and to preserve and inrich the indigenous cultural values of the mountains."
>
> The paper goes ahead to state that the students are trained as labor organizers and that Mr. Dombrowski, "who has traveled to Russia," will tell all about his impressions of the Soviet and its accomplishments.
>
> Of course, I declined the invitation in courteous, but vigorous terms. This enterprise of destruction requires no comment from me. It is about the boldest and most insulting thing to the Anglo-Saxon South that has yet been done. (Edgerton 1)

This attack—with its emphasis on foreign sounding names, on textual traces of alien enterprises, on links to Russia and "the Soviet" and suspect supporters, on the threat to social purity and harmony, always sarcastic about Highlander's educational nature—epitomizes the assaults faced by the Highlander Folk School throughout its history. From its inception as a labor education school to its educational role in the Civil Rights movement, Highlander only grew more bold and insulting in its affront to what Edgerton elsewhere called "the normal relationships between employers and the employed in our homogenous section." Investigated by the FBI, attacked by the Ku Klux Klan and the White Citizens Council; targeted for closure by local, statewide, regional, and national political figures; lambasted in editorials and news-articles; and ultimately shut down by the state of Tennessee on fabricated charges, Highlander rarely went a year without having to devote extensive time, energy, and finances to refuting charges that became, through acts of accumulation and identification, authoritative. Highlander's social agenda, emphasizing first labor education and later, integration, always became proof enough, most commonly, of its Communist mission.

Highlander, it should be noted, was certainly not affiliated with Communism, but the school, to some, was a clear threat, openly and intentionally. Highlander did seek to disrupt standing—if not, in Edgerton's words, "normal"—relations between employers and the employed. Highlander did seek to promote integration and the political, social, and economic equality of African Americans. Highlander did protest racist state and federal policies and governments. Highlander advocated higher wages, improved working conditions, equal treatment across racial lines, voting rights, educational rights, civil rights in general. Highlander brought African Americans and Whites together for weeks at a time, sharing sleeping quarters, dinner tables, bathrooms, and classrooms at a time when such activities inspired violence and even murder. As Horton noted in a 1967 speech, "When 'white' and 'property' are combined with 'law and order,' we have a sacred trinity that only heretics dare question" ("The Place of Whites" 6). Highlander's questioning certainly granted it the cultural status of heretics. The issue for Highlander, then, was not that some people found them threatening; the issue became how to define that threat. Highlander provides a fascinating case study of what happens when educational literacy practices go beyond a socially acceptable limit, when they push the boundaries of what counts as an educational project so far that they must be stopped.

Returning to Bernstein's discussion of pedagogic discourse, we might restate this dynamic as follows: the regulative discourse, "the discourse of the social order," became so overtly oppositional in the case of the Highlander Folk School that it represented a coherent and obvious danger to the dominant political and social powers in Tennessee and throughout the South. As I have noted, there was nothing hidden about the regulative discourse at Highlander; dramatic social change was an open aspect of their educational mission. Its 1950 "Statement of Purpose, Program and Policy" stated this quite clearly:

> We reaffirm our faith in democracy as a goal that will bring dignity and freedom to all; in democracy as an expanding concept encompassing human relations from the smallest community organization to inter-

> national structure; and permeating all economic, social, and political activities. (1)

Highlander's commitment was to "assist in creating leadership for democracy. Our services are available to labor, farm, community, religious, and civic organizations working toward a democratic goal." By 1955, they had added to this:

> We hold that democracy has been outlawed wherever Negro and white children are prevented [sic] by segregation or discrimination from receiving a public school education which teaches the dignity and worth of all children through the everyday experience of growing and learning together. (1)

At a time when some Southern states were abolishing public education altogether as a way of defying *Brown v. the Board of Education*, Highlander was bringing Blacks and Whites to residential programs on the Monteagle farm with the specific intent of challenging and ultimately destroying segregation in the South. With such a mission—part of a goal, Horton called it, "of having a revolutionary change in this country and in the world" (*Long Haul* 108)—Highlander required constant official surveillance and, in regular and dramatic bursts, legally sanctioned harassment and intimidation. Highlander's labor agenda and the socialist background of many of its staff already made it open to the charge of communism, but as transgressive was their open attachment of political goals to an educational enterprise, acknowledging, in effect, the centrality of the regulative discourse that guided the school. Such an attachment violates a sort of educational code by which the supposed neutrality of schooling becomes part of its justification; anything else becomes a kind of brainwashing. So, attacks on the school used that openness as a way to attach Highlander to a project understood as anti-American and anti-Southern, treasonous and outrageous, hateful and undemocratic. Highlander's own discourse could not be used against it, for that would amount to attackers having to represent themselves as undemocratic and against the interests of laborers and African-Americans (though certainly overt racism had particular political capital in the region during this period). Rather, attackers used the openly political nature of Highlander's discourse to bolster an argument that the school had Communist designs, that it was, in effect, sponsored by Communists. At the heart of the controversy over Highlander, then, is the issue of sponsorship; determining (or, more pointedly, repeatedly alleging) communism as, in Brandt's words, "the cause [ ] into which people's literacy . . . gets recruited" effectively defined the regulative discourse of Highlander as inherently dangerous and subversive.

I have argued throughout that central to educational literacy practices is a vision of the future, but as Brandt suggests, that vision comes from somewhere, acts in service of something or someone. Highlander's ongoing project, as I read it, was to foster a sort of partnered sponsorship; that is, they sought to create a framework by which local communities could begin to work together toward the democratic society that Highlander envisioned. It would be wrong to call Highlander the only sponsor of those literacies, though they certainly were one. Horton's conception of crisis education, which could only occur "when people want help with solving their own problems or in carrying out an urgently needed program" (Horton "Statement" 2), directly affirms the necessity of community sponsorship of their own literacy practices. Success required extensive study of the communities in which Highlander sought to develop programs, because "the place to attack a problem is at the point at which the people concerned are aware of it" (ibid 2). The archives of the school contain hundreds of documents indicating the extent to which Highlander staff studied various communities, including transcribed interviews with community leaders, detailed logs of lengthy visits, demographic, economic, historical, and cultural analyses of the community, and extensive on the ground work to determine community concerns. Thus, although Highlander staff came to a community with a broad social agenda, their vision of a more democratic society, they also knew that in order to succeed, they had to tie that vision to the local community. What develops in this model is a sort of communal sponsorship of literacy. A more democratic society had to start somewhere, and the staff at Highlander never presumed to know exactly where that was. The Citizenship Schools, for example, began only after several other projects to increase voter registration on the Sea Islands proved unsuccessful, after Horton and other staff members involved in developing the project—in particular Septima Clark—realized the depth of Esau Jenkins's initial observation in 1954 that what people on Johns Island needed was to learn to read and write so that they could vote. This meant that Highlander's project could never have a predetermined shape, one of the reasons that Horton was famously dismissive of identifying a Highlander method. The method, he insisted, although important, was not the basis of Highlander's program, which came from a dynamic relationship between current conditions and future goals, as Horton explained in conversation with Freire:

> . . . it's essential that you start where people are. But if you're going to start where they are and they don't change, then there's no point in starting because you're not going anywhere. So while I insist on starting where people are, that's the only place they could start. *I* can start somewhere else. I can start where *I* am, but they've got to start where *they* are. But then if you don't have some vision of what ought to be or what

> they can become, then you have no way of contributing anything to the process. (Horton and Freire *We Make the Road* 99–100)

Thus, working toward what ought to be always entailed careful collaboration with, but never subordination to, students where *they* are. This is a sort of communal sponsorship of literacy, literacy in this case being recruited both for the immediate world of the students and the long-term vision of the educators.[31] With a model like this, determining sponsorship demands an understanding of what is happening within local communities.

For its opponents, Highlander is granted the status of school only insofar as it promotes a limited agenda of Communist training. Identifying Communists as sponsors of the school means that anything else the school might say or do is beside the point, a dodge of their ultimate goal to destroy the American way of life. So, for example, an image recreated throughout the South in the 1950s and 1960s, depicts Martin Luther King, Jr. attending a "Communist Training School." The picture, reproduced on billboards and in pamphlets attacking the Civil Rights movement, was taken at the twenty-fifth anniversary celebration of Highlander in 1957, and first appeared in a broadsheet, also headlined "Communist Training School," distributed by the Georgia Commission on Education chaired by Governor Marvin Griffin.[32] As the Georgia Commission on Education claimed, "The meeting of such a large group of specialists in interracial strife under the auspices of a Communist Training School, and in the company of many known Communists is the typical method whereby leadership training and tactics are furnished to the agitators" (Georgia Commission on Education n.p.). Teachers, here, become "specialists in inter-racial strife," learning is something "furnished to the agitators," and the process is one in which the schooling is wholly a matter of reproducing Communist doctrine and ideals. So, according to the caption under a picture of Horton and John Thompson, a chaplain at University of Chicago, in the Georgia broadsheet, both "have long been regarded as useful aids to the Communist apparatus." In effect, the charge of communism attempts to suggest Highlander as, primarily, a tool in service of a dangerously subversive social agenda.

Most commonly, Highlander's threat manifests itself in its alleged goal of covertly popularizing Communist doctrine and allegiance throughout the South and the nation. Highlander appears within many of the attacks as more a propaganda tool than a school, something like a Southern version of a re-education camp, where waves of agitators come and go, learning to wreak havoc on good government. A 1939 attack on Highlander, written as a series of articles in the *Nashville Tennessean* and subsequently used as evidence for later attacks on the school, claimed that Highlander "is a center, if not the center, for the spreading of communist doctrine in 13 southern states," and that Highlander faculty "spreads communism, approves this red doctrine, and sends its alumni into labor organizations, mostly in the south, where they maintain contact with their alma mater and spread its teachings over a wide area" (Burns "Using Grundy"). In 1940, the Grundy County Crusaders assembled with the express purpose of shutting Highlander down, or at least evicting them from the community. Under the leadership of C.J. Kilby, a secretary for the Tennessee Consolidated Coal Company (which ran mines in Grundy County and had extensive political power in the county), the Crusaders launched charge after charge detailing the school's communistic impulses. A description by Leon Wilson, then the secretary of Highlander, who attended a public meeting of the Crusaders, provides an example of the absurd quality these attacks could take on. Wilson describes a somber Kilby apologizing to his audience for the anti-American symbolism he had to demonstrate:

> Kilby: "I have in my possession five affidavits showing that there are communistic teachings at the Folk School. I have three affidavits stating that a song about the Russian Red Flag is sung at the end of each class and that then the students line up and give the Russian red salute." Kilby then demonstrated the salute, apologising for having to show his loyal, red-blooded American patriots such an awful thing: elbows close in to the body, the forearms raised smartly up until the opened and stiffened hands are palms outward at the shoulders. Kilby repeated this extraordinary antic several times, his Crusaders taking it in deadly seriousness. (L. Wilson "Statement" 1)

Kilby's performance, according to Wilson prompting shock and fear from some and open guffaws from others, represents Highlander as teaching a subservience to Communist ideology and to an imposing foreign power.[33] Highlander becomes, in such representations, something more like a political cult than a school.

Listing the charges launched against Highlander during this thirty year period, while entertaining and instructive, could take up a chapter in itself (in fact, they do take up a chapter in Glen's history of the school). Add to this the insinuations and direct charges of free love, public intercourse, and interracial sex (the Georgia broadsheet, under a picture depicting Black and White swimmers relaxing on a platform at the lake on Highlander's farm, intoned "BOTH THE DAY AND NIGHT LIFE at Highlander Folk School Labor Day Weekend were integrated in all respects" [Georgia Commission on Education n.p.]), the accusations of public drunkenness, the claims that students sang the "Internationale" almost constantly, the more or less total disregard allegedly shown by the staff and students for any sort of moral code and social convention, and Highlander does begin to appear less like a school and more like, in Edgerton's memorable phrase, "the boldest and most insulting thing to the Anglo-Saxon South that has ever been done." Indeed, this fictional Highlander is more of an assault, an act of cultural violence, than any sort of school.

The most vociferous opponents of Highlander presented very little in the way of credible evidence for their claims of Communist sponsorship. More typically, evidence was on the order of Kilby's pantomime salute, or opponents simply pointed to Highlander's open work toward integration. In the case of the Georgia broadsheet, for example, a two-page center photographic spread had as the most prominent photograph an uncaptioned picture of a Black man and a White women in a semi-embrace, dancing in a community dance. However, the overt concern with sponsorship acknowledges that the educational literacy practices have a social meaning beyond a particular context, and it suggests that the primary concern in responding to practices that are a social threat is to fix the popular perception about what that wider social meaning is. The point, always, was to brand Highlander as subversive not by pointing out the practices of the school, but by using those alleged practices as evidence of Communist sponsorship.

The educational literacy practices within the Highlander Folk School, then, and those within the representations disseminated by its opponents, have almost no line of connection. At Highlander, educational literacy practices mattered in terms of developing individuals and communities that worked toward social change through increased participation. Skills such as, say, graphic design and journalism were important insofar as they helped laborers to win a strike or establish unions, projects valuable because they fostered "democracy as a goal that will bring dignity and freedom to all" (Highlander Folk School "Official Statement" 1). The ability to read, design effective posters, or debate the finer points of legal philosophy were not intrinsically valuable from the perspective of Highlander. They mattered only if they acted in service of a larger democratic social project. Under such a model, educational literacy practices, like the curricula of the school, privilege flexibility, diversity, and openness to change in order to meet shifting community demands and pressures. For Highlander's opponents, literacy practices became simply and insidiously a matter of transferring a Communist agenda from some kind of nebulous central organization into the brains and actions of people too weak or foolish to resist. These arguments implicitly rely on the most transparent form of banking education, in which not only knowledge but a rigid and predetermined ideological framework and a submission to outside authority were deposited first from the Communist Party to the teachers and then from the teachers to the students, who would, in turn, as one Highlander staff member wryly put it, try to spread communism "over the South like a diner spreading butter on his cracker" (Buttrick 2). As threatening as the actual Highlander apparently was (demanding, as I have noted, sustained attacks for several decades), it could only be named as a threat through an educational model that was diametrically opposed to its actual practice.

There is an almost comic element, then, about throwing the FBI into this swirling controversy, because the FBI accepted, with a discursive straight face, the possible truth of these Communist charges. Most of the attackers in the history of the school seem clearly uninterested in actually verifying the truth of the charges; as I have indicated, Highlander's threat (at least to powerful interests), although not based on a Communist mission, was part of its public discourse, and the goal seems to have been to stop the school from expanding its potential audience and effect. The FBI, however, truly set out to determine whether the school was attached to the Communist Party or other subversive organizations that sought to overthrow the American government. Thus, the FBI entered with a model for studying literacy practices that emphasized the power of a particular sponsor: The goal of its investigation was to determine the degree to which that sponsor controlled the school. The only way to construct Highlander as an actual threat, then, was to present it as the tool of a more powerful and secretive organization.

I am tempted, tongue-in-cheek, to refer to the FBI as early ethnographers of literacy, setting out to study literacy practices at Highlander with a goal of determining their ideological significance. For the FBI, this meant implicitly accepting a model of educational literacy practices that emphasized an authority transferring a subversive and anti-American will directly into students; in the theory of schooling that the FBI used to collect and analyze their data, then, what mattered were the texts that students were reading and the position of the people who supported the school either as staff or financial contributors. In order to prove that Highlander was an actual threat, then, the FBI worked with a theory of educational literacy practices that had nothing to do with actual practices at the school.

For the FBI, understanding literacy practices meant first and foremost identifying their sponsors, which they did by studying literacy in a particularly narrow framework that defined practices primarily in relation to the texts that appeared in the school, and the background of people who provided the material resources to acquire them and operate the school. Proving sponsorship meant examining not what Highlander was doing, but who was telling them what to do. The FBI eventually cleared Highlander, determining that it was not a Communist facility, but my point in presenting a reading of the files is not to repeat that absolution. My point is to show that attempting to understand Highlander by identifying its sponsors misses completely the actual significance of the school and defines educational literacy practices in ways that do not reflect the literacy practices of the school. Through the lens of the FBI, what Highlander is matters only in terms of what it is not.

EARLY STUDENTS OF LITERACY: THE FBI GOES TO SCHOOL

On April 10, 1941, the Knoxville Office of the FBI submitted the first document of the official investigation on the Highlander Folk School, with the notice that "Numerous complaints received in the Knoxville Office concerning Communist activities at the Highlander Folk School made it desirable to investigate the school and its personnel" (FBI 61-7511-20 April 20, 1941 01 1). This report sets out the early case against Highlander by attempting to establish a record of Communist activity surrounding the school, a record based primarily on an analysis of literacy events and practices. A paragraph about James Dombrowski, for example, notes a letter written in 1940 that alleges that Dombrowski "signed a bulletin issued by the Revolutionary Policy Committee of the Socialist Party in 1934" (ibid. 3) The proported document, the original of which seems never to have been found, is quoted as readying for "the victorious revolution by arming the workers and by preparing the working class to turn imperialist war into class war" (ibid. 3) The letter alleges that Zilla Hawes, another early and important staff member at Highlander, "reported to have been especially strong in her teaching of Communist principles and how they can be used in labor agitation," also signed this document. (The letter itself is noted as "Exhibit No. 1" but appears to have been expunged from the official release. The files do include, however, many other letters warning the FBI about Highlander's Communist menace.)

From the opening pages of the investigation, then, the FBI seeks to establish a connection between particular literacy events—the alleged (and never verified) signings of a subversive document seven years earlier—and the educational literacy practices of the school. In describing Dombrowski, the agent notes that he "is the person who signs all of the mail sent out by the school requesting contributions and designates himself on these letters as chairman, without saying what he is chairman of" (ibid. 3). What matters about Dombrowski, then, is what he has signed, and the FBI seems to be drawing an implicit comparison between these acts of signing. The report also seems to doubt Dombrowski's credibility, as though he is somehow hiding something in calling himself chairman, even though these letters went out on Highlander Folk School letterhead. The point of this is not only to discredit these staff members, of course, but to introduce the possibility that Dombrowski's revolutionary agenda and Hawes's Communist principles are inherent to the folk school, that the presence of people who would participate in such dubious literacy events suggests the school's malicious intent. In other words, establishing Communist sponsorship by analyzing the alleged literacy events and practices participated in by particular members of the school suggests, in this report, a corresponding educational agenda.

The report also attaches numerous affidavits collected by C.J. Kilby, reported as "extremely interested in getting the Highlander Folk School out of Grundy County." Although the writer notes that "this matter has almost reached the point of being an obsession with him," he also notes that "In all contacts in this investigation, the persons interviewed were questioned regarding Mr. KILBY and they were uniformly of the opinion that he is a reputable citizen and that his feeling toward the school is a patriotic desire to rid the county of a subversive influence"[34] (ibid. 4). The agent notes that Kilby has collected numerous artifacts highlighting the school's Communist menace, including several affidavits which "in almost every instance . . . mention the Communist flag being displayed on the platform of the school, teachings of a definite Communist nature, and attempts on the part of several of those connected with the school to get others to join the Young Communist League"[35] (ibid. 4). They even note the photographic record of a Young Communist League Membership Card Kilby has in his possession, even though "it is not possible to determine the origin of this card and the names on it are not known in Grundy County."

As part of an attempt to establish the accuracy of these and other charges, John J. Lynch, a special agent from the Knoxville office, visited Monteagle and the surrounding region in early October of 1941, interviewing members of the community who had experience with Highlander. W.M. Murphy, the Special Agent in Charge in Knoxville, wrote in a direct letter to J. Edgar Hoover on October 12, 1941 that the purpose of Lynch's ongoing visit was "to interview those persons who have either attended the Highlander Folk School, in an effort to secure information from them concerning the doctrines and principles advanced at this institution, or persons in the locality who have either visited the premises or been informed by enrollees concerning any Communistic or subversive activities thereat" (FBI 61-7511-50 2a 1).

Lynch's visit soon became common knowledge. Leon Wilson, Highlander's secretary, wrote on October 11 that "We have been hearing rumors of an FBI man in the county since about October 1st. For several days I have been hearing the neighbors talking about the 'investigator' in the community and the green *chevrolet* that looks like ours." Staff at the school had heard of several particular visits, and even Wilson had seen "A spectacled dark man of between 30 and 40" moving about Monteagle conducting his inquiries. "We guess that this man has gotten Kilby's stuff 'on' the school, since he's been seeing the people Kilby used to see" (1941 L. Wilson "Notes" 1). In an effort to set the record straight, while the agent was interviewing a woman about the possible Youth Communist League membership of her son (which she alleged and her son denied), Wilson left a note on the seat of the agent's car. I take up the narrative of the following events from Murphy's letter to Hoover (the name deleted in the FBI files is Lynch):

> Agent [deleted] upon entering his car, observed the note on the seat of his car stating, "We have been hearing quite a bit of your interest in the Highlander Folk School. Why don't you pay us a visit and get your dope first hand. Come about 6:00 and you'll get a good supper. Resp. yours, for Highlander, Leon Wilson."
>
> The original of this note is being retained in the Knoxville file.
>
> Agent [deleted] did not acknowledge receipt of this note, nor did he communicate in any way with the Highlander Folk School.
>
> Upon returning to his hotel room, at 10:30 P.M., the same evening, Agent [deleted] had delivered to him in his room at the Monteagle Hotel, by a hotel employee, a letter on Highlander Folk School stationary, stating as follows:
>
> "Knowing how much time you have spent talking us over with our neighbors, we are, frankly, disappointed that you haven't been to look at us first hand.
>
> "Some very good friends of the school are members of your organization, and to date our relations with the F.B.I. have been of the pleasantest.
>
> "Our cook was disappointed you were unable to accept my hasty invitation to supper and she insists that I deliver the accompanying slice of home-baked applesauce cake. Cordially yours, for HIGHLANDER FOLK SCHOOL, Leon Wilson."
>
> This communication was not acknowledged by Agent [deleted]. (FBI 65-7511-50 October 12, 1941 2)

The next day, Wilson wrote, "Myles and I cornered Lynch as he drove into his hotel," where they talked for an hour. According to Wilson, Lynch "Said the FBI would only conduct such an investigation if the evidence tended to show Highlander had subverted the U.S. government; and then only if the charges or complaints against the school were pretty strong: inference being that he was investigating us on this basis." After Lynch refused another invitation to the school or a meeting with the executive council of the school ("You want to have it like a nice big tea party with those people telling me what fine fellows you are" ["Notes" 2]), they questioned him and he refused to commit to any number of issues. "He thanked us for the cake, after I reminded him of it, and we told him to ask Kilby to demonstrate his idea of the Russian salute, for a laugh" ("Notes" 3). One local correspondent to Highlander wrote the next week that Lynch had offered to pay his tuition for the next term, "to see if there was any communism taught, or any communists at the school, and to report to them" (Brown n.p.).

Lynch's reluctance to visit the school and talk to teachers and students at the campus, preferring instead to send an undercover student to attend classes and report, suggests the model of educational literacy practices that the FBI operated with. For the FBI, the Communist agenda at the school could not be directly established by a government agent, because the agenda (the claims about Communist flags on the platform or a Russian salute ending every class notwithstanding) was by definition covert and required covert means to uncover. Highlander officials could never be trusted, because they are possibly Communists, and Communists could never be trusted for candor about their intentions. Highlander's historic openness to outsiders visiting and examining the school, then, was immaterial. What mattered were the inferences of Communist sponsorship that the investigation could establish.

As ethnographers, the FBI's main method was the interview. They interviewed anyone they could think of that had an opinion or experience with the school, except those people actually working for the school at the time, who they avoided for several months into the investigation. Anyone mattered, and agents all over the country looked for the Communist connections of people who had visited or worked for Highlander in the past. From Detroit to Denver, Minneapolis to Miami, reports came in about the ties of individuals—most of their names deleted—who had appeared at the school or worked on their staff at one point or another. Thus, from San Antonio came the report that one individual connected to Highlander "has been reported to the office as being a member or sympathizer of the Communist Party" (FBI 61-7511-52 Oct. 13, 1941 2a 1). Another man in Birmingham who occasionally did printing for Highlander "associates with Communists only in business matters and shares none of their beliefs and no information developed to the contrary" (FBI 61-7511-44 Sept. 18, 1941 2a 1). From San Francisco came the report that Mr. And Mrs. [deleted] "were reported to this office as individuals with possible radical tendencies" (FBI 65-7511-55 Oct. 16, 1941 2a 1). One man, interviewed by the Memphis office, gave information on Dr. Lillian Johnson, who donated the land for the Highlander Campus in 1931, stating that "DR. JOHNSON is in no way associated with the Communist party as far as he knows; that her ideas do not lean directly toward Communism but more toward Socialism but she is very interested in educating the ignorant. He stated that she has been completely deceived by Horton" (FBI 64-7511-56 Oct. 17, 1941 2a 2). One member of the executive board is reported by the Knoxville office as "considered one of the most dangerous communist [deleted] having repeatedly stated that he was against the Government of the United States and would do anything to bring about its downfall" (FBI 64-7511-72 Dec. 30, 1941 2b 13).

The Knoxville Office, of course, led the investigation, and they sought as much information about the past and present actions as they could. As I have noted, because they were seeking evidence of sponsorship, the FBI focused not on the literacy practices that had marked Highlander as suspect in the first place—most notably their commitment to linking education to community and labor organization—but operated with a considerably more passive model of literacy practices, presumably accepting the notion that evidence of outside influence would come in the form of texts connected, however peripherally, to the school, and the experts who impart their knowledge to the students. In essence, the FBI focuses on literacy as a mode of consumption.

Note, for example, the focus on text and outside influence in the FBI report of an interview with a police officer about a man who visited Highlander employees at the scene of a 1936 strike at a hosiery mill in Rockwood, Tennessee.[36] Both the officer's name and the man's name have been deleted from the files. Where I write "the officer" or "the man," picture a thick line of black ink, a distinguishing feature of the released files:

> [The officer] related that one day during the strike, he sighted [the man] driving in an automobile in Rockwood and took out after him in an attempt to arrest him. [The man] was driving a car with Virginia license plates on it and had been seen frequently with MYLES HORTON for several days preceding this incident. [The officer] followed [the man]'s car out into the country where he succeeded in stopping [the man] and arresting him. The back seat of [the man]'s car was completely filled with literature. [The officer] remembers that some of this literature contained the following statement: "Down with the American flag, up with the Red flag." Other parts of this literature advocated equal rights for negroes, marriage between whites and negroes, the adoption of Communism in this country, and free love. [The officer] stated that he kept some of this literature for a long time but believes that it has all been destroyed. However, he will search his records in an effort to find some of this. [The man] stated at the time of his arrest that he was on his way to the Highlander Folk School to deliver series of lectures. [The officer] later learned that upon his release, [the man] went to the Highlander Folk School and remained there for about two weeks. (FBI 61-7511-23 June 1, 1941 01 27–28)

In this excerpt, the significance is not the participation of Highlander in the strike at the Rockwood Hosiery Mills, part of their extension program that provoked death threats and police harassment, but the ideological leanings of the texts in the car owned by a man with a peripheral connection to the school.

The FBI also conducted interviews with people who had visited the school for the most mundane reasons, and these too typically focus on texts. One man, for example, "stated that he made a delivery of lumber to the

Highlander Folk School in 1939. He went into the main building of the school in search of somebody to take delivery of the lumber. He noticed charts on the wall of one of the downstairs rooms depicting how to organize a meeting by parliamentary procedure and how to get control of a meeting. He saw no evidence of mountain craft work" (ibid. 24). As well as seeming like a feeble attempt to make something subversive out of a poster about Roberts Rules of Order, this comment suggests a sort of hypocrisy in the name of the school, focused, according to this authoritative witness, on matters unconnected to community folk crafts, though this was not a contradiction to staff at the school. Another man, sent to the school in connection with the Forestry department to plant trees on the school property, received a tour of the campus from James Dombrowski, another staff member: He "noted that the library in DOMBROSKI'S [sic] room contained copies of the works of KARL MARX, a biography of LENIN, and other Communist books. One of the books was entitled 'Workers of the World Arise.' DOMBROSKI stated to [him] that these Communist books in the library were used as background for labor education" (ibid. 29). In another report, a Special Agent inventoried the contents of a box of books left at a hotel for delivery to Highlander, "most of which were children's stories, and fiction books of an innocuous nature. Included in the box were a few books of interest because of their radical labor or political character" (FBI 64-7511-20 April 10, 1941 01 17). Their list of eight books meeting this standard includes *The Social Principles of Jesus* by Walter Rauschenbusch and *The Road Ahead (A Primer of Capitalism)* by Harry W. Laidler. Significantly, near the end of the investigation, on one of the FBI's rare visits to the school (two reported, by my count, over the two year period), the texts on the wall became evidence of Highlander's patriotism. The agent noted that "a great many magazines and recent publications, as well as posters which decorated the walls of the school, contained slogans that were extremely anti-Fascist and anti-Nazi, that everywhere democracy and the war effort was stressed" (FBI 61-7511-106 July 7, 1942 3e 10). Texts, initially sought as evidence of Highlander's corruption, became important indicators of its loyalty to American interests.

The FBI files also reprint a great deal of material from Highlander documents, in many cases transcribing extensive excerpts of material they saw as relevant into the report. In a December 30, 1941 report, the writer notes that "this office obtained a mimeographed booklet from C.H. [sic] KILBY . . . entitled 'The South Tomorrow'," published by students attending the previous spring. For the most part, the agent only identifies the name of the writer, "however, in cases where the student writing the article is indicated to be radical or uses language usually associated with communist [sic], those parts of the article are quoted" (FBI 61-7511-72 2b 19). One student, Paul Berthiaume, "President of the United Furniture Workers, CIO, New

Orleans," gets a good portion of his "Experiences of a Union Man" transcribed, a piece which describes his involvement in as a twelve-year-old in a 1929 strike, already an "active sympathizer," often "in the midst of riots" during which he helped pile bricks for strikers to throw at the police. He writes against "crooked politics" and "the stuffed shirt bosses" and about helping workers "get better living wages for their work" (ibid. 21), all projects he attaches to Highlander as well. In a long excerpt, Gatha Mae Lee discusses coming of age in Paris, Arkansas, where a Presbyterian minister named Claude Williams preached social justice issues as part of his ministry, and writes of her work with radical unions in California. "After attending Highlander Folk School, I know better than ever before that working people all over must unite and fight to maintain the gains in economic security and civil rights that we have won; to stay out of this imperialist war; to prevent the growth of fascism in this country" (ibid. 23). The excerpt taken from "The Farmer is the Man" by Joel Matthews contains only the following, which is identified as the platform of a publication he was involved with:

> 1–Government of the people, by the people and for the people. 2–Complete separation of church and state. 3–Freedom of conscience, press, speech and assemblage. 4–Economic, political, and racial justice for all. 5–The right of every group or class to its own collective bargaining agency. 6–Equality of all men before the state and before God. 7–Cooperation and brotherhood in everyday life. 8–Not a drop of American blood shed on foreign battlefields. (ibid. 24–25)

Excerpts from another student publication, "We Know the Score," are "handled in the same way as 'The South Tomorrow'" (ibid. 39). One piece is summarized but not quoted, because "although [the writer] is strong for labor unions, he does not believe in any radical change in our form of Government" (ibid. 39). T.G. Vanlandingham receives praise from the writer for his temperance and for being "conservative and American in his views" (ibid. 40). The FBI does not highlight what makes the quoted excerpts "pertinent," but the most recurring theme in their selected passages is a willingness to engage in ongoing struggle against capitalist interests in order for the working class to gain more power and greater economic and social security.

In 1951, Highlander staff once again learned that FBI agents were interviewing people about the school, this time, according to letters Horton sent to United States Attorney General Howard McGrath, Senator Estes Kefauver and others, "about the attendance of Negroes at Highlander and implying that our non-discrimination policy was communistic and immoral" (FBI 61-7511-158 March 12, 1951 46 4). Horton complained that one agent had suggested to him that Highlander's mission would be communistic to most people in the South, and Horton demanded to know whether the FBI was again investigating him for being a Communist. (They were not.) This time, Horton's ire became public, and news stories appeared detailing the story and the alleged connection between interracial education and Communist intent. Hoover received letters from the director of the ACLU and several politicians asking about the controversy, and he demanded an accounting from the Knoxville Office, which had not been authorized to investigate. At one point, the Knoxville Special Agent in Charge, D.M. Ladd, wrote that "the Highlander Folk School is not a school in the normal sense but merely has short session labor and social study classes usually of a two weeks' duration." Hoover's irritation is evident in his scrawled annotation: "We won't argue about this. It is a *school* whether in a normal or abnormal sense" (FBI 61-7511-166 April 7, 1951 4c n.p.).

That issue, about what sort of educational institution Highlander could possibly be, lies at the heart of many discussions about the school. Numerous attackers disparaged Highlander's label as a school as a simple pretense, but Horton noted that even supporters of the school who believed in its goals and politics often did not accept them as educational:

> people inside the school system almost unanimously said Highlander had nothing to do with education. They said we did organizing, we did propaganda. Even the people who financed and supported Highlander didn't claim we were doing education. They just liked what we were doing, but it wasn't education. And the truth about the matter is that very few people in the United States were calling what we did at Highlander education. Practically no educational institutions invited any of us to talk about education. We were invited to talk about organizing, civil rights, international problems—but education, no. We were not educators . . . We were not neutral. (Horton and Freire 200–201)

That argument, that Highlander could not be educating because they were not neutral, lies behind much of my analysis in this chapter. When Highlander openly declared the political ambitions of their educational program, it was as if they had given up credibility as educators and were suddenly agitators and propagandists, intent not on teaching but on persuading people to think and act in a particular unified way.

CONCLUSION

The rhetorical ability to paint Highlander as a Communist menace—or, conversely, as an enlightened group of social activists—rather than as educators stemmed from their open embrace of the regulative discourse that guided the school. A regulative discourse, however named, is not something most teachers accept comfortably. This is, in part, what makes Bernstein's model so compelling: He argues that not only is this discourse always present, it is always primary. Horton (*We Make the Road*) claimed that Highlander disavowed neutrality in its education, but he also called neutrality "an immoral act" (102), making clear his argument that neutrality in education was impossible, "an excuse . . . a refusal to oppose injustice or take sides that are unpopular" (102). The claim of neutrality, then, is cover for anything but neutrality. However, Highlander also suggests the risk involved in openly naming the political and moral mission of an educational approach; to disavow neutrality in education immediately calls into question the legitimacy of an educational enterprise.

In part, this can be highlighted by exploring the idea of expertise, an idea that lies at the heart of traditional educational perceptions. Understood as a process of acquiring knowledge from experts, an education that openly seeks to challenge the social order would be, by definition, one in which outside experts told students how and what to think about their world, their country, their work. Framing the attacks on Highlander as reaction against a Communist threat plays into this model. Most approaches to schooling, I daresay then and in the present, accept the notion that experts control the dissemination of knowledge, from the organization of material in a particular subject area to the ways in which students demonstrate capability through standardized measurement systems. Adult education, in many of its theoretical discussions, has historically challenged this notion, arguing in part that a reliance on experts increases dependency and decreases the ability of students to choose wisely in the future. Eduard Lindemann, for example, argued that relying on specialists to address the "equation of our lives when meanings have become confused or lost" (134) signifies a lack of courage in taking an uncertain step. "The expert cuts the cord of uncertainty" (134), perhaps, but the end result is that, "When we next confront a similar difficulty, another expert will need to be consulted; in the end, if this were the essence of expert service, life would become a chronic succession of consultations in the presence of specialists. The only meanings possible would be those purchasable from experts" (135). The distinction between Highlander as represented by the continuous attackers and Highlander in its developing theories and practices can be encapsulated in these different conceptualizations of the notion of expertise.

As a way of describing how Highlander used, but did not rely upon, experts, Horton told a story in an interview about a group of African Americans who wanted to bring a lawsuit against a school that was reluctant to become fully integrated. Horton knew this was a bad idea, that "it could drag on for years and they'd probably lose it," but the students didn't know this.

> We didn't say in our great wisdom 'It'll kill the situation,' because it was their idea. We said, it's a legal question—a technicality of whether you have a case or not. Would you like us to get a lawyer to talk to you?
>
> . . . within two hours we had a Civil Liberties lawyer from Knoxville. I told him to explain the whole thing—how long it would take for everything. First, he told them he didn't think they had a case, and even if they did have a case, it would cost a lot of money. He didn't know what the expenses would be. He couldn't get to it for two or three months. It would probably be another two or three years before they got an answer.
>
> That wasn't what they had in mind. . . . So we told the lawyer to go home. We were through with him. He'd served his purpose. We don't let a person ride in on expertise and stay and take over. (Kennedy 109)

This kind of relationship to outside authority is visible, too, in this excerpt from the FBI files, regarding the visit to the school of two known Communists:

> When asked about the purpose of their visit Horton stated that, although he knew these men to be Communists, they were well versed in labor problems and were invited to give lectures at Highlander Folk School as long as they made no mention of Communism or tried to influence any members of the student body to become members of the Communist Party. (FBI 61-7511-96 April 11, 1942 3d 3)

The value of experts here is balanced by a sense of caution about experts' ability to take over in a pedagogical situation, and by every account Highlander worked hard to prevent this.

I cannot characterize the attacks on Highlander as a failure to imagine a different possibility for education, because I have no way of knowing how much the attackers believed their own stories about Highlander, stories that in many cases were demonstrably fictitious and apparently created to increase sensation. Certainly the FBI took those stories seriously enough to devote enormous resources to their investigation, and the sheer power of the narrative itself suggests its seeming plausibility, a plausibility that relies on a model of education diametrically opposed to Highlander's practice. Educational literacy practices, in the representation of attackers of Highlander and FBI investigation, emphasize the transference of knowledge from expert to novice and the straightforward reproduction of a rigid and dangerous ideology that seeks to destroy the American way of life. Regardless of whether attackers believed this construction, they understood it to be compelling, and I argue that part of its compelling nature lay in the fact that it grafted a dominant model of schooling onto Highlander. The goals of schooling, after all, are typically determined by outside experts who decide what students should know, when they should know it, and what they should know it for. In one way or another, these educational literacy practices become represented as objective and neutral (the most common contemporary approach being a reliance on their scientific nature), but as Horton argued they can never be. Still, the privileging of an apparent neutral stance makes any educational approach that denies neutrality immediately vulnerable to the sorts of charges launched against Highlander.

From the point of view of the school, as I have noted, its successes in programs like the Citizenship schools existed in precise relation to that disavowal of neutrality. Students did not want to learn to read and write for nothing, simply for its intrinsic value. They wanted to vote, to participate, to actively challenge a legal and social system that refused to grant them fundamental human rights. That this powerful force is also dangerous from an official point of view is evident in the sustained opposition to the school, a sign that to embrace the work of teaching as inherently a political and moral project not only makes people tremendously uncomfortable but is actually threatening. Of course, in Highlander's case, a good part of its threat lay in the school's ongoing advocacy of what amounted to dramatic social upheaval, but it was also threatening, I think, because its commitment to political and social aims for education challenged fundamental assumptions about the objectivity and neutrality of dominant approaches to learning. Given the continued strength of those assumptions and the seeming necessity to keep them in place, that aspect of Highlander's threat seems as significant and relevant as their advocacy of integration and workers' rights. Aside from the particular political aims of the moment, Highlander threatens the very nature of how we understand education in the United States. That's as dangerous and as important as anything else it could do.

CHAPTER 5

Conclusion

Teaching With the Cannon

I begin my conclusion in a trap.

I return to the cannon in the classroom, aimed at students from the teaching platform in the Walnut Street Jail. It is not the teacher who places the cannon there, but the warder of the jail, who uses that cannon to mark both the institutional context of instruction and the ways that, whatever claims the teacher might make about what happens and who it happens to, the classroom is still institutional space in which institutional prerogatives hold sway. That cannon remains a visible reminder, not only for students, but for teachers as well.

The moment the cannon appears in the classroom, of course, particular institutional relationships become overt. It is no longer possible, for example, for teachers or students to imagine themselves independent and outside an institutional context. Cannon or not, I have argued that one of the most provocative aspects of the discourse of correctional education is the overtness with which the institution itself shapes the concerns of that discourse. It is that overtness, however, and not the shaping itself, that sets aside correctional education, just as it is Highlander's overt claim that it teaches toward a world that ought to be, rather than the fact that is does so, that sets the school apart. Educational rhetoric appears to sidestep politics by claiming that it simply seeks to assist students in a world as it is; likewise educational rhetoric does well to hide the cannon in the classroom, to claim that the cannon, in fact, isn't present at all. To use a term broadly applied by Bourdieu and Passeron, educational rhetoric and action regularly rely on a process of "misrecognition."

This concept forms the teeth of my trap. For Bourdieu and Passeron, misrecognition serves a critical function in schooling: It allows all involved to misrecognize schooling as legitimate and progressive when its primary function, they argue, is to reproduce social power relations. They argue that all pedagogic action (PA, in their acronym-laden prose) is, by definition, "*the imposition of a cultural arbitrary by an arbitrary power*" (5, all italics in original) and thus an act of "*symbolic violence.*" The pedagogic authority (PAu) of the agent (in schools, the teacher) relies on representing that arbitrary as legitimate and natural, even universal. As Lewis Hyde notes in another context, "The well fed take the artifice of their situation and pass it off as an eternal verity" (69). Obviously, admitting the artifice behind the verity is not a viable option:

> a PA which aimed to unveil, in its very exercise, its objective reality of violence and thereby to destroy the basis of the agent's PAu, would be self-destructive. The paradox of Epimedes the liar would appear in a new form: either you believe I'm not lying when I tell you education is violence and my teaching isn't legitimate, so you can't believe me; or you believe I'm lying and my teaching is legitimate, so you still can't believe what I say when I tell you it is violence . . . every PA requires as the condition of its exercise the social misrecognition of the objective truth of PA. (12)

For Bourdieu and Passeron, there is no way out of this paradox. Dominant forms of pedagogic action, they argue, necessarily project what they call "*legitimate culture, i.e., the culture endowed with the dominant legitimacy, [which] is nothing other than the dominant cultural arbitrary insofar as it is misrecognized in its objective truth as a cultural arbitrary and as the dominant cultural arbitrary*" (23). Restated, schools pass off an artifice, a cultural construction, as a legitimate and eternal verity. The effective result of this, they argue, is a tight and inescapable system of cultural reproduction, by which

> *the system of PAs, insofar as it is subject to the effect of domination by the dominant PA, tends to reproduce, both in the dominant and dominated classes, misrecognition of the truth of the legitimate culture as the dominant cultural arbitrary, whose reproduction contributes towards reproducing the power relations.* (31)

The act of education insists upon such misrecognition; meaningful recognition of the arbitrary nature of its authority and the power relations sustaining it would, in effect, delegitimate it.

A great deal follows from this critical claim. Bourdieu and Passeron argue that dominated cultures learn, through pedagogic work and within educational systems, to misrecognize their own culture and ways of knowing as illegitimate, just as dominant cultures come to accept their own legitimacy. Educational systems always exist in service of social and cultural reproduction, just as the agents (i.e. the teachers) within those systems demonstrate a "self-reproductive tendency" (61). Institutions and their agents produce and reproduce those conditions that ensure their survival and the functioning of the educational system. Furthermore, "institutional legitimacy *dispenses the agents of the institution from having to endlessly win and confirm their PAu*" (63), at the same time that that legitimacy is misrecognized, most crucially by the agents, as "*based on nothing other than the agent's personal authority*" (65). In other words, teachers derive their authority from the institutions in which they teach, but they presume, along with their students, that their authority is personal. This fosters "*the illusion that the [work of schooling] is carried on independently of its institutional conditions (the paradox of professorial charisma)*" (66). As Bourdieu and Passeron argue,

> Nothing is more likely to enhance the authority of the institution and of the cultural arbitrary it serves than the enchanted adherence of teacher and taught to the illusion of an authority and message having no other basis or origin than the person of a teacher capable of passing off his delegated power to inculcate the cultural arbitrary as a power to decree it. (66–67)

It is impossible to display the complexity and layers of Bourdieu and Passeron's argument; I can only present it in these overly broad terms. I emphasize the critical role misrecognition plays within educational systems and the work of schooling, a misrecognition that all parties—teachers, students, and society at large—engage in. Cultural arbitraries appear legitimate, as do dominant cultural practices (*habitus*, to use the term so central to Bourdieu's overall work) and dominant power relations. Bernstein (2000) summarizes their model as such:

> the school disguises and masks the way power relations, external to the school, produce the hierarchies of knowledge, possibility, and value within the school. In disconnecting its own hierarchies from external hierarchies, the school legitimates inequalities between social groups deriving from differential school attainment. This is the essence of what Bourdieu calls 'la violence symbolique.' (*Pedagogy, Symbolic Control* xxiii)

Teacherly authority seems, to both students and teachers, to emanate from teachers, while it instead emanates from an educational system enabled in large part by the continual processes of misrecognition. The end result of this series of misrecognitions, of course, is social reproduction. In short, regardless of what teachers and students *think* they're doing in school, they are necessarily, inevitably, inescapably reproducing social and cultural power relations.

Richard Miller highlights something akin to misrecognition in exploring the historic appeal of Paulo Freire's work for composition teachers. Miller argues that Freire's central claim—that the authentic work of teachers is to liberate students, to raise their consciousness, to help them resist the oppressors assaulting them in many guises—

> is so attractive because it covers over our more primary role as functionaries of the administration's educational arm . . . I would argue that the prevailing desire to reconstruct the scene of instruction as a site where authenticity is forged and layers of false consciousness are peeled away indicates a general commitment in our profession to imagine that the power dynamic in the teacher-student relationships can, under ideal conditions, be erased. (18, 19)

The "ideal teacher," Miller argues, "is . . . typically cast as the one who works against the system, critical of its movements, free of its impurities, allied with science and reason rather than myth and folklore" (19). In other words, one of the appeals of Freire is the degree to which he supports the act of misrecognition, so that teachers see themselves as opposing the systems in which they teach, rather than being "functionaries of the administration's educational arm" commissioned to put students in rank order for institutional processing, or, in Max Weber's memorable phrasing (quoted by Bourdieu and Passeron), "little prophets in the pay of the State" (20). Teachers align themselves with students, here, as a sort of act of professional self-preservation, for to do anything else is to cop to the inherent complicity of working for the state.

My argument thus far in this book clearly highlights acts of misrecognition, ways in which the cannon in the classroom has been effectively disguised. Certain strands of correctional education, such as those based on social cognition, do away with the prison as a setting that fundamentally shapes teaching and learning practices. In the process, teachers represent their work as detached from the penal system, the criminal justice system, and social conditions in general. Teachers correct the social cognitive deficits of individual offenders. Exeunt the cannon. Likewise, I argue that a dominant trend in vocational education hinges on misrecognition. Competency-based education asks students to internalize workplace control, representing management strategies such as teamwork and job training as individual and measurable skills; control becomes essentially invisible in the discourse.

Even my discussion of Highlander suggests the official threat represented by an educational practice that refuses to pivot on misrecognition; somehow, Highlander appears more agitative than educative—often even to its own supporters—because the school openly promotes change in the status quo. And Horton's determined separation from the control of other institutions, educational, labor, and civil rights, emphasizes his sense that such institutions would inherently limit the school's agency. Such determined independence also means that, however tempting (à la Miller's Freireans), Highlander is not a model that educators working within official institutions can enact, not the least because those institutions fundamentally shape the regulative and thus the instructional discourses guiding the works of the teachers within them.

Where does this leave teachers, then? The model constructed by Bourdieu and Passeron effectively provides no option but for teachers to work in service of social and cultural reproduction. Once their model is understood, that is, it cannot simply be dismissed, because it lays such complete claim to the work of teachers that it must be considered, responded to, dealt with in some manner. This is especially the case because most teachers, in my experience, are not drawn to teaching in order to enable social and cultural reproduction; often, in fact, they are drawn for precisely the opposite reasons. But Bourdieu and Passeron close off the possibility of action in resistance to the system by placing any resistance in the context of the paradox invoked by Epimedes the Liar: A teacher might point out that his teaching is a process of symbolic violence, but for students to fully accept that would delegitimate the teacher's authority. To proclaim it and still maintain authority actually strengthens the process of misrecognition; misrecognition becomes effectively misrecognized. Miller notes that borrowing from Freire allows teachers to separate themselves from the system that they support simply by putting students in rank order, by grade, at the conclusion of the class. Misrecognition becomes stronger as soon as it is defined.

For me and for the new teachers and teachers in training I have worked with, Bourdieu and Passeron's model of education as a project of symbolic violence is as compelling as it is troubling, and for the same reason; in its extraordinary structure and layers of complexity, it makes sense. As I consider my own teaching, it is impossible for me not to accept fundamental aspects of the claims they make. I squarely stand, in my position as a university professor, in a system predicated on social and cultural reproduction, and my work serves that system. Every act of teaching and learning within state-structured and regulated institutions can be accounted for within the model. Teachers who claim to teach resistance to the system simply strengthen the degree to which misrecognition actually supports reproduction; students who rise beyond their social level of birth accept the legitimacy of the "dominant cultural arbitrary" and the illegitimacy of their own culture. "[T]he most hidden and most specific function of the educational system consists in hiding its objective function, that is, masking the objective truth of its relationship to the structure of class relations" (Bourdieu and Passeron 208). Any action that serves to further mask that truth simply strengthens the disguise.

In part, Bourdieu and Passeron are arguing for boundaries that cannot be crossed, for a process that cannot be altered, for a model that determines outcomes even when the model is named, especially when it is named. There is no escape, no movement, no way out. It's in that trap that I begin my conclusion.

TRICKSTER MAKES THIS CLASSROOM: TEACHING IN THE APORIA OF CULTURAL REPRODUCTION

In a fascinating passage from *Trickster Makes this World*, Lewis Hyde describes how tricksters in tales from around the world create a porous environment, noting the etymological link of *pore*—through the Greek *poros* meaning *passageway*—to *opportunity*. In these stories, tricksters create burrows with more than one entrance, providing multiple tunnels for escape. They also are expert at sealing up those entrances, thus turning escape routes into traps for what they prey upon, or for what preys upon them, in the burrow. They close up pores, in other words; Hyde notes that humpback whales create a net of bubbles to confuse prey, and that the octopus clouds water with an ink to enable escape, linking natural history to these trickster stories. What these tricksters do "is turn an escape route into a trap, a hole into a snare, a *poros* into an *aporos*, a clear medium into an aporia" (49). Hyde connects the rhetorical meaning of *aporia*—"a contradiction or an irreconcilable paradox"—to these trickster stories: "To experience aporia is to be caught in a tunnel with a fire at either end, to be bewildered by clouds of ink or encircled by a net of bubbles. No matter how many times you reverse yourself, you're still caught. Aporia is the trap of bafflement, invented by a being whose hunger has made him or her more cunning than those who only think to travel forward through a transparent world" (49).

Bourdieu and Passeron, in their description of reproduction in schooling, perform an amazing feat of sealing up multiple exits in an argument that, while adroitly dodging a mechanistic model, manages to make a stunning case for the notion that under all circumstances, in all cultures, in all cases, under any pedagogical model, officially sponsored schooling functions primarily as a means of reproduction, and any notion otherwise is a misrecognition serving that reproduction. Thus, school, first and foremost and always, irreversibly, reproduces and justifies existing class divisions in society; teachers can do no more and no less in their classes. The exits are sealed, and we can feel our skin begin to sear from the fires coyote has built to keep us in. By *we* I mean especially teachers of literacy practices, whose actions by Bourdieu and Passeron's model are especially vital in service of cultural and social reproduction. They note that "no one acquires a language without thereby acquiring a *relation to language*" (116), a version of my argument that all literacy teachers are better understood as teachers of literacy practices, teachers of the "values, attitudes, feelings, social relationships" (Barton and Hamilton 7) that attend academically sanctioned uses of literacy. To experience the structure Bourdieu and Passeron describe as something other than a trap, perhaps we can utilize a sort of trickster consciousness, use hunger and cunning to foster something besides "travel forward through a transparent world." The ends of such a process should not be to escape, but to work in service of covert, situationally grounded, and always constrained action.

At this point, my metaphor of the trap might have outlived its discursive usefulness, itself becoming a conceptual snare. The trap Bourdieu and Passeron describe no doubt exists in some strong fashion (few would suggest that the state has no interest in shaping the educational and social futures of the schooled) but a trickster consciousness invites us to consider how inviolate that trap may be. One of the reasons, perhaps, that Bourdieu and Passeron's model provokes anxieties for teachers is exactly that they themselves represent it as a trap, and traps, like prisons, provoke in turn a desire for release or even escape. From another perspective, though, this trap is nothing more than an acceptance of constraints, constraints imposed by descriptions of the world as it is. *Trap* becomes too heavy-handed, too conspiratorial, too unidimensional. If in some places the constraints on teachers of literacy practices are greater than in others (think, say, of the difference between that first class in the Walnut Street Jail and Bernice Robinson's first Citizenship class), it would be wrong to suggest that they are ever absent, that teaching without constraints is ever a viable goal. Instead, working effectively within any institution means understanding constraints, pushing against them when possible and useful or necessary, working to rebuild them, recognizing that the only constant will be the existence of constraints, not the particularity of them. Rather than hope for escape from "ceaselessly oppressive and instrumentalist" classrooms into ones "radically liberating and empowering", teachers instead must work in "the fraught, compromised world where all of our classes are convened" (R. Miller 23).

A sort of trickster consciousness facilitates action in that world. Hyde argues that trickster figures operate in places of moral ambiguity, and that there is a particular danger in any pretence to act outside of that ambiguity: "We may well hope our actions carry no moral ambiguity, but pretending that is the case when it isn't does not lead to greater clarity about right and wrong; it more likely leads to unconscious cruelty masked by inflated righteousness" (Hyde 10–11). One way of claiming to act with no moral ambiguity, of course, is to separate oneself from the ambiguities of the present world by aligning wholly with a morally impeccable but unrealized (and unrealizable) ideal of a world that ought to be—Miller's argument about the usefulness of engaging in Freirean composition instruction. If, however, we teach in morally ambiguous places, rife with multiple and contradictory impulses, then we must recognize the ambiguity inherent in our own actions. We must recognize that what we do is shaped fundamentally by the institutions and discourses within which we teach, that we live, not in some future world, but in the present, with everyone else.

Teachers, then, need theories that allow for reasoned action within morally ambiguous situations, and I don't think they find this in Bourdieu and Passeron's model of reproduction. Their model requires constant misrecognition by all parties, provoking simultaneously the desire to escape and something akin to despair at the inability to escape. This is the genesis of my argument in resistance to Bourdieu and Passeron. I resist their argument, that is, not because I find it flawed, but because in order to teach where I teach, I have to resist their argument, even as I accept many of their central claims. Moore and Jones argue that theories of competency-based education are officially valuable, not due to their "intrinsic viability," but because they are "well-suited to fulfil a particular set of policy objectives" (81); I would suggest that the ability for teachers to work with any theory must be a central criterion in any assessment of that theory's "intrinsic viability." It is in that regard that I have found the work of Basil Bernstein so compelling, because although his description of the pedagogic device always accepts the official constraints dramatically shaping the work of teachers, he also claims that "the device is not deterministic in its consequences" (38), that "it is possible to have an outcome, a form of communication which can subvert the fundamental rules of the device" (*Pedagogy, Symbolic Control* 28).

Hyde recounts a Russian legend about a trickster who attacks the knees, the weak spot of an otherwise invulnerable hero, thus cutting him down. "[T]he eternals," he uses the story to illustrate, "are vulnerable at their joints. To kill a god or an ideal, go for the joints" (253). In educational rhetoric, I would argue, such joints are especially visible where discourses move from one field to another, where ideology is at play. Bernstein's criticism of "the Parisian version" of cultural reproduction suggests that one of its shortcomings is its lack of attention to the internal structure of pedagogic discourse, an examination of which reveals certain vulnerabilities invisible in Bourdieu and Passeron's model. In their theory,

> pedagogic discourse becomes a carrier for something other than itself. It is a carrier of power relations external to the school, a carrier of patterns

> of dominance with respect to class, patriarchy, race. It is a matter of great interest that the actual structure which enables power to be relayed, power to be carried, is itself not subject to analysis. Paradoxically, what is missing from theories of cultural reproduction is any internal analysis of the structure of the discourse itself, and it is the structure of the discourse, the logic of this discourse, which provides the means whereby external power relations can be carried by it. (*Pedagogy, Symbolic Control* 4)

Bourdieu and Passeron define a pedagogic discourse primarily in terms of the external power relations it serves. By exploring instead the internal structure of pedagogic discourse, Bernstein suggests the presence of joints at which the dominant cultural ideal of reproduction becomes vulnerable.

Bernstein's model of the pedagogic device, briefly introduced in the first chapter, explores the internal structure of pedagogic discourse, seeking to understand "the means whereby power relations can be carried by it." In Bernstein's model, there are three fields within the pedagogic device: the field of production, the field of recontextualization, and the field of reproduction. I discussed recontextualization in some detail in Chapter 1, and here I will introduce more fully the other fields as a way of exploring those joints where the drive to social reproduction through education becomes vulnerable, where scholars and teachers might do something other than "travel forward through a transparent world" (Hyde 49).

As I noted in my introduction, the field of production encompasses those sites in which knowledge is created. Bernstein's typical example is physics, and the field of production in physics exists in academic and research institutions in which physics as a science is practiced. There, legitimate methods and objects of study are determined and pursued. The field of production—mostly under the purview of "institutions of higher education and private research organizations" (Singh 574)—is structured by what Bernstein calls distributive rules, which "create a specialised field of production of discourse, with specialised rules of access and specialised power controls . . . The distributive rules mark and distribute who may transmit what to whom and under what conditions, and they attempt to set the outer limits of legitimate discourse" (*Pedagogy, Symbolic Control* 31). By setting limits on what is legitimate discourse, distributive rules provide a way of defining what is acceptable and unacceptable knowledge. Within the pedagogic device, this amounts to an attempt to regulate access to sites of knowledge and to limit the range of discourses available to be pedagogized (that is, turned into pedagogic discourse).

Central to Bernstein's entire model is the notion that the movement of discourses from one field to another fundamentally changes those discourses. So, when a discourse within the field of production is recontextualized into a pedagogic discourse—when the discipline of physics becomes transformed into teaching physics—it becomes something other than what it was. As Bernstein argues, "The transformation takes place because every time a discourse moves from one position to another, there is a space in which ideology can play. No discourse ever moves without ideology at play. As this discourse moves, it becomes ideologically transformed; it is not the same discourse any longer" (*Pedagogy, Symbolic Control* 33). Pedagogic discourse, as I noted in the introduction, consists of an instructional discourse embedded within the regulative discourse. When the discourse of physics is transformed into the pedagogic discourse of physics, the pedagogic discourse becomes defined by issues irrelevant to the primary discourse of physics: It takes on issues focused on instruction, such as who teaches it, to whom, in what settings, and in what order, as well as issues central to a regulative discourse, such as who has access to such knowledge, what are acceptable relationships between teachers and students, what social order the discourse seeks to project.

This movement from the field of production into the field of recontextualization becomes for me the first joint within the pedagogic device, the first place in which it becomes vulnerable. As I will discuss, movement from the field of production into the field of recontextualization is highly charged, because the discourse created decides what knowledge should be available to students, what counts as legitimate and what does not matter. For example, legitimacy in dominant discourses of vocational education comes from business leaders and politicians, whose descriptions of the high-performance workplace and the competencies required within it become the most important knowledge about the future of work and employment. Certainly, dominant discourses of vocational education do not legitimate the vast discourses produced as criticism of a post-Fordist capitalism in the late twentieth and early twenty-first centuries; students in vocational schools, for example, rarely learn about sweatshops and the effects of international trade agreements and policy on a well-paid domestic labor force. Such knowledge, in effect, is not legitimated in this circumstance. In current official discourses surrounding reading within No Child Left Behind and other federal educational initiatives, legitimacy in the field of production increasingly relies on narrow definitions of *science*; thus, research that cannot be validated as scientific becomes unacceptable as useful for recontextualizing into pedagogic discourse. Officially, the movement from the field of production into the field of recontextualization is vital to control, because as a joint in which "ideology is at play" other possibilities for legitimate knowledge must be discounted (labeled unscientific) or simply ignored altogether.

The second potential joint that challenges the determinism of Bourdieu and Passeron's model exists in the movement from the field of recontextualization into the field of reproduction. Within Bernstein's model, reproduction becomes something quite different than what it means within Bourdieu and Passeron's. In the terms of the pedagogic device, what is reproduced is the knowledge that was produced and then recontextualized, thus becoming the second of "two text transformations": "Privileged and privileging pedagogic texts created in the field of recontextualization, such as curricular schemes and textbooks, are transformed again as they appropriated (sic) by teachers and converted into modes of common or shared classroom knowledge in interaction with students" (Singh 577). Descriptions of, for example, the high-performance workplace become recontextualized into pedagogic discourses considering how to prepare students to work in such a workplace; reproduction begins to occur within particular classrooms. Given the discursive gaps between the field of production and the field of reproduction, the knowledge reproduced will necessarily be different from the knowledge produced, which means, in turn, that reproduction under the terms of Bernstein's model is a slippery and variable concept.[37] The necessary changes due to such gaps—gaps between what is initially produced and what is ultimately reproduced—also suggest avenues for action by scholars and teachers, because reproduction in education can never be understood as seamless. Instead, reproduction in education requires at least two transformations where discourses cannot be wholly controlled, where scholars and teachers, however necessarily embedded within systems predicated on reproducing social power relations, might also act to resist that reproduction, to limit and redirect it, if never to detach themselves from it.

I turn to a specific example of what I would call a joint within educational rhetoric, a place where a discourse moves from one field to another. The tightly structured curriculum Gerald Coles describes here, extreme yet representative of the pressures elementary school teachers face, simultaneously demonstrates the official power in shaping teachers' work and, by its very presence, official anxieties about the limits of that power:

> "M – M – M – M." "Ma – Ma – Ma – Ma." "Mad – Mad – Mad – Mad." Chanted in unison, these exercises were part of the reading lessons in classroom after classroom in an elementary school in Sacramento City, California. Additional chants responded to questions about what letters were needed to change *mad* into *made*, *made* to *make*, and *make* to *Mike*. The lessons were part of a new reading program called Open Court, the hope of many educators and parents in the Sacramento City school district who wanted to reverse "years of substandard achievement" caused primarily, they believed, by whole language teaching. In contrast, Open Court was described as "a systematic, phonics-based language arts teaching program" that used heavily scripted instructional guides complete with daily lesson plans. In the words of one teacher, the teachers manual "is so specific, you really can't miss it." The program was especially good for new teachers, said one principal, because

> "they need much more scripting" than had been provided by previous programs. For principals, the program made supervision easier because instruction was uniform. (Coles *Misreading* 31)

At its most extreme, this is the logical response of an educational system bent on eliminating the contingencies inherent in pedagogical practice. The construction of education as the script of an extremely tedious, very long, and plotless play ("I seriously doubt," Elaine Garan writes of Open Court, "that a single adult could endure what we require of children" [31]) turns teachers into extensions of, in this case, a commercial product, but it also attempts to do away with the messiness of teaching, to control the contingencies and personalities that shape every classroom regardless of the theories guiding individual teachers. Both students and teachers act as inarticulate puppets of a soundly debunked, but still oddly compelling, educational method, variations of which have become the backbone of federal educational literacy policy.

Such a script replaces contingency with a drive toward essence, a term I use to recall the Aristotelian distinction between accidentals and essences, paraphrased here by Hyde: "Accidentals are present by chance, essentials by design. Accidentals are changeable and shifting; essentials are stable. The real significance of a thing lies with its essences, not its accidentals" (97). Using the image of the Open Court classroom as an example, I suggest that the method seeks to protect the "essence"—a narrow phonics-based literacy instruction promoted as scientific and research based—from the "accidents" inherent in particular classrooms due to the variety of teachers and students within them. There will always be institutional and political conflicts involving the relationship between educational accidents and essences, and it is in the tension between these two poles, and not in the prioritizing of one over another (capitulation versus escape), that pores appear in the project of reproduction.

The need for the control represented by a script, which teachers and students will literally and simply recite as their primary educational literacy practices, demonstrates an anxiety that Bernstein suggests is necessarily present in the movement from one pedagogic field to another. Given the vulnerability inherent in the shift from the field of recontextualization, in which pedagogic discourse is created, to the field of reproduction, which occurs in particular classrooms, it should be no surprise that programs like Open Court would appear. Such a program seeks to do away with that transformation altogether, so that nothing is at play in the movement from one field to another. In fact, one could argue this as a significant factor in many manifestations of pedagogic discourse, that built into it are explicit directions on its proper use. Certainly, when I used the I-CANS materials, described in Chapter 3, during the year of the pilot project, one of the complaints of the project coordinators had to do with the fact that we didn't use the materials as they had specified.[38] My argument about that at the time was that we chose not to follow directives we recognized as unproductive for our own students and situations. My argument now, following Bernstein, is that regardless of how we felt about the material (most of us had several critiques), direct correspondence between instructional guides and actual practices is probably impossible. Still, inscribed into pedagogic discourses like Open Court and I-CANS is a desire to police the boundary between the two fields.

Likewise, given Bernstein's argument that "The recontextualising field has a crucial function in creating the fundamental autonomy of education" (*Pedagogy, Symbolic Control* 33), we should expect a similar attempt to police what and how things are recontextualized, to control the discourse as it moves from the field of production to the field of recontextualization. He argues that within the recontextualizing field exist two related but still distinct fields. There is always, he claims, "an *Official Recontextualizing Field* [ORF], created and dominated by the state for the construction and surveillance of state pedagogic discourse," and "usually (but not always) a *Pedagogic Recontextualizing Field* [PRF] consisting of trainers of teachers, writers of textbooks, curricular guides, etc., specialized media and their authors" (ibid. 115):

> If the PRF can have an effect on the pedagogic discourse independently of the ORF, then there is both some autonomy *and* struggle over pedagogic discourse and its practices. But if there is only the ORF, then there is no autonomy. Today, the state is attempting to weaken the PRF through its ORF, and thus attempting to reduce relative autonomy over the construction of pedagogic discourse and over its social contexts. (ibid. 33)

In other words, Bernstein argues that the boundary between the field of production and the field of reproduction is also the site of official attempts to control and fix pedagogic discourse, to limit—and perhaps to entirely suppress and reshape—oppositional perspectives shaped in the Pedagogic Recontextualizing Field.

Those attempts by the state to weaken the PRF are evident, I think, in the sorts of initiatives and curricula I examine in chapter three, but they are also evident in current struggles to define the correct literacy pedagogies for elementary school children. The official response to these struggles is evident within Bush's "No Child Left Behind," which provides funding for reading instruction billed as "scientific," but such attempts to control reading pedagogies certainly predate the Bush administration. Coles traces official reliance on "scientific research" in support of reading pedagogies to

Jeanne Chall's criticism, in the late 1960s, of the neglect of phonics in reading textbooks. The growing power of the movement, Coles argues, should be understood in opposition to other educational changes also developing in the 1960s, including "more power for teachers and students, such as giving students greater voice in formulating the direction of instruction, reducing school and classroom hierarchy and increasing democratic decision making, encouraging students' critical thinking, and giving greater classroom attention to issues of equality and justice" (*Reading* 11). As Coles and several commentators have noted, these official recommendations for reading instruction defend their claims by invoking essence over accident; in the words of Laura Bush, "We now know—because science tells us—what teaching methods are most effective" (qtd. ibid. 125). Coles notes several other instances where officials have used the phrase "science tells us" or "research has taught us" to support "skills-emphasis" reading instruction: "The use of the phrase 'what science tells us' is extraordinary insofar as it reconceptualizes what is no more than a doctrine based on biased beliefs into what is continually described as objective, independent findings based on impartial pursuits. Pure science conveys its truths to us: we tell it nothing; it 'tells us'" (*Reading* 125–126). We have been in the arena of objectivity and truth before, in the discussion of competency-based education, which also claims empirically verifiable facts as the solid basis of its educational philosophy. Both work to a similar rhetorical effect, I would argue; they dismiss the sort of expertise represented within the Pedagogical Recontextualizing Field and replace it with, in the case of competency-based education, common sense and officially constructed descriptions of what people need for success in the high-performance workplace and, in the case of mandating narrow and skills-based reading instruction, science. Both, in other words, work to create solid descriptions of the world as it is that brook no argument, educated or otherwise.

The work of the National Reading Panel (NRP) aptly demonstrates this attempt to regulate the boundary between the fields of production and recontextualization, because the panel worked specifically to determine what sorts of research could be recontextualized into pedagogic discourse. Organized by the National Institute for Child Health and Human Development (NICHD) in 1997, the National Reading Panel, made up of fourteen members (only two of whom had experience teaching reading to children), assembled with the mandate to review the voluminous research concerning how children learn to read and determine how best to apply it. As one of their first actions, the NRP developed criteria to evaluate and discriminate among the roughly 100,000 published studies of reading, going back to 1966, submitted for consideration. They began by cutting all studies not about reading development within school-age children and all studies dealing with "key aspects of reading development such as motivation and reading, writing and reading, and children's interests and reading" (Coles *Reading* 41). They allowed only studies that met their definition of scientific research, which was "limited to quantitative, experimental studies, the kind that have a research and a control group, quantitative outcomes, and statistical analyses" (ibid. 41), thus eliminating, for example, studies based on observations of specific classrooms and other qualitative studies vital for teachers. Finally, the studies were culled according to how well they "adequately described the subjects, instruction used, outcome measures, data, statistical analyses, and other basic aspects of the research" (ibid. 41). At the conclusion, the panel accepted slightly over 300 studies, defined by their process as scientific. Conclusions drawn from these studies, then, could be considered based on science.

Coles and many others have worked through several of the particular studies deemed scientific by the Panel to demonstrate their shortcomings as research (see also Garan, Allington, Larson, Smith). For my purposes here, however, I simply want to present this as an explicit example of the Official Recontextualizing Field at work, defining in minute and narrow terms what is allowable for recontextualization. The "how" which follows from this initial culling, perhaps not surprisingly, advocates pedagogies that overwhelmingly emphasize skill-based instruction—sound-letter correspondence, letter blends, and so forth—and leaves out educational literacy practices like sustained silent reading and any sort of writing instruction. This is a clear attempt to control what passes over that discursive boundary, to define the terms by which pedagogic discourse can be formulated, by which discourses from the field of production can be included as valid in the field of recontextualization. It is an attempt, in short, to control what is thinkable, for teachers and for students.

It's possible, even common, to react to such institutional and political attempts to control the thinkable with what Herbert Kohl calls "Stupidity that leads to tears." This type of stupidity

> is not a matter of people lacking intelligence, or making clumsy or thoughtless decisions, or acting in ways that make them the butt of jokes. It is not a matter of ignorance. Rather, it is a form of institutional and social coercion that traps people into acting in ways they consider to be stupid and, in the context of teaching, counter to the work they feel they must do to help their students . . . [I]t can be a form of confinement to insane norms of educational programs that restrict creativity and clearly have not worked. Being stupid can be demoralizing. But it can also be a call to resistance and the rebirth of teacher militancy. (Kohl 11)

Most of us as teachers have probably felt this kind of stupidity and will likely feel it again during our careers. It is the stupidity that comes when there seems to be no escape, when the only option appears to be to act counterproductively to our sense of what we should do. But those attempts to control the thinkable are acts of power that simultaneously demonstrate their own limits by revealing the anxieties that provoke them. Those attempts, then, mark vulnerabilities as much as they mark power.

An attempt to control the thinkable, after all, is most likely to come in those places where what might become thinkable is indeterminate, under threat. It's the inherent indeterminacy of those boundaries that I want to foreground here as the gaps within which scholars and teachers can operate, if not independently, at least perhaps other than in the specific interests of the systems for which they are employed. I accept Bourdieu and Passeron's argument that we are always in part determined by the systems within which we teach and that as teachers in officially sanctioned and regulated sites we are necessarily complicit in a project of cultural reproduction; my interest, however, is in exploring those ways in which we are other than wholly determined, to create not a free space, not an unambiguous space, but a pore, an opportunity to act within the seeming aporia of that project.

Bernstein's model of the pedagogic device suggests the places where official attempts at control are most likely to be their strongest as well as the places in which scholars and teachers can enact a sort of trickster consciousness. That consciousness resists accepting official claims of transparency that rely on what science tells us or straightforward descriptions of the world as it is. That consciousness not only allows for movement within the constraints of the systems we find ourselves in, it often requires that movement, as Kohl suggests. However, this is a movement of construction, not a movement of escape; rather than seeking a release from constraints altogether, in other words, we try to rebuild them, a political process that is necessarily ongoing.

LEGIBILITY, CONTEXT, AND THE STRUGGLE FOR DEFINITION

In a 1991 article in the *Journal of Correctional Education*, Glendel D. Love declares that inmates in prison are not properly served by andragogical approaches to education, especially those relating to self-directed learning. Because "the typical adult male inmate students will have a marked external locus of control, . . . the andragogical assumption of self-directedness is not valid" (37–38). Inmates, in other words, are not psychologically prepared for self-directed learning and need considerably more shaping; "externally oriented individuals appear to be more attuned to what the leader wants and are more willing to allow themselves to be influenced by the leader's subtleties" (38). Love argues other distinctions between internals and externals as well, each supporting a particular teaching strategy appropriate to a classroom dominated by externals: "The autocratic or authoritarian leader uses extrinsic rewards for which the group members endeavor. While this leadership style has received unfavorable commentary, it is effective and appropriate for those with a strongly external locus of control such as male inmate students" (38). By defining particular characteristics of the offender-student, Love provides a constraint on effective teaching within prisons.

I point out Love's argument not to argue with it, though, as should be clear from my chapter on correctional education, I do not accept it. What interests me here is the way in which the construction of context simultaneously describes the constraints with which a teacher operates. Those constraints operate in shaping both the world that is—by defining the type of student that teachers will encounter in the classroom—and in the world that ought to be—by suggesting that a primary goal of correctional education should be to "systematically shift the inmate student's locus of control beneficially" (39). The definition of the world as it is justifies and allows movement toward the world as it ought to be. If the world as it is revolves around a particular kind of high-performance workplace for which the labor pool is unprepared, then the world that ought to be is one in which the labor pool is ready to function at high levels of performance; if the world as it is relies on the systematic disenfranchisement and oppression of particular social groups, then the world as it ought to be works for the alleviation of that oppression.

In effect, this is the sort of dialectic Myles Horton referred to in his address to teachers of the Citizenship Schools:"We have kept our eyes firmly on the *ought to be*, and it seems to me that in our schools we have succeeded in making a pattern of procedure so that all the things that are needed down here, the specifics in the 'is' circle—begin to move in the direction of what *ought to be*—and this is the difference" ("Myles Horton's Talk" n.p.). Playing a role in shaping the constraints teachers teach within—constraints both on the world as it is and the world as it ought to be—requires an active role in defining the contexts of teaching. In my introduction, I argued that something is always at stake in discussions of educational literacy practices, and so it is with discussions of context, which become central sites of conflict within educational rhetoric.

Context presented by educational rhetoric is never the same as the world as it is. Context is a rhetorical device always shaped by particular people for particular purposes, always a construction. That construction is necessarily a simplification, a term I borrow here from James Scott, who discusses its necessary role in any process of state intervention: "No administrative system is capable of representing any existing social community except through a heroic and greatly schematized process of abstraction and simplification" (22). Necessarily, he argues, that simplification includes a legibility that provides particular definitions to a social structure:

> Legibility is a condition of manipulation. Any substantial state intervention in society—to vaccinate a population, produce goods, mobilize labor, tax people and their property, conduct literacy campaigns, conscript soldiers, enforce sanitation standards, catch criminals, start universal schooling—requires the invention of units that are visible. The units in question might be citizens, villages, trees, fields, houses, or people grouped according to age, depending on the type of intervention. Whatever the units being manipulated, they must be organized in a manner that permits them to be identified, observed, recorded, counted, aggregated, and monitored. The degree of knowledge required would have to be roughly commensurate with the depth of the intervention. In other words, one might say that the greater the manipulation envisaged, the greater the legibility required to effect it. (Scott 183)

Certainly, interventions like those involved in mass education require a legibility that attempts to define terms central to the pedagogic device: knowledge, students, teachers, evaluation, and so forth. Any educational process requires such legibility in order to function, so the simplification itself is not grounds for critique (though it always allows for critical questioning). However, when what is legible becomes an official synonym for what is true, for what, in Bourdieu and Passeron's terms, is legitimate, it helps to look again at the scribbling that legibility attempts to conceal.

Perhaps one legible unit at stake in the educational discourses I examine here could be understood as the citizen. All of the educational discourses have a perspective on the proper role of the citizen, a role that lines up in part with some of the conflicts that circulate, as I pointed out in Chapter 1, around the meaning of the word *adult* in *adult education*. Citizens might be understood as employable, a labor force useful for the maintenance of both state and corporate economic superiority; in this definition, a first-class citizen is one who serves the state economically. Closely related to this is one definition of citizen emphasized within the discourse of correctional education, whereby a citizen is a person who abides by the laws of the state and lives according to the contemporary social requirements, most fully by holding a job, paying taxes, and assuming proper family roles. Thus, citizens become citizens precisely because they assume identities useful from a state and administrative perspective. Highlander's insistence that first-class citizenship accommodate not the state but the wants and needs of people, especially those people the state has most closely attempted to silence and disable, directly challenges the principle of legibility emphasized from a state's perspective: Citizenship requires in the work of Highlander an always skeptical view of the work of the state, of the ways in which the state seeks to shape social identities. Highlander's conception of citizenship requires constant work to change, improve, make the state more democratic; citizens necessarily and constantly challenge social and political constraints, likely making those citizens, from a state perspective, a social and political threat, because those constraints often directly serve official purposes.

If developing citizens, variously defined, becomes a goal for the educational process, it becomes necessary as well to make legible the student who will attain citizenship through education. As indicated by Love's claims about the external locus of control of male inmate students, defining the student makes the educational process itself legible, provides a way to create pedagogic discourses because that student provides their proper focus, the subject and starting and ending points of their narrative structure. In order for students to be fixed (in both senses of the word), "complex reality must be reduced to schematic categories" (Scott 77). Such reductions include, I would argue, claiming that particular students lack the sorts of competencies necessary for success in the twenty-first century workplace, or that they have cognitive and moral deficiencies that make them overly vulnerable to criminal behavior. Scott notes that the simplifications imposed by the state have direct consequences on the individuals whose identities are thereby simplified:

> State officials can often make their categories stick and impose their simplifications, because the state, of all institutions, is best equipped to insist on treating people according to its schemata. Thus categories that may have begun as the artificial interventions of cadastral surveyors, census takers, judges, or police officers can end by becoming categories that organize people's daily experience precisely because they are embedded in state-created institutions that structure that experience. (82–83)

Regardless of the accuracy or complexity of any given act of simplification, then, how pedagogic discourse defines the student will likely matter a great deal to students.

Who the student is also works to define what counts as knowledge within a particular pedagogic discourse, the content that will be taught. Knowledge is what the student needs to drive the narrative, to make the student become what the student is not yet: employable, noncriminal, socially active. Within pedagogic discourse, there is no such thing as knowledge for knowledge's sake, learning simply for the intrinsic value of learning, a concept that fosters heady misrecognitions in numerous pedagogical settings. Just as students become simplified into sets of characteristics that educational practice can concisely address and assess, so must particular settings become simplified. In the dominant discourse of vocational education, the most obvious simplification is that of the high-performance workplace, by which workplaces become easily identified by their team-oriented social structures, their consequent lack of hierarchy, their need for a flexible and creative and highly skilled workforce. In the dominant discourse of correctional education, the most obvious simplification is the elision of the prison as a context that matters; the prison is not so much simplified as it is done away with as a significant educational factor.

A compelling simplification throughout the discourses of vocational and correctional education occurs regarding race, which essentially disappears as a significant contextual factor surrounding employment or criminality. In her discussion of one of the classic works in literacy studies, *Ways With Words*, Catherine Prendergast argues that Shirley Brice Heath faced the question of how to account for race in her ethnography of community language practices. Heath intended her analysis to facilitate better teaching in school systems trying to contend with the pressures of desegregation. She was not only celebrating linguistic diversity in a call for teachers to be more aware; she hoped to help enable an educational reform that would allow equal (and, in the term Heath uses, Mainstream) education for all students, a reform she candidly admits was largely unsuccessful. The central insight in Heath's book, that differences in language practices do not signify differences in intelligence or capacity, is critical for any teacher to understand regarding her students. Prendergast claims, however, that Heath steps back from a crucial contextual factor in her argument by avoiding a direct discussion of the effect of institutional racism, using a racially imbalanced interchange between a Black student and a White teacher (described in a paper by a teacher from Heath's class) to argue that

> While Heath's research might be seen as an attempt to create a shared community between home and school where all the rules of language use are understood by all, the interaction between the student and teacher suggests that there is already a shared community, one in which some of the rules involve allowing people with certain skin color to dictate the terms of interaction. (Prendergast 91)

Prendergast argues that "*Ways* has within its analytical structure a lacuna around the topic of race" (59), a lacuna that shapes the context of the book directly: To introduce racism as a problem would add an element that teachers in the community did not want to confront. Couching the problem as a difficulty in understanding differences in language practices suggests a world as it ought to be in which those differences do not hold students back, a world in which teachers intellectualize and correct their biases about language use. If racism enters as a significant factor, it, too, changes the world that ought to be, because it means that educational practice will have to engage, in some way, with racism as an institutional and interpersonal problem facing educational reform. In other words, Heath's definition of the world that is implies the educational goal; Prendergast suggests the necessity of directly acknowledging racism as central concern in cultural constructions of literacy, an acknowledgement that would immediately change understandings of the world that ought to be that education should work to enact. If educational literacy practices exist within institutions with extensive histories of racist action, then educational literacy practices need to work in service of addressing that history.

Working to address that history, of course, dramatically alters the terms of educational action. As Joe Kincheloe argues, silence around race allows for approaches to education relentlessly focused on student inability:

> In our color-blind and power-erased microcosm, teachers have no way of appreciating the complex issues that lead African-Americans, Latinos, Native American, or poor people from all backgrounds to score lower in IQ tests or achievement tests and to be placed in remedial and vocational curricula. In the culture of racial silence, white-dominated educational institutions have nothing to do with the low station of the poor and nonwhite. Individuals are entirely responsible for their own fate, as the social context in which one grows is deemed 'inadmissible evidence' in the everyday world of educational evaluation. In this world, the consideration of individuals in terms of the social aggregate of which they are a part is forbidden by the grammar of race silence. (Kincheloe 218–19)

When the discourse of vocational education defines the students it addresses as unskilled, the mission of vocational education hinges on teaching skills. If inmates are imprisoned largely as a consequence of their social cognitive deficits, then the educational solution is to correct those deficits. To include substantial discussions of race would require a frank acknowledgement of the racial and social imbalance in vocational classes and in prisons, which demands another explanation than low-skills or external orientation. As soon as that happens, however, as soon as poverty and unemployment, criminality and imprisonment, are understood as reflecting complex social dynamics and not simply individual shortcomings, curricula based on transforming individuals are no longer sufficient. To be successful, educational action must engage with more than the students; it must seek to change as well the societies and institutions in which it takes place. The threat Highlander represented to official institutions resulted from the school's consistent belief that economic and racial disparities were matters of injustice that required social action. Highlander scared the state, that is, because it steadfastly argued that the ultimate goal of educational work was not to create skilled and capable adults but to fundamentally change unjust social structures. The African Americans on the Sea Islands did not suffer from their inability to read. Instead, they were systematically and intentionally oppressed and disenfranchised by a racist state. Addressing the conditions of that oppression, not improving the literate abilities of individuals, became the ultimate goal of educational action.

In conversation with Freire, Horton noted that "the going practice is to fall back on telling people that if they learn to read and write they'll get a job. I said, 'Anyone that's dumb enough to believe that is too dumb to learn to read.' But yet they still tell poor people that" (Horton and Freire 92). When the context of educational work becomes simplified to exclude systematic racial and social injustice, then economic and racial disparities must be accounted for by simplicities such as an inability to read or write. The lofty ambition suggested by the name "No Child Left Behind" will be achieved, under the Act, by ensuring that all students gain proficiency on a battery of standardized tests. This makes economic and racial disparities understandable as failures to teach poor and non-white students how to do well on machine-scored exams. To include in the context of educational work such realities as the vast difference in resources between schools in wealthy communities and schools in poor communities would require a different approach to leaving no child behind, one that acknowledged ongoing racial and social injustice as a significant factor. If an inability to find work stems from an individual's poor education, then the blame is on that person and that person's teachers; if the inability results from systematic injustices, then addressing it requires changing society and those who most powerfully shape it. Government and economic authorities are either empowered to take greater control of teachers and curricula or required to focus on their own roles in a history and present of inequality and discrimination. It's easy to see why one approach would appear more officially palatable than the other.

The simplification of context is not in itself the central problem, however, because any time contexts are named and defined, they become, by that process, constructions, simplifications. This is necessary for educational action; Bernstein defines the pedagogic device as acting to define, from limitless possibilities, what becomes the object of pedagogic action. This is a rhetorical move, given that pedagogic discourses name the proper goals and procedures of pedagogy. The problem comes, I think, when those contexts acted upon, within, and toward are fixed, pinned down, totally defined. Those contexts, then, become constraints theoretically impervious to teachers, constraints intended to wholly shape their practice.

It's useful at this point to turn to Highlander's practice in their community education programs, such as the Citizenship Schools they developed on Johns Island in South Carolina. It was nearly three years between the moment when, in 1954, Esau Jenkins mentioned, during a Highlander workshop on the school campus, the desirability of a literacy program for African Americans, and the moment when, in 1957, Bernice Robinson taught the first group of adults there. The time between those events was spent learning about the island and the other Sea Islands, a process that involved regular extended visits by numerous members of the staff and extensive interviewing of islanders by staff, especially Septima Clark, regarding their living conditions and their particular needs. It involved a comprehensive knowledge of the history and culture of the islands, the climate, the soil conditions, the relationships between employers and employees, the history of race relations, the patterns of daily movement throughout the islands and between the islands and the homeland. It also involved an initial attempt by Highlander to direct projects not in the way Jenkins suggested, but toward projects like public school desegregation, the forming of cooperatives, the establishment of a credit union. Only after several years of work and study of context did the Highlander staff return to Jenkins's initial insight as a necessary first step.

This process reflected a central philosophy at Highlander, that what mattered was not what staff and teachers at the school thought a community needed, but how the community itself perceived its needs. Determining this, then, became a central goal in the development of Highlander's educational outreach programs. Building context, then, was not a matter of imposing an educational agenda on groups of simplified students (as, for example, offenders) or working toward sites that could be defined universally (as in the high-performance workplace); rather, it required extensive ethnographic research in specific places and with specific populations of people. It meant that Highlander determined not to define its students (or potential students) in terms those students would not recognize or would resist. To put this in Scott's terms, students, goals, and contexts had to be legible first to those students. Given that any attempt to name and shape reality requires some sort of simplification, in this case Highlander sought simplifications that the students themselves could accept.

But this process never involved a capitulation of Highlander's own social agenda. The context within which Highlander acted, in other words, always required a compatibility with Highlander's long-term vision of a more democratic society, a vision tied in the period I examine to union and civil rights education. The extraordinary level of research and questioning served the construction of an openly biased, not an objective and true, context. Horton noted that Highlander relied on a "a goal or direction based on value judgement," on a "philosophy and purpose which is of an unfolding nature and is difficult to define" (*Long Haul* 217). Immediate activities had to work in service of that philosophy and purpose. That Highlander's construction of context is more complex than, say, generic descriptions of the high-performance workplace does not make it something other than a rhetorical simplification; rather, it is a simplification invoked to serve a particular political and social end.

As I noted in Chapter 4, Highlander's definition of context in service of their radically democratic agenda provoked constant official and quasi-official attacks throughout the first three decades of their operation. This brings me back to my argument about the struggle for the rights to define context. Highlander's independence in defining the educational contexts they worked within rejected the state's own formulations except insofar as the school worked in express opposition to them. Few teachers operate with such independence, of course. Increasingly, as Bernstein argues, the Official Recontextualizing Field works to narrowly define educational contexts and thus the worlds that ought to be, which those contexts invoke. Rather than respond with a "stupidity that leads to tears," however, teachers and scholars of pedagogy must steadfastly work to retain the right to define context as well, understanding that engaging in this process will mean, at best, "both some autonomy *and* struggle over pedagogic discourses and its practices" (33) within the Pedagogic Recontextualization Field. To assume a voice in defining the contexts for teaching means teachers also assume an active role in constructing both the world as it is and the world that ought to be. It also suggests that a goal of discourses emanating from the Official Pedagogic Field will be to limit the degree to which teachers and scholars can assume that voice.

TEACHING AS MÉTIS AND THE CONSTRUCTION OF CONTEXT

This points out, of course, a particular anxiety within pedagogic discourse, and thus the site of extensive attempts at simplification, regarding the role of the teacher. My chapter on vocational education highlights the ways in which pedagogic discourse works to define and evaluate what teachers do. Certainly, when teachers are assessed on the basis of their students' performance regarding a standard ideal, that standard functions as much, if not more, to shape the work and evaluation of teachers as it does the learning and assessment of students. The more contexts can be universalized and objectified, the easier it is to define the proper role of the teacher. Once the most effective reading instruction for all students is proven scientifically, teachers can deliver it according to a script or a predetermined curriculum, from which deviation is objectively misguided. When pedagogic discourse functions to strictly limit and define the role of individual teachers in shaping the particular context of their own classrooms, teaching becomes deprofessionalized, a matter of acting solely in standard ways to address standard students for standard purposes.

That this doesn't work is never really the point. As Moore and Jones argue about competency-based education, the usefulness of particular approaches as policy instruments often matters more than their academic acceptability: "The logic of competency is located within the politics of practice, not in social theory" (84). Theories of competency are valuable not because they have credibility, but because they allow for particular educational policies. In effect, the ORF ignores the PRF; criticism of the ORF from the position of the PRF will likely be summarily ignored as well. From a policy perspective, the power of local contexts to shape educational practice is threatening, regardless of the viability of that power within social and educational theory. So it seems likely that there will always be a determined tension between theoretical approaches that privilege that power of local contexts and official desires to efface context to the point where the practice of teachers and the goals for individual students can be universalized and objectively defined, independent of any particular local situation.

Shaping the constraints in which we teach requires that we negotiate this tension, not attempt the impossible act of escaping or doing away with it. To suggest how teachers might deal with this tension, I turn to another useful concept from Scott, one he borrows from the ancient Greek tradition and one that embodies, I think, a particular kind of trickster consciousness, the idea of métis. Métis, that defining characteristic of Odysseus, emphasizes contingencies over essence, local over universal, particular knowledge over objective fact. As Scott explains,

> Métis is most applicable to broadly similar but never precisely identical situations requiring a quick and practiced adaptation that almost becomes second nature to the practitioner. The skill of métis may well involve rules of thumb, but such rules are largely acquired through practice . . . and a developed feel or knack for strategy. Métis resists simplification into deductive principles which can successfully be transmitted through book learning, because the environments in which it is exercised are so complex and nonrepeatable that formal procedures of rational decision making are impossible to apply. In a sense, métis lies in that large space between the realm of genius, to which no formula can apply, and the realm of codified knowledge, which can be learned by rote. (315–16)

Scott contrasts métis to techne, or technical knowledge, expressible "precisely and comprehensively in the form of hard-and-fast rules . . . , principles, and propositions" (319). Techne is "universal, . . . settled knowledge, . . . characterized by impersonal, often quantitative precision and a concern with explanation and verification" (320). Techne specifies "how knowledge is to be codified, expressed, and verified, *once* it has been discovered" (320). Most importantly, Scott argues, techne "is characteristic . . . of self-contained systems of reasoning in which the findings may be logically derived from the initial assumptions. To the degree that the form of knowledge satisfies these conditions, to that degree it is impersonal, universal, and completely impervious to context" (320).

Scott does not discuss métis in regard to teaching, but I would argue that teaching is one of those professions that most demands the skills of métis, that teachers become better teachers not simply by learning theories and methods of teaching (as much as these can help) but by the act of teaching in particular and always changing local contexts.[39] This is self-evident to anyone who has taught, of course, but its self-evidence seems lost on educational policy makers for whom an ideal of techne, of formally definable practice, seems paramount. Scott argues that it is perfectly reasonable to "speak of the art of one loom, the art of one river, the art of one tractor, or the art of one automobile" (318); I would add that it is likewise reasonable to speak of the art of one student, or the art of one classroom. In that regard, the art of teaching requires a particular sort of interpersonal métis.

Scott's distinction between métis and techne also points out ways in which it becomes possible to denigrate the profession of teaching. Because it is locally grounded, métis gets in the way of truth: "The spheres of human endeavor that are freest of contingency, guesswork, context, desire, and personal experience . . . came to be perceived as man's highest pursuit. They are the philosopher's work" (321). In contrast, the findings of métis are always tainted because they are "practical, opportune, and contextual rather than integrated into the general conventions of scientific discourse" (323). Teaching as métis resists measurement, quantifiable assessment, quick determination of effectiveness, truth; teaching as techne is scientific, verifiably effective, universally applicable.

Scott argues that the widespread loss of the ideal of métis is not simply attributable to economic and social changes:

> The destruction of métis and its replacement by standardized formulas legible only from the center is virtually inscribed in the activities of both the state and large-scale bureaucratic capitalism . . . The logic animating the project . . . is one of control and appropriation. Local knowledge, because it is dispersed and relatively autonomous, is all but unappropriable. The reduction, or more utopian still, the elimination of métis and the local control it entails are preconditions, in the case of the state, of administrative order and fiscal appropriation and, in the case of the large capitalist firm, of worker discipline and profit. (335–36)

This project is widely evident in many of the discourses I have explored here, of course. When pedagogic discourses point to universal descriptions of contexts such as the high-performance workplace or generalizable characteristics of students such as offenders who are cognitively deficient, they seek to define teaching as techne. Resistance to these discourses typically highlight aspects of métis. Simon, Dippo, and Schenke for example, recommend that vocational education students focus on particulars of workplace practices. For example, teachers should encourage students to discuss disparities and practices of pay in the workplace, challenging conventions of vocational education that pay is a personal, private matter and "that for students, especially 'lower-level' students who are presumed to be headed for lower-level jobs, talk of pay only adds insult to injury" (*Learning Work* 165). Their curriculum "encourages an understanding of the historical, cultural, and economic character of work as an exchange relation" (8) and requires that teachers deal with their particular students, not with a generalized potential worker. Stephen Duguid's call for a model of democratic prisoner education, run not by prison staff but by definably outside educators and the prisoners themselves, requires identifying student-inmates as rich and varied subjects, rather than as objects, offenders. When Myles Horton argues that the "how" of educational practice matters less than the "why," he is arguing for a reliance on particular contexts to guide practice, poking fun at the notion that there might be a Highlander method—a Highlander techne—applicable in any situation.

Invoking the priorities of métis, then, becomes a way for teachers to resist the push toward techne emphasized by official educational discourses. It means insisting that métis is the proper attitude with which to approach teaching: "It is the mode of reasoning most appropriate to complex material and social tasks where the uncertainties are so daunting that we must trust our (experienced) intuitions and feel our way" (Scott 327). I use my reading of Bernstein to suggest that the most effective places to exercise métis are those places where official discourses attempt most strongly to control or do away with it, at the boundaries between fields in the pedagogic device. Stephen Duguid is only the most prominent example of theorists within correctional education who attempt to exercise métis at the boundary between the field of production and the field of recontextualization within correctional education; he argues for a vastly different kind of pedagogic discourse than the dominant one based within social cognition. Any teacher who has disregarded an institutional mandate, modified a required lesson plan, or suddenly questioned goals that at one time seemed self-evident and necessary, understands the power of métis at the boundary between the fields of recontextualization and reproduction. In officially sanctioned and regulated institutions, there will always be a fundamental tension between teaching as métis and teaching as techne.[40] I argue that the play in that tension provides a fruitful site for the action of teachers and scholars.

Likewise, the idea of métis asserts the particular urgency of defining educational work according to the particulars of local context rather than to universal abstractions and narrowly defined future outcomes. John Dewey points out the short-sightedness of imagining education only in terms of the future in his discussion of childhood.[41] He argues that a dominant and flawed perspective on the education of children revolves around defining children, not by what they are, but by what they should become. From that perspective, the proper role of education, then, exists entirely in preparing children

> for the responsibilities and privileges of adult life. Children are not regarded as social members in full and regular standing. They are looked upon as candidates; they are placed on the waiting list. The conception is only carried a little farther when the life of adults is considered as not having meaning on its own account, but as a preparatory probation for "another life." (54)

This conception stems in part from what Dewey refers to as a negative definition of immaturity, "the absence of powers which may exist at a later time" (42). The tendency to understand immaturity in these terms, he argues, stems from a comparative and not intrinsic regard of childhood: "We treat [immaturity] as a privation because we are measuring it by adulthood as a fixed standard. This fixes attention upon what the child has not, and will not have till he becomes a man" (42). Such a perspective effectively dehumanizes the child: "Since life means growth, a living creature lives as truly at one stage as at another, with the same intrinsic fullness and the same absolute claims" (51). To teach otherwise treats the child's life as valuable only in terms of her future, and means that educational ideals such as development, process, and progress "possess significance only as movements *toward* something away from what is now going on. Since growth is just a movement toward a completed being, the final ideal is immobile. An abstract and indefinite future is in control with all which that connotes in depreciation of present power and opportunity" (57).

I introduce Dewey's notion here because he is arguing for the importance of a particular perspective regarding the world as it is. The world as it is cannot be defined solely in terms of what it is not; rather, the world as it is must be embraced as a fully realized present. To define childhood against the ideals of adulthood, so that education becomes defined as a preparation for that adulthood, essentially defines childhood in terms that make the individual child nearly irrelevant, given the necessary "substitution of a conventional average standard of expectation and requirement for a standard which concerns the specific powers of the individual under instruction." A child is measured by "a vague and wavering opinion concerning what youth may be expected, upon the average, to become in some more or less remote future," a process that "fails just where it thinks it is succeeding—in getting preparation for the future" (55). Dewey argues that only by understanding education as an act grounded firmly in the present can education effectively prepare for the future:

> The mistake is not in attaching importance to preparation for future need, but in making it the mainspring of present effort. Because the need of preparation for a continually developing life is great, it is imperative that every energy should be bent to making the present experience as rich and significant as possible. Then as the present merges insensibly into the future, the future is taken care of. (56)

As I noted in my introduction, adults in settings of adult education are typically defined in negative terms, as adults who cannot read, who are not capable of living productive lives (whether as, for examples, noncriminals or useful employees) because they are cognitively deficient or lack particular competencies. This is essentially a comparative view of the present, a present that only matters in the terms of some distant ideal, an ideal, moreover, usually set not by particular students but by educational and social institutions.

Dewey is not arguing that the future doesn't matter, only that the necessary way to get to that future is by means of the ongoing present, that any movement toward a world that ought to be has to start in a full acceptance of the world as it is. I have emphasized the limits of using Highlander as a pedagogical model for those of us who teach within officially sanctioned and regulated institutions, but, following Dewey, I would suggest that one way we can apply the theories that guided Highlander is in negotiating the dialectic between the world as it is and the world that ought to be. We do our students and ourselves a disservice when we define them in negative terms, in terms of what they are not capable of, of what they cannot do. This negativity, however, remains a dominant force in education, especially in the education of adults. To see students in terms of their potential, of what they might become, requires seeing them first in terms of who they are, of what they can do. It requires a positive understanding of potential, not as a "merely dormant or quiescent state," but as "potency, force" (Dewey 40). When Highlander staff spent such energy at understanding the needs and wants, the social conditions and histories, of the communities in which they teach, they demonstrated this power without ever taking their eyes off the ought to be. When Horton argues that the goals of Highlander—"brotherhood, democracy, a kind of *world, in which we need to live*"("Myles Horton's Talk" n.p.)—are impossible to realize, he is arguing for continued grounding in a present which will always need changing, for the necessity to be always where we are while we work toward where we ought to be. Most of us, of course, are grounded in morally ambiguous places, where the ethical consequences of our actions are impossible to project. To pretend otherwise would be to attempt the impossible act of teaching somewhere besides where we are.

WHAT WE TEACH ABOUT WHEN WE TEACH ABOUT LITERACY

I opened each of my earlier chapters with an embedded image, educational literacy practices located or represented within something else: an educational program located within a jail; literacy programs embedded within, and thus shaped by, the goals of a workplace; and the radical educational practices of the Highlander Folk School as projected within the records of an FBI investigation. One point of that construct is the rather simple but still crucial recognition that educational literacy practices exist somewhere and for some purpose, that beyond particular classrooms or individual teacher goals, educational literacy practices are fundamentally shaped and determined by where they are, that location understood as a discursive as much as a physical location.

Literacy programs existing within the workplace, then, must be understood in relation to the businesses that sponsor them and that determine their value in the first place. The educational literacy practices promoted within those programs are an intrinsic aspect of that relationship. They matter at least in part because the organization has decided that they matter, which immediately ties those educational literacy practices to issues critical for any business, namely, profit, employee-employer relations, efficiency, and so forth, all of them related in some way to issues of control on the workplace. To note that those educational literacy practices are fundamentally tied to workplace control, then, is not to condemn them or indict them as ideologically flawed or weak; rather, it is simply to highlight that educational literacy practices always have a relationship to something else, that they are always in service of something beyond the particular classrooms in which they are taught.

Schools within prisons likewise highlight this relationship; educational literacy practices become valued precisely because they direct themselves toward central questions surrounding the practice of incarceration in the United States and other Western countries. It is impossible, then, to teach literacy practices within a prison without considering the relationship of those practices to issues of criminality, rehabilitation, justice, and the prison itself. Thus, although approaches to and theories about education within prison have vastly different stances about these matters, they all, necessarily, have stances toward them, making them central considerations in their discussions of education.

Similarly, my opening of the Highlander chapter (Chapter 4) served, in effect, two purposes: The notes from Dombrowski's speech act as an excellent introduction to the work and philosophy—the praxis—of Highlander, and the fact that I first saw those notes as part of the FBI file on Highlander highlights the official threat that praxis represented. However, the educational literacy practices of Highlander are embedded in other contexts as well, most centrally the history of civil rights and union education in the United States. In fact, the frame one puts around Highlander's educational literacy practices has everything to do with what those educational literacy practices are said to mean. Read through Highlander's literature and archives, the educational literacy practices are directly associated with Horton's vision of "brotherhood, democracy, a kind of *world, in which we need to live*"; read, however, through official and quasi-official attacks on the school, the educational literacy practices are part of an insidious effort to spread communism and communists throughout the South and the nation. Even the act of reading and attributing meaning to the educational literacy practices, then, requires a theoretical and rhetorical frame.

It is this rhetorical observation that guides my analysis in this book. I argue here that educational literacy practices must be understood and explored in ways that go beyond specific local contexts, in this case, typically, but not only, particular classrooms, by examining the educational rhetoric that justifies, sustains, even invokes those educational literacy practices. What those practices mean, on a rhetorical level, is as vital as the literacy events that enact those practices, and it is my argument that literacy studies, in its attempts to address educators, has not attended enough to this relationship.

Literacy studies certainly has addressed literacy as a rhetorical device. One could argue that the shape of the field has developed largely as a resistance to rhetorics of literacy that have routinely generalized in comprehensive and ultimately unsupportable ways about the powers of literacy. Early claims about what literacy caused culturally and psychologically became the foil for studies which contextualized literacy in particular settings. Challenges of the claims made for literacy by scholars such as Jack Goody and Ian Watt, Walter Ong, and others developed, in large part, from empirical observations of how people actually used literacy, what it meant to them in particular settings. These studies have proven enormously important, in part because they have demanded identifying literacies as multiple, varied, and impossible to pin down as any one thing.

In the process, though, I would argue that a potentially unwieldy division has surfaced, one analogous to the division Brandt and Clinton point out about local perspectives on literacy. As I noted in Chapter 1, they argue that a resistance to seeing literacy as having a particular agency has led to an overemphasis on studying local meanings of and uses for literacy. In other words, in order to demonstrate the shortcomings of research that claimed literacy as having extensive, universal, and overwhelming independent agency, literacy studies has determinedly demonstrated literacy's local meanings. The distinction, as Brandt and Clinton argue it, is between "how readers and writers mediate their social world through literate practice (i.e., literate action as part of our action)" and "how literacy acts as a social agent, as an independent mediator (i.e., literacy, itself, in action)" (349). They argue that as a field, literacy studies has emphasized the former at the expense of the latter. Empirical studies of "literate action as part of our action" have relied on a critique of approaches to literacy as capable of action in its own right.

For teachers, however, this critique does not address a central issue, which is that, in any classroom, literacy and the teaching of literacy is supposed to do something to (or if you prefer, for) students within those classrooms. It is not enough to understand and identify the myriad literacy practices that students have when they enter a classroom, because the point of any classroom is almost never to simply validate and celebrate that variety of literacy practices. Rather, the classroom is a place in which the learning of other and new literacy practices is prioritized because those practices are understood by a teacher to have a particular value. Just as Bernstein argues that within any pedagogic discourse a regulative discourse is primary, so I would argue that any classroom in which literacy practices are taught—which I presume includes most of the classrooms occupied by teachers reading this book—necessarily attaches a particular agency to those literacy practices. Educational literacy practices are supposed to take students beyond the literacy practices already familiar to them when they enter the classroom. Why else would we presume to teach?

As with literacy studies, I argue here, in my call for an understanding of teaching as métis, that local contexts matter fundamentally in any teacher's praxis. However, I also place the educational idea of context in a temporal dialectic; within pedagogic discourse, context implies a future. Teachers of literacy practices need ways of defining context, not only geographically, socially, or culturally, but temporally. Teachers of literacy practices require descriptions of context that assume the desirability of an intentional reshaping, through educational practice, of that context. What we teach about when we teach about literacy always involves a vision of the present inextricably tied to a vision of the future. As I have noted repeatedly, an attempt to define education as a politically neutral act is often central within educational rhetoric, which typically does away with bias by grounding action and goals squarely within an empirically or scientifically grounded description of the world as it is. And as academics, we work within a professional field founded on ideas of reason and truth that privilege objectivity as a goal. More often than not, bias appears as a problem; rarely is it openly embraced as a scholarly goal. Rather, it is something that usually needs to be excused, accounted for, used to qualify claims.

Teaching, however, requires bias, a bias that should be understood not as a problem but as a goal. Teachers have to train their biases. They have to shape them and critique them and question them. But most of all, they have to teach with them. To teach without biases is a ridiculous, an incredible concept. To accept as a practical guide educational rhetoric that claims objectivity and neutrality as its guiding principle doesn't change this. Bias is a problem when we proclaim as a goal the possibility of teaching without bias; once this is acknowledged as impossible for meaningful (or even meaning-empty) teaching, the informed development of bias should become a central intellectual goal for teachers, a development that can only take place in particular places with particular students.

In one of his last pieces, a video address to a symposium regarding his work, Bernstein mentioned that "a triumphant silence of the voice of pedagogic discourse" is central to official projects of pedagogy in the present. He argues during questioning after his talk that "only by systematically revealing the voice of this silence can we actually make this pedagogy enabling rather than disabling" ("Video Conference" 380). A critical aspect of that silence is an attempt to deny the regulative discourse primary within pedagogic discourse. His opposition to recent official educational mandates in the United Kingdom—mandates analogous to those well underway in the United States—has to do with his argument that

> pedagogy is simply seen as a technology, that a group of people can now put together a discourse aimed at producing changes in individual experiences, knowledges, and competency, in a quite, almost mechanical way. This pedagogy they produce is completely decontextualised from the rest of the acquirer's life span. The notion that pedagogy must be meaningful, not simply relevant, how to combine relevance and meaningfulness, I think, is the challenge of pedagogy and to put these two together . . . means that you cannot actually design a pedagogy without making explicit the regulative discourse which generates it. (ibid. 380)

Bernstein's distinction between relevance and meaningfulness seems to me here a distinction between the goals of the state to produce subjects relevant to state projects and the desire on the part of "acquirers"—learners, students, people—to engage in a pedagogical process meaningful in the context of "the rest of . . . [a] life span."

I am reminded here of Duguid's (*Can Prisons Work?*) critique of the cognitive-skills approach to correctional education: "In the prison, . . . we are not offering a life of subjectness—the life of a citizen—to a mere object—a criminal. Instead we are trying to persuade a subject disguised to our eyes as an object to, in fact, switch subjectivities—a much more complicated task" (69). When pedagogic discourse defines a student as an object who might become relevant, it is always a disguise for a subject whose rights to a meaningful education become severely constrained. For most of us, there will always be a tension between these approaches, if only because, as Bernstein notes, "education is a state-generated activity and any attempt to make changes in the system can only be done with the approval, in the end, of the State and its various agents and agencies" ("Video Conference" 382). There is no method that will allow us to treat students—and ourselves as teachers—as subjects rather than objects. How we do that will always revolve around why we do that, and that why will always be a site of conflict and struggle. To teach should mean to engage directly and intentionally in that struggle, and training teachers should involve training them to engage in that struggle as well. We can do better than simply misrecognize our work as primarily other than State-sponsored, just as we need not attempt to gnaw off our own feet in order to escape a trap of cultural and social reproduction. For most of us, moral ambiguity will always be a condition of action, one that will never be resolved; this does not preclude the necessity, however, for intentional moral action.

I began this conclusion in a trap; do I also end in one? An honest answer to that question would be, "I don't know." I know that, at times, the institutional and bureaucratic constraints around my own teaching can feel suffocating, even as I also recognize that the constraints on teachers of literacy practices in countless other settings are even stronger. I cannot offer a way out of those constraints, nor can I suggest that teachers can always resist successfully official impulses to limit their agency. The most appropriate words to conclude with, then, are not an inspiring call to action full of evocative rhetorical flourishes (the words I have tried, and failed, to write). Rather, I want to represent this ending instead as a beginning; I address teachers and scholars who read this book in the words of Myles Horton, who spoke them at the conclusion of a somewhat despairing talk he gave to a Memphis Unitarian Universalist congregation in 1972, wondering if there had been any meaningful social progress in his lifetime, and whether such social progress was even possible. The contradictions and challenges I discuss are central to the ways I understand and struggle over my own goals and practices as a teacher, but I know that I neither can nor want to figure out how to deal with them on my own:

> If I had some prescriptions here I would dish them out, but what I have is a problem. My experience is that when you have a problem that you cannot solve, instead of talking about it, crying about it, you share it with other people. Maybe together you can get some answers, and that is what I would like to do. You may question my analysis of the situation, fine: I would like to discuss it. (Jacobs 233)

Notes

1. For more analysis of the work at Goodwill, see Branch "From the Margins," "In the Hallways."
2. I have saved all this student writing, an extraordinary collection of work that I wish I could reproduce throughout this book; I made the deliberate choice, however, not to seek permission up front from my students because I did not want them, or me, to understand that class in terms of a research opportunity. Given the extreme power and eloquence of so many of these pieces, I often regret not approaching individual students for permission. Their inclusion would significantly enrich this book.
3. I discuss the Citizenship Schools at length in Chapter 3.
4. For a sample of various claims made for literacy's transformative power, see Finnegan 17–24.
5. Street's edited collections (*Cross-Cultural, Literacy*) provide several examples of these types of approaches. Other ethnographic explorations include Guerra, Cushman, and Barton and Hamilton. For historical discussions of literacy in contexts, see Graff, Gere, Brandt.
6. I learned to ask this question from Moore and Jones, who ask why the discourse of competencies continues to have such official appeal. I explore their response in Chapter 3.
7. As a scholar of literacy and rhetoric, I am concerned in this book with the representation of literacy and transformation within particular sites of adult education. I do not write this as a scholar of adult education, which would not reflect my training or disciplinary interests, and I am not trying to take or position myself within a particular theoretical perspective within that field. This section by no means should be read as an introduction to the field of adult education, nor as an adequate summation of its concerns; the literature of adult education is vast and widely diverging, and the materials I examine in this book represent

only a fraction of its scholarship and theories. What I am more interested in here are ways in which adult education sets itself apart from other (usually, in the discourse, more traditional) approaches to education.

8. Bernstein makes clear that his discussions of pedagogy go well beyond schooling to "include the relationships between doctor and patient, the relationships between psychiatrist and the so-called mentally-ill, the relationships between architects and planners" (*Pedagogy, Symbolic Control* 3). I use this example with that in mind.
9. I am puzzled by Bernstein's notion of an "unmediated discourse" here, because discourses cannot be unmediated as I understand them. Because I take his distinction between "actual" and "imaginary" discourses to reflect his emphasis on the operation of the pedagogic device (that is, the recontextualized discourse is imagined as closely resembling the discourse it recontextualized), perhaps he also means "unmediated" by the terms of the pedagogic device.
10. Within the section of NCLB titled "Reading First," scientifically based reading research is defined as research that
    (A) applies rigorous, systematic, and objective procedures to obtain valid knowledge relevant to reading development, reading instruction, and reading difficulties; and
    (B) includes research that–
        (i) employs systematic, empirical methods that draw on observation or experiment;
        (ii) involves rigorous data analysis that are adequate to test the stated hypotheses and justify the general conclusions drawn;
        (iii) relies on measurements or observational methods that provide valid data across evaluators and observers and across multiple measurements and observations; and
        (iv) has been accepted by a peer-reviewed journal or approved by a panel of independent experts through a comparably rigorous, objective, and scientific-review.

    The fourth criterion under (B) provides a way to determine the sorts of research officially available for use within teacher education and within classrooms themselves. Research that such "panel(s) of independent experts" (such as, for example, the National Reading Panel) determine as "scientific" becomes the basis for what counts as valid for scholars of education and for teachers to rely upon.
11. When I went through the volunteer orientation at the Douglas County Jail, the program director told us that many officers labeled volunteers at the jail with the blanket and, in this case, disparaging term "social worker." He also noted that we should refer to the staff as "officers" not "guards" as a mark of respect.
12. As Nolan Jones notes, the baseball metaphor driving the three-strikes-and-you're-out policies requires several questions: "What does 'you're out' really mean? Is it for the remainder of the game, and if so, how long is the game? What counts as a strike? What is the strike zone?" (56) As he shows, these questions have been answered quite differently by states enacting this policy.
13. Interested readers can find extensive references to such studies by visiting websites for The Sentencing Project (www.sentencingproject.com) and www.prisonsucks.org. Also, the Bureau of Justice Statistics (www.ojp.usdoj.gov/bjs/) provides extensive statistics regarding changes in incarceration and punishment.

14. Arthur McClure, James Riley Chrisman, and Perry Mock note, in their history of vocational education in the United States, that most vocational programs have traditionally focused on particular trades or occupations. Although these programs dealt with general job skills, they were more concerned with particular job requirements, and they certainly had no lists of general skills comparable to the ones I discuss here. As such, this attention to general skills represents an important shift in the discourse of vocational education.
15. Bernstein notes in great detail that particular versions of competence models can be considerably opposed to other versions of competence models (and likewise for performance models), but for my purposes here, the initial distinction between competence and performance is sufficient. For further discussion, see Bernstein (*Pedagogy, Symbolic Control* 50-56).
16. The notebooks in which this *System* appears are otherwise unpublished, as far as I have been able to ascertain. In referencing it, I have attempted to identify the notebook in which it appears, because page numbers are often unavailable. Notebook 1 (N. 1) is titled *Trainer's Manual and Curriculum Resource Guide*; N. 2, *Assessment Guide, Part I*; and N. 3, *Assessment Guide, Part II.*
17. Were I to provide a pragmatic analysis of this *System*, in addition to the official analysis in this chapter, I would have to indicate that it met with a great deal of resistance from teachers and administrators who refused to implement it exactly as required by the designers, or who failed to give the tests on schedule or in the correct manner. Most of the ten instructors, including myself, found the *System* unwieldy to teach and overly directive, and test designers grew frustrated with our reluctance to follow their guidelines as they provided them to us. I have not been able to find any evidence that this program was developed past this pilot stage. Northwest Regional Educational Laboratories remains a valuable voice and resource for teachers at all levels in the Northwest, and by critiquing their *System* I by no means intend to critique the organization in general.
18. This is not the only time that SCANS has fun with the rhyme between *earn* and *learn*, as indicated by their pamphlet *Learning a Living*.
19. This opening sentence, from a SCANS-based ESL teacher's guide in California (Marshall), reminds us that no matter what their philosophy, educators might feel compelled to teach such competencies because unemployed students face the threat of losing welfare benefits: "California's version of welfare reform involves lifetime limits for receipt of welfare and an emphasis on short-term, intensive employment training, including ESL. English training instructors must make instruction more of an overt job-training tool that prepares students for the first available job" (1). Whether educators like it or not, this suggests, students often face an economic need to take any job they can get.
20. William Covino points out that the definitions of SCANS competencies "are presented without human nouns or pronouns; there are no grammatical subjects, only behaviors. People charged with these behaviors have been abbreviated away, or at best standardized into ciphers—owner, client, worker, supervisor, operator, whose skills are entirely operational" (112). See also my earlier reference to the job descriptions for further evidence of this.
21. This assessment appears in System N. 3, a reprint of a 1991 CASAS document called "Critical Thinking Assessment Items for Employability: A Resource for Teachers." The exercise I cite appears on page 9 of that document.

22. Carnevale et al. provide a helpful chart detailing various theories about learning to learn (behaviorist, structuralist, functionalist, and humanist). About the humanist assumptions, they write: "Being a better human being is considered a valid learning goal." One disadvantage to this approach, however, is that it "[c]an be a very inefficient, time consuming process"(44).
23. The testlet does not come with correct answers. Rather, the test taker is to be encouraged to write down as many possible solutions to the problem as he can, or, with the aid of the teacher, to state them verbally. To elicit more answers, the test administrator is instructed to ask "And what would you do if that didn't work?" or "What would you do if you couldn't do that?" Students demonstrate "limited ability" if they can only come up with one "reasonable" solution, "competency" if they come up with two or three, and "proficiency" if they can generate more than three ways to deal with the lack of sugar.
24. "Fast Schools" is Robertson's term for schools operating under paradigms structured by "fast capitalism," which she names as "a descriptive and metaphoric category to point to a number of different but related aspects of the changed socialist relations of capitalist production and consumption that are part of the new social settlement" (111). For further description, see Robertson, pp. 111-124.
25. My friend Laura Hines used to tell my young son (helpfully), when my wife or I would tell him that he had a choice between, for example, "the red hat or the blue hat," that we were offering him a false choice, since he didn't have the option of no hat at all. The idea of flexibility in NCLB is similar: schools can choose to spend whatever federal funds they receive on a range of federally sanctioned programs, though that funding will dry up if they do not meet the very narrow standardized-test-driven accountability standards for achievement set by the federal government.
26. Harold Berlak notes that Harold McGraw III is a confidant and "generous campaign contributor" to George Bush; he is also CEO of McGraw-Hill, "the nation's largest producer of standardized tests, school textbooks, and instructional materials, including two of the best known highly scripted phonic programs, *Open Court* and *Reading Mastery*" (281).
27. In chapter 2, in which I explore correctional education, I examine a situation in which the educational discourse is primarily about the institution it is located within; likewise, in my chapter on the Highlander Folk School, I examine an institution that challenged dominant views of education by remaining largely outside of state-sanctioned educational settings and goals.
28. The FBI files are available on-line at the Federal Bureau of Investigation website in 19 parts: 01, 2a, 2b, 3a, 3b, 3c, 3d, 3e, 4a, 4b, 4c, 5a, 5b, 5c, 6a, 6b, 6c, 7a, and 7b. Highlander's FBI case number was 61-7511. Each document added to the file received a number, beginning with 61-7511-1 and proceeding sequentially. I have included in my in-text citations the number of the document, the exact dates it was entered into the file (unless that is referenced in the text), and the correct part of the FBI website, listed in the works cited. When possible I have concluded with a page number. An example reference is (FBI 61-7511-106 July 7, 1942 3e 10). Because the files are so unwieldy and unreliably paginated, this strikes me as the most accessible method of citing here.
29. The best detailed history of Highlander is John Glen's *Highlander: No Ordinary School*, which has been the basis for a good deal of this brief history. More cele-

bratory and anecdotal than Glen's work, Frank Adams' *Unearthing the Seeds of Fire: The Idea of Highlander* presents a vivid portrait of the personalities and conflicts that shaped the school. Glen's book includes an extensive bibliographical essay for numerous other citations related to the school.

30. I will reference, in this discussion, three different versions of a workbook produced for students in the Citizenship Schools. The first, "My Reading Booklet," is dated 1959 and was developed primarily for use in South Carolina and the Sea Islands. The second, "My Citizenship Booklet," dated 1961-1962, emphasizes Tennessee requirements for registration and voting as well as more standard discussions of government and citizenship (some of which appear in *MRB* as well). The third, "Citizenship Workbook," is a slicker mass-produced booklet, undated but presumably around 1965, put out by the Southern Christian Leadership Conference. It was used for classes throughout the South and so does not include references to state or local government. I will discuss the three of these together.
31. Other organizations that played a sponsoring role during Highlander's history were labor unions, farmers unions, and civil rights organizations (such as King's SCLC). Highlander, however, never defined themselves by the goals of these organizations, which was one reason for their official break with organized labor in the early 1950s.
32. The story of this photograph itself suggests a collusion between a journalist from the Communist newspaper *The Daily Worker*, Abner Berry, and a photographer sent by the Georgia Commission on Education, who waited until Berry had crouched in front of Horton, King, and Aubrey Williams to take the soon infamous picture. Together with Berry, these three were labeled "the 'four horseman' of racial agitation." Although Berry denied any collusion and apologized to Horton for the trouble he caused, Horton continued to believe the school had been deliberately set up.
33. The affidavits Kilby mentions here had counter-affidavits, one signer, who had "a good job on the government construction project at Tullahoma," attesting that Kilby had cornered him in a popular Monteagle bar at 2:30 in the morning, questioned him extensively about the school, and threatened him if he refused to sign a statement condemning the school (Marlowe, B. n.p.). The signer's uncle confirmed the threat, noting in another affidavit that he visited Kilby at the offices of the Consolidated Coal Company and instructed him not to use his nephew's name in any statement against the school: "Mr. Kilby said if Bill denied his statement he would lose his job" (Marlowe, W. n.p.).
34. Only six months later, when the investigation already seemed to be producing few useful leads, a report notes that Kilby had threatened to ensure that the foundation of a new Highlander building "will never be laid and that he will not restrain the Grundy County Crusaders but indicated that he would probably be with them. It is not believed that KILBY meant what he said . . . but the incident is reported to indicate the type of mind that KILBY has" (FBI 61-7511-72 Dec. 30, 1941 2b 119).
35. See note 33 for a further affidavit on how Mr. Kilby collected these charges.
36. "The strike," Glen notes, "was doomed from the start" (47). After a ten-hour a week increase in work with no corresponding wage increase, strikers walked out. Highlander staff supported the strikers by operating food drives and running

workshops, but as Zilla Hawes noted, "every authority in the county lined up behind the company with not even any outside chance for redress of any kind" (qtd. Glen 48). Punctuated by violence on the part of deputized mill guards against union leaders, the strike was broken within two months. "Once more," Glen writes, "striking workers had been powerless before the overwhelming onslaught of anti-union forces" (48).

37. Bernstein's model, in fact, presents a number of ways that, in Michael Apple's words, "ruptures and cleavages . . . impede the effectivity of education" in working for official interests. Complicating the discursive gaps I note are often conflicting agents that play a role in shaping discourse in every field. Thus, reproduction never occurs in straightforward or obvious ways, and official interests cannot simply be said to appear in the classroom. For a more detailed examination of this, see Apple and Wong and Apple.
38. Such deviation from the proscribed practice also provides an explanation for the failure of particular curricula to meet the expectations set for them: teachers used them improperly.
39. Karen Kopelson also explores the relationship of métis to teaching, arguing that it might be necessary for a "determinedly progressive educator . . . to be sneakier" in dealing "with an audience of resistant students" (121). She calls for a "performance of neutrality" whereby teaching might actually be heard rather than immediately rejected as politically biased and narrowly self-interested. For Kopelson, métis becomes a tool of cunning so that teachers speak in the guise of someone students might listen to. She is particularly interested in métis as a tool for introducing issues of difference—race, sexuality, class, and such—into classrooms in which even raising such issues can be grounds for immediate resistance. Kopelson's essay emphasizes métis as a necessary tool for teachers in working through—rather than simply bemoaning—the constraints established by student tendencies for such resistance. In my discussion, I am interested in métis as a tool for dealing with institutional and discursive constraints.
40. Kopelson notes that one tool of métis might be to act according to the norms of accepted techne: "performing the more disinterested, academic, authoritarian role" (127) students expect from a professor, she argues, might be a cunning project reflecting "the honest desire and honest effort . . . to keep students open, keep students learning, keep students open *to* learning, so that they may engage with rather than shut out difference" (135).
41. I am grateful to Nathan Jenkins for suggesting this reading of Dewey.

References

Adams, C. F., E. L. Godkin, and J. Quincy. "Report of the Committee on Composition and Rhetoric (1892)." in *The Origins of Composition Studies in the American College, 1875-1925: A Documentary History*, Ed. John Brereton. Pittsburgh: University of Pittsburgh Press, 1997.

Adams, F. with Horton, M. *Unearthing Seeds of Fire: The Idea of Highlander.* Winston-Salem: John F. Blair, 1975.

Allington, R. *Big Brother and the National Reading Curriculum: How Ideology Trumped Evidence.* Portsmouth, NH: Heinemann, 2002.

Apple, M. "Does Education Have Independent Power? Bernstein and the Question of Relative Autonomy." *British Journal of Sociology* 23(4) (2002): 607–16.

Arbenz, R. "In Our Lifetime: A Reformist View of Correctional Education." *Journal of Correctional Education* 45(1) (1994): 30–37.

Ball, S., A. Kenny, and D. Gardiner. "Literacy, Politics and the Teaching of English." in *Bringing English to Order: The History and Politics of a School Subject,* Eds. Ivor Goodson and Peter Medway. London: The Falmer Press, 1990.

Barton, D. and M. Hamilton. *Local Literacies: Reading and Writing in One Community.* London and New York: Routledge, 1998.

Beckett, K. *Making Crime Pay: Law and Order in Contemporary American Politics.* New York: Oxford University Press, 1997.

Berlak, H. "From Local Control to Government and Corporate Takeover of School Curricula: *The No Child Left Behind Act* and the *Reading First* Program." in *Critical Social Issues in Education: Democracy and Meaning in a Globalizing World*, Eds. H.S. Shapiro and D.E. Purpel. Mahwah, NJ: Lawrence Erlbaum, 2005: 267–286.

Bernstein, B. "From Pedagogies to Knowledges." in *Towards a Sociology of Pedagogy*, Ed. A. Morais. New York: Peter Lang, 2001.

Bernstein, B. "Video Conference with Basil Bernstein." in *Towards a Sociology of Pedagogy*, Ed. A. Morais. New York: Peter Lang, 2001.

Bernstein, B. *Pedagogy, Symbolic Control and Identity: Theory, Research, Critique.* rev. ed. Lanham, Maryland: Rowman and Littlefield, 2000.

Blinn, C. "Teaching Cognitive Skills to Effect Behavioral Change Through a Writing Program." *Journal of Correctional Education* 46(4) 1995: 46–54.

Boudin, K. "Critical Thinking in a Basic Literacy Program: A Problem-Solving Model in Corrections Education." *Journal of Correctional Education* 46(4) 1995: 141–45.

Bourdieu, P. and J.C. Passeron. *Reproduction in Education, Society and Culture.* 2nd ed. London: Sage Publications, 1990.

Bowles, S. and H. Gintis. *Schooling in Capitalist America:Educational Reform and the Contradictions of Economic Life.* New York: Basic Books, 1976.

Boyle, M.-E. *The New Schoolhouse: Literacy, Managers, and Belief.* Westport and London: Praeger Publishers, 2001.

Branch, K. "In the Hallways of the Literacy Narrative: Power in the Lives of Adult Students." in *Multiple Literacies in the 21st Century*. Eds. Charles Bazerman, Brian Huot and Beth Stroble. Cresskill, NJ: Hampton Press, 2004.

Branch, K. "From the Margins at the Center: Literacy, Authority, and the Great Divide." *College Composition and Communication* 50(2) 1998: 206–231.

Brandt, D. *Literacy in American Lives.* Cambridge: Cambridge University Press, 2001.

Brandt, D. and K. Clinton. "Limits of the Local: Expanding Perspectives on Literacy as a Social Practice." *Journal of Literacy Research* 34(3) 2002: 337–56.

Buckingham, D. and M. Scanlon."Parental Pedagogies: An Analysis of British 'edutainment' Magazines for Young Children." *Journal of Early Childhood Literacy* 1(3) 2001: 281–99.

Bureau of Justice Statistics (U.S. Department of Justice). "Prison and Jail Inmates at Midyear 2003." U.S. Department of Justice: Washington, D.C., 2004.

Burns, J. M. "Using Grundy County As Laboratory, School Spreads Communist Doctrines in State." typewritten copy in Highlander Archives, box 33, folder 3, 1939.

Buttrick, W.. "Statement on the article about the Highlander Folk School, printed in the *Nashville Times*, October 18, 1939" typewritten copy in Highlander Archives, dated October 16, 1939, Box 33, folder 3, 1939.

Carey, G. "A View From Higher Education." in *Higher Education in Prison: A Contradiction in Terms?* Ed. Miriam Williford. Phoenix: Oryx Press, 1994.

Carnevale, A., L.J. Gainer, and A.S. Meltzer. *Workplace Basics: The Essential Skills Employers Want.* San Francisco: Jossey-Bass, 1990.

Chambliss, W. "Drug War Politics: Racism, Corruption, and Alienation." in *Crime Control and Social Justice: The Delicate Balance*. Eds. D. Hawkins, S. Meyers, and R. Stone. Westport, CT: Greenwood, 2003.

Cobb, A. "The Sea Island Citizenship Project." Highlander Archives, box 38, folder 4, 1939.

Coles, G. *Reading the Naked Truth: Literacy, Legislation, and Lies.* Portsmouth, NH: Heinemann, 2003.

Coles, G. *Misreading Reading: The Bad Science That Hurts Children.* Portsmouth, NH: Heinemann, 2000.

Collins, J. "Bernstein, Bourdieu and the New Literacy Studies." *Linguistics and Education* 11(1) 2000: 65–78.

Conover, T. *Newjack: Guarding Sing Sing*. New York: Random House, 2000.

Covino, W. *Magic, Rhetoric, and Literacy: An Eccentric History of the Composing Imagination.* Albany: SUNY Press, 1994.

Cushman, E. *The Struggle and the Tools: Oral and Literate Strategies in an Inner City Community.* Albany: SUNY Press, 1998.

Darrah, C. "Workplace Skills in Context." *Human Organization* 51 1992: 264–73.

Davidson, H. *Schooling in a "Total Institution": Critical Perspectives on Prison Education.* Westport, CT: Bergin and Garvey, 1995.

Dewey, J. *Democracy and Education: An Introduction to the Philosophy of Education.* New York: The Free Press (reprinted 1997).

Downes, D. "The Macho Penal Economy: Mass Incarceration in the United States – A European Perspective." in *Mass Imprisonment: Social Causes and Consequences*. Ed. D. Garland. London: Sage, 2001. 51–69.

Duguid, S. "Confronting Worst Case Scenarios: Education and High Risk Offenders." *Journal of Correctional Education* 44(4) 1997: 153–159.

Duguid, S. *Can Prisons Work? The Prisoner as Object and Subject in Modern Corrections.* Toronto: University of Toronto Press, 2000.

Duguid, S. "Subjects and Objects in Modern Corrections." *Journal of Correctional Education* 51(2) 2000: 241–55.

Edwards, R. *Contested Terrain: The Transformation of the Workplace in the Twentieth Century.* New York: Basic Books, 1979.

Edgerton, J. "STOP! LOOK! LISTEN!" Highlander Archives, box 33, folder 1, 1934.

Egerton, J. "The Trial of the Highlander Folk School." *Southern Exposure* 6(1) 1978: 82-89.

Eggleston, C. and T. Gehring. "Democracy in Prison and Prison Education." *Journal of Correctional Education* 51(3) 2000: 306–10.

Eldred, J. C. and P. Mortensen. "Reading Literacy Narratives." *College English* 54(5) 1988: 512–39.

Engel, M. *The Struggle for Control of Public Education: Market Ideology Vs. Democratic Values.* Philadelphia: Temple University Press, 2000.

Fabiano, E. "How Education Can be Correctional and How Corrections Can be Educational." *Journal of Correctional Education* 42(2) 1991: 100–106.

Faith, K. "Santa Cruz Women's Prison Project, 1972–1976." In H. Davidson: 1995.

Federal Bureau of Investigation. (1939–1960). Highlander File, 65-7511. <http://foia.fbi.gov/foiaindex/hfschool.htm>.

Finnegan, R. *Literacy and Orality: Studies in the Technology of Communication.* Oxford, England: Blackwell Publishers, 1988.

Fox, T. A. "The Necessity of Moral Education in Prisons." *Journal of Correctional Education* 40(1) 1989: 18–25.

Garan, E. *Resisting Reading Mandates: How To Triumph With the Truth.* Portsmouth, NH: Heinemann, 2002.

Gee, J. P., G. Hull, and C. Lankshear. *The New Work Order: Behind the Language of the New Capitalism.* Boulder: Westview Press, 1996.

Gehring, T. "Recidivism as a Measure of Correction Education Program Success." *Journal of Correctional Education* 52(2) 2000: 197–205.

Gehring, T. "Characteristics of Correctional Instruction, 1789–1875." *Journal of Correctional Education* 46(2) 1995: 52–59.

Gehring, T. "A Change in Our Way of Thinking" *Journal of Correctional Education 40*(1) 1989: 166–73.

Georgia Commission on Education. "Communist Training School." Highlander Archives, box 34, folder 2, 1957.

Gere, A. R. *Intimate Lives: Literacy and Cultural Work in U.S. Women's Clubs, 1880–1920*. Chicago: University of Illinois Press, 1997.

Glen, J. M. *Highlander: No Ordinary School.* 2nd Edition. Knoxville: University of Tennessee Press, 1996.

Goffman, E. *Asylums: Essays on the Social Situation of Mental Patients and Other Inmates*. New York: Anchor Press, 1961.

Gonczi, A. "Competency Based Assessment in the Professions in Australia." *Assessment in Education: Principles, Policy, and Practice*, *1*(1) 1994. 27 – . *Academic Search Premier*. EBSCO. Montana State University Bozeman. 15 Nov. 2003. <http://search.epnet.com/login.aspx?direct=true&db=aph&an=9512190089&loginpage=Login.asp>

Goodman, K. "NCLB: A Tool in the Neoconservative Movement to Privatize Public Education." in Goodman et al.: 51–65.

Goodman, K., P. Shannon, Y. Goodman, and R. Rapoport eds. *Saving Our Schools: The Case for Public Education Saying No to "No Child Left Behind."* Berkeley: RDR Books, 2004

Goody, J. and I. Watt. "The Consequences of Literacy." in *Literacy in Traditional Societies* Jack Goody (ed). Cambridge: Cambridge UP, 1968.

Gordon, B. *Congressional Record*, April 20, 1994.

Gowen, S. G. "The 'Literacy Myth' at Work: The Role of Print Literacy in School-to-Work Transitions." *Critical Education for Work: Multidisciplinary Approaches.* Ed. Richard D. Lakes. Norwood, NJ: Ablex Publishing, 1994.

Graff, H. *The Labyrinths of Literacy: Reflections on Literacy Past and Present.* 2nd ed. London: Falmer, 1995.

Graff, H. *The Literacy Myth: Literacy and Social Structure in the Nineteenth-Century City*. New York: Academic Press, 1979.

Guerra, J. *Close to Home: Oral and Literate Practices in a Transnational Mexicano Community*. New York: Teachers College Press, 1998.

Heath, S. B. *Ways With Words: Language, Life, and Work in Communities and Classrooms*. Cambridge: Cambridge University Press, 1983.

Highlander Folk School. "Highlander Folk School Report to William Roy Smith Memorial Fund." Highlander Archives, Box 1, folder 3, 1939.

Highlander Folk School. "Statement of Purpose, Program and Policy." Highlander Archives, box 1, folder 2, 1950.

Highlander Folk School. "This We Believe—at Highlander." Highlander Archives, box 1, folder 2, 1955.

Highlander Folk School. "Conversation between Justine Wise Polier, Septima Clark and Myles Horton at the Highlander Folk School, May 1959" Highlander Archives, Box 38, folder 14, 1959.

Highlander Folk School. "My Reading Booklet, 1959-1960." Highlander Archives, Box 67, folder 10, 1959.
Highlander Folk School. "My Citizenship Booklet." Highlander Archives, Box 38, folder 11, 1961.
Highlander Folk School. "Training Leaders for Citizen Schools: Outline of Training Workshop." Highlander Archives, Box 38, folder 2, n.d.
Highlander Folk School. "A Plan for Furthering the Citizenship Potential of the Southern Negro." n.d.
Highlander Research and Education Center. *Records: 1917–1999.* Wisconsin State Historical Society Archives.
Hill, Adams Sherman. "An Answer to the Cry for More English. (1879)" in *The Origins of Composition Studies in the American College, 1875–1925: A Documentary History,* Ed. John Brereton. Pittsburgh: University of Pittsburgh Press, 1997.
Horton, M. "Myles Horton's Talk at Experimental Citizenship School Workshop, February 19-21, 1961." Highlander Archives, Box 40, folder 4, 1961.
Horton, M. "College Workshop Devotion." Highlander Archives, Box 78, folder 9, 1960.
Horton, M. "Statement by Myles Horton for Saugeen Seminar" dated August 11–20, 1960. Highlander Archives, box 31, folder 5, 1960.
Horton, M. "The Place of Whites in the Civil Rights Movement." Highlander Archives, box 40, folder 4, 1967.
Horton, M., with J. Kohl and H. Kohl. *The Long Haul: An Autobiography.* New York and London: Teachers College Press, 1990.
Horton, M. and P. Freire. *We Make the Road by Walking: Conversations on Education and Social Change.* Eds. Brenda Ball, John Gaventa, and John Peters. Philadelphia: Temple University Press, 1990.
Houk- Cerna, F. "What the Dibels is That?" in Goodman et al.: 2004, 129–31.
Hull, G. "Critical Literacy and Beyond. Lessons Learned from Students and Workers in a Vocational Program and on the Job." *Anthropology and Education Quarterly* 24(4) 1993: 357–72.
Hull, G. "Hearing Other Voices: A Critical Assessment of Popular Views on Literacy and Work." *Harvard Educational Review* 63(1) 1993: 20–49.
Hyde, L. *Trickster Makes This World: Mischief, Myth, and Art.* New York: Farrar, Strauss, and Giroux, 1998.
Hyslop-Margison, E. J. and B. Welsh. "Career Education and Labour Market Conditions: The Skills Gap Myth." *Journal of Educational Thought* 37(1) 2003: 5–22.
Jacobs, Dale, ed. *The Myles Horton Reader: Education for Social Change.* Knoxville: University of Tennessee Press, 2003.
Jacques, Roy. *Manufacturing the Employee: Management Knowledge from the 19th to 21st Centuries.* London: Sage Publications, 1996.
Jarvis, P. *Adult and Continuing Education: Theory and Practice.* London: Routledge, 1995.
Jones, N.E. "Three Strikes and You're Out: A Symbolic Crime Policy?" in *Crime Control and Social Justice: The Delicate Balance.* Eds. D. Hawkins, S. Meyers, and R. Stone. Westport, CT: Greenwood, 2003.

Kantrowitz, S. *Ben Tillman and the Reconstruction of White Supremacy.* Chapel Hill: University of North Carolina Press, 2000.

Kazemek, F. E.. "'In Ignorance to View a Small Portion and Think that All': The False Promise of Job Literacy." *Journal of Education* 173(1) 1991: 51–65.

Kim, Joyce. "Challenges to NLS: Response to 'What's "New" in New Literacy Studies.'" *Current Issues in Comparative Education* [online], 5(2). 5 pars. 16 August 2003 <http://www.tc.columbia.edu/cice/vol5nr2/al152.htm>

Kincheloe, Joe. *How Do We Tell the Workers? The Socioeconomic Foundations of Work and Vocational Education.* Boulder: Westview Press, 1999

Kirsch, I. S., A. Jungeblut, L. Jenkins, and A. Kolstad. *Adult Literacy in America: A First Look at the Results of the National Adult Literacy Survey.* Washington DC: U.S. Department of Education, 1993.

Knowles, M. *The Modern Practice of Adult Education: From Pedagogy to Andragogy.* New York: Association Press, 1980.

Kohl, H. R. *Stupidity and Tears: Teaching and Learning in Troubled Times.* New York: New Press, 2003.

Kopelson, Karen. "Rhetoric on the Edge of Cunning; or, The Performance of Neutrality (Re)Considered as a Composition Pedagogy for Student Resistance." *College Composition and Communication* 55(1) 2003: 115–46.

Lakes, R. D. "Is This Workplace Democracy? Education and Labor in Postindustrial America." *Critical Education for Work: Multidisciplinary Approaches.* Ed. Richard D. Lakes. Norwood, NJ: Ablex Publishing, 1994.

Larson, J. *Literacy as Snake Oil: Beyond the Quick Fix.* New York: Peter Lang, 2002.

Levine, K. *The Social Context of Literacy.* London: Routledge and Kegan Paul, 1986.

Lindemann, E. *The Meaning of Adult Education.* New York: New Republic, 1926 .

Lindsay, Margaret. "Competency-Based Teacher Education and Certification in New York State: An Overview." *Teachers College Record* 77(4) 1976: 505–16.

Lockwood, A. "Highlander's Concept of Education for Social Action." Highlander Archives, Box 38, folder 2, 1960.

Love, G. D. "Consideration of the Inmate Student's Locus of Control for Effective Instructional Leadership." *Journal of Correctional Education* 42(1) 1991: 36–41.

Lu, Min-Zhan. "An Essay on the Work of Composition: Composing English Against the Order of Fast Capitalism." *College Composition and Communication* 56(1) 2004: 16–50.

Lynch, O. R. "An Analysis of Achievement Scores and Types of Crimes Among Arizona's Adult Male Prison Population." *Journal of Correctional Education* 44(1) 1993: 32–36.

MacCormick, A. *The Education of Adult Prisoners: A Survey and a Program.* New York: National Society of Penal Information (reprinted 1976).

Marks, A. "One Inmate's Push to Restore Education Funds for Prisoners." *Christian Science Monitor* 27 March 1997: 3.

Marlowe, B. "Affidavit." Highlander Folk School Archives. Box 33, folder 5, 1940.

Marlowe, W. "Affidavit." Highlander Folk School Archives. Box 33, folder 5, 1940.

Marshall, B, compiler. "English Language Training for Employment Participation: Resource Package." Sacramento: California State Department of Social Services, 1998.

Martinson, Robert. "What Works: Questions and Answers About Prison Reform." *The Public Interest* 35 1974: 22–54.

Matthews, R. *Doing Time: An Introduction to the Sociology of Imprisonment.* New York: St. Martin's Press, 1999.

Matthews, S. "Each Day is a Challenge: Paving the Way for Success in the Prison Classroom." *Journal of Correctional Education* 51(1) 2000: 179–82.

Mauer, M. *Race to Incarcerate.* New York: The New Press, 1999

McClure, A. F., J.R. Chrisman, and P. Mock. *Education for Work: The Historical Evolution of Vocational and Distributive Education in America.* Cranbury, NJ: Associated University Presses, 1985.

Meier, D. and G. Wood, eds. *Many Children Left Behind: How the No Child Left Behind Act is Damaging Our Children and Our Schools.* Boston: Beacon Press, 2004.

Miller, R."The Arts of Complicity: Pragmatism and the Culture of Schooling." *College English* 61(1) 1998: 10–28.

Miller, T. *The Formation of College English: Rhetoric and Belles Lettres in the British Cultural Provinces.* Pittsburgh: University of Pittsburgh Press, 1997.

Montross, K. J. and J. F. Montross. "Characteristics of Adult Incarcerated Students: Effects on Instruction." *Journal of Correctional Education* 48(4) 1997: 179–86.

Moore, R. and L. Jones. "Appropriating Competence: The Competency Movement, the New Right and the 'Culture Change' Project." *British Journal of Education and Work* 8(2)1995: 78-92.

Moss, G. "Informal Literacies and Pedagogic Discourse." *Linguistics and Education* 11(1) 2000: 47–64.

Moss, G. "Literacy and Pedagogy in Flux: Constructing the Object of Study From a Bernsteinian Perspective." *British Journal of Sociology of Education* 23(4) 2002: 549–58.

Moyers, B. "The Adventures of a Radical Hillbilly: An Interview with Myles Horton." *Appalachian Journal* 9(4) 1982: 248–85.

National Center for Education Statistics. *Literacy Behind Prison Walls: Profiles of the Prison Population from the National Adult Literacy Survey.* Washington, D.C.: U.S. Department of Education, 1994.

National Commission on Excellence in Education. *A Nation at Risk: The Imperative for Educational Reform.* Washington, D.C.: United States Department of Education, 1983.

Newman, A.P., L. Warren and C. Beverstock. *Prison Literacy: Implications for Program and Assessment Policy.* Philadelphia: National Center on Adult Literacy, 1993

No Child Left Behind Act of 2001. P. Law 107–110 Jan. 2002. Stat. 115.1425.

Norris, N. "The Trouble With Competence." *Cambridge Journal of Education* 21(3) 1991.

Northwest Workplace Basics. (1992). *Curriculum Management and Assessment System.* Portland: Northwest Regional Educational Laboratory, 1992.

Ohmann, R. "Literacy, Technology, and Monopoly Capital." *College English* 50(6) 1985: 675–89.

Ong, W. *Orality and Literacy: The Technologizing of the Word.* London and New York: Routledge, 1982.

Papen, U. "Literacy—Your Key to a Better Future"? Literacy, Reconciliation and Development in the National Literacy Programme in Namibia" *Literacy and*

Development: Ethnographic Perspectives. Ed. Brian Street. London and New York: Routledge, 2001.

Peramba, A. "Appendix One: The Federal Pell Grant Program." in *Higher Education in Prison: A Contradiction in Terms?* Ed. Miriam Williford. Phoenix: Oryx Press, 1994.

Prendergast, C. *Literacy and Racial Justice: The Politics of Learning after* Brown v. Board of Education. Carbondale: Southern Illinois University Press, 2003.

Pullin, D. "Learning to Work: The Impact of Curriculum and Assessment Standards on Educational Opportunity." *Harvard Educational Review* 64(1) 1994: 32–54.

Robertson, S. L. *A Class Act: Changing Teachers' Work, Globalisation and the State.* New York and London: Falmer Press, 2000.

Rogers, A. *Teaching Adults* 3rd ed. Buckingham: Open University Press, 2002.

Ross, R. and E. Fabiano. *Time to Think: A Cognitive Model of Delinquency Prevention and Offender Rehabilitation.* Chattanooga, TN: Institute of Social Sciences and Arts, 1985.

Samenow, S. *Straight Talk About Criminals: Understanding and Treating Anti-Social Individuals.* Northvale, NJ: Jason Aronson, 1998.

Samenow, S. "Correcting Errors of Thinking in the Socialization of Others." *Journal of Correctional Education* 42(2) 1991: 56–58.

Sampson, G. *English for the English: A Chapter on National Education.* Cambridge: Cambridge University Press, 1971.

Scholes, R. *The Rise and Fall of English: Reconstructing English as a Discipline*. New Haven: Yale University Press, 1998.

Scott, J. *Seeing Like a State: How Certain Schemes to Improve the Human Condition Have Failed.* New Haven and London: Yale University Press, 1998.

The Sentencing Project. Schools and Prisons: Fifty Years After Brown v. Board of Education. The Sentencing Project: Washington D.C., 2004.

Shannon, P. "What's the Problem for Which No Child Left Behind is the Solution?" in Goodman et al.: 2004. 12–26.

Silva, W. "A Brief History of Prison Education in the United States." in *Higher Education in Prison: A Contradiction in Terms?* Ed. Miriam Williford. Phoenix: Oryx Press, 1994.

Simon, R. I., D. Dippo, A. Schenke. *Learning Work: A Critical Pedagogy of Work Education.* New York: Bergin and Garvey, 1991.

Singh, P. "Pedagogising Knowledge: Bernstein's Theory of the Pedagogic Device." *British Journal of Sociology* 23(4) 2002: 571–82.

Smith, F. *Unspeakable Acts, Unnatural Practices: Flaws and Fallacies in "Scientific" Reading Instruction.* Portsmouth, NH: Heinemann, 2003.

Southern Christian Leadership Conference. "Citizenship Workbook." Highlander Folk School Archives. Box 38, folder 14, 1962.

Southern Christian Leadership Conference. "Citizenship School Training Program." Highlander Folk School Archives. Box 38, folder 14, 1962.

Spear, Karen. "Controversy and Consensus in Freshman Writing: An Overview of the Field." *Review of Higher Education* 20(3) 1997: 319–44.

Street, B., ed. *Literacy and Development: Ethnographic Perspectives.* London and New York: Routledge, 2001.

Street, B. *Cross-Cultural Approaches to Literacy*. Cambridge, England: Cambridge University Press, 1993.

Svensonn, S."Imprisonment—A Matter of Letting People Live or Stay Alive? Some Reasoning from a Swedish Point of View." *Journal of Correctional Education* 47(2) 1996: 69–72.

Taylor, J. M. "Appendix Two: Pell Grants for Prisoners." in *Higher Education in Prison: A Contradiction in Terms?* Ed. Miriam Williford. Phoenix: Oryx Press, 1994.

United States Department of Education. *No Child Left Behind: A Desktop Reference.* Washington D.C.: U.S. Department of Education, 2002.

United States Department of Labor. Secretary's Commission on Achieving Necessary Skills. *Learning a Living: A SCANS Report for America 2000.* Washington D.C.: U.S. Department of Labor, 1992.

United States Department of Labor. *Skills and Tasks for Jobs: A SCANS Report for America 2000.* Washington D.C.: Department of Labor, 1991.

United States Department of Labor. *What Work Requires of Schools: A SCANS Report for America 2000.* Washington D.C.: Department of Labor, 1991.

United States Department of Labor and U.S. Department of Education. *The Bottom Line: Basic Skills in the Workplace.* Washington D.C.: U.S. Department of Labor and U.S. Department of Education, 1988.

Valli, L. *Becoming Clerical Workers.* Boston: Routledge and Kegan Paul, 1986.

Warner, K. "The 'Prisoners are People' Perspective—and the Problems of Promoting Learning Where this Outlook is Rejected." *Journal of Correctional Education* 49(3) 1998: 118–32.

Welsh, M."The Effects of the Elimination of Pell Grant Eligibility for State Prison Inmates." *Journal of Correctional Education* 53(4) 2002: 154–58.

Whitty, G. and E. Willmott. "Competence-Based Teacher Education: Approaches and Issues." *Cambridge Journal of Education* 21(3) 1991: 309–18.

Williams, G. "The Pedagogic Device and the Production of Pedagogic Discourse: A Case Example in Early Literacy Education." in *Pedagogy and the Shapiong of Consciousness: Linguistics and Social Processes.* Ed. Frances Christie. London and New York: Continuum, 2000.

Wilson, A. "'Speak Up—I Can't Write What You're Reading": The Place of Literacy in the Prison Community." *Journal of Correctional Education* 47(2) 1996: 94–100.

Wilson, L. "Notes." Highlander Archives, Box 33, folder 6, 1941.

Wilson, L. "Statement by Leon Wilson." Highlander Archives, Box 33, folder 5, 1940.

Winters, C. A. "The Therapeutic Use of the Essay in Corrections." *Journal of Correctional Education* 44(2) 1993: 58–60.

Wong, T. H. and M. Apple "Rethinking the Education/State Formation Connection." *Comparative Education Review* 46 2002: 182–210.

Wright, M. "Pell Grants, Politics and the Penitentiary: Connections Between the Development of U.S. Higher Education and Prisoner Post-Secondary Programs." *Journal of Correctional Education* 52(1) 2001: 11–16.

AUTHOR INDEX

SUBJECT INDEX